The Rough Guide to

Babies

Miranda Levy

ROUGH GUIDES

Rough Guide Credits

Text editor: Orla Duane
Design/layout: Dan May and Pradeep Thapliyal
Illustrations: Murray Wallace
Cover design: Chloë Roberts
Production: Aimee Hampson
Reference Director: Andrew Lockett
Series Editor: Mark Ellingham

Publishing Information

This first edition published May 2006 by Rough Guides Ltd.
Distributed by the Penguin Group:
Penguin Books Ltd, 80 Strand, London WC2R 0RL.
Penguin Putnam, Inc. 375 Hudson Street, New York 10014, USA.
Penguin Books Australia Ltd, 487 Maroondah Highway,
PO Box 257, Ringwood, Victoria 3134, Australia.
Penguin Books Canada Ltd, 10 Alcorn Avenue,
Toronto, Ontario, Canada M4V 1E4.
Penguin Books (NZ) Ltd,
182–190 Wairau Road, Auckland 10, New Zealand.

Typeset in Myriad and Minion to an original design by Dan May.
Printed in Italy by LegoPrint S.p.A..

© Miranda Levy, 2006
352pp includes index
A catalogue record for this book is available from the British Library.

ISBN 10: 1-84353-522-X
ISBN 13: 978-1-84353-522-5

The publishers and authors have done their best to ensure the accuracy and currency of all the information in The Rough Guide to Babies, however, they can accept no responsibility for any loss, injury or inconvenience sustained by any traveller as a result of information or advice contained in the guide.

Contents

Introduction

When I had my daughter Annabel three years ago, I was desperate for a book that really told me how it was. I wanted reassurance that the devastation wreaked on my body wasn't permanent; to be told that my utter failure to follow a routine meant I was still qualified to be a mother, and that my baby wasn't defective because she refused to eat and sleep when she was "meant to". I also needed to know (whisper it) I wasn't the only person who found life with a new baby exhausting, yet rather boring at the same time. Mostly, I wanted a book that made me feel normal.

They were all out there, the volumes that told you how to breastfeed, change a nappy, encourage your baby to sleep through the night. Others were fun to read, sharing the experiences of the author and her friends. What I really needed was a mixture of the two: a book that gave the answers to real questions – can I breastfeed and still drink alcohol? Which is the right formula for my baby? When do most people start having sex again? Will I ever fit back into my jeans? Is a nursery better than a childminder? – backed up with stories from real parents who had been there themselves. All this combined with more serious sections on illness, development, and where to go for further help.

So, when my new son Jacob was days old I started scribbling some notes. This book has the benefit of being written as I was going through it all, without the rosy tint of hindsight. It's set in a very British world of busy labour wards, statutory maternity leave and community midwives who make you stay in all day waiting for a visit, so you won't find reference to "choosing your own paediatrician" (as if!), like in some of the other books out there. It's also set in the very real world of grumpy partners, competitive fellow parents, and nipples that squirt embarrassingly in public places.

I certainly learned a lot during the process of researching this *Rough Guide*. Hope you enjoy reading it as much as I enjoyed writing it!

Miranda Levy

Dedication

To Annabel and Jacob, and my husband Mark Holland, without whom they would not have been possible.

Acknowledgments

A large cast of invaluable people have helped me write this book. First, there are the baby professionals, credited in every chapter. However, special thanks must go to midwife Teresa Driver, health visitor Lynda Skilton, *Relate*'s Christine Northam and postnatal exercise teacher Meg Walker, also to doula Pru Guthrie who guided me through a sleep-deprived fog during the early chapters. Particular mention also to GP Sarah Davey and consultant paediatrician Dr Mike Greenberg, who found time and patience in their busy schedules to answer my endless medical queries. Next, thank you to Kerry Smith who kicked my butt into making my vague idea a reality, and to Andrew Lockett at Rough Guides for having the faith that this pregnant woman who polished off a plate of scampi and chips in five minutes during our first meeting, would actually have what it takes to write a book. Rebecca Bocchetti, thanks for your brilliant research and Orla Duane, for your sensitive copy editing. Finally, a big merci to my friends including Hermione, Justine, Leah, Mel, Sarah and Anna – sorry, it's impossible to mention all of you - for putting up with my endless calls and emails with plaintive requests for baby-related stories.

1

After the birth

1

After the birth

So, here you are: you, your baby and a Pampers newborn disposable. Did you ever really imagine yourself here – on a postnatal ward, in a baggy old T-shirt, or perhaps in tasteful post-C-section surgical stockings, staring at the tiny, red, helpless bundle that's your new son or daughter. For most pregnant women, so all-consuming is the prospect of labour pain, pushing and something medieval-sounding called an *episiotomy*, that the thought of actually having a baby is just secondary to the main event. Yes, you've bought the buggy, the breast pump and "The Bag", sat packed by your bed for three weeks, but did you honestly ever think you'd use all that stuff? Now, your baby, the "it" that has been a biological curiosity for the past forty weeks is a very real, very dependent "he" or "she" that needs to eat, sleep and stay clean. And that's all down to you. So what next?

Chances are, you're exhausted. Or shocked, numb, baffled, euphoric and sore – most likely a mixture of all of these. You may be surrounded by a proud partner or dazed grandparents, or you may choose to cocoon yourself away, drinking in the sheer wonder of those first moments with your newborn.

Never could you have imagined quite so many surprises in one day. That it would really, really hurt as much as it did. That it would make such a mess "down below" (or that you'd walk like Quasimodo if you've had a Caesarean). That the thought of emptying your bowels ever again fills you with complete dread. That you really would make use of those hilarious paper knickers. That you'd be so pleased to see a plate of NHS toast. And most of all, that you could never, ever have dreamt of having created something so precious, so special, and so truly miraculous.

The reason you couldn't have imagined all of this is because it is simply impossible. No books, videos or NCT courses even come close to the real thing. You have to experience it all yourself to believe it. Well, you've done it now – you're there. You're a mother. Welcome.

Your new baby

However exhausted, shocked, numb, baffled etc … you may be, your baby will be feeling rather more so. And what better way to deal with this than to sleep though the whole lot, until it all becomes a bit easier to deal with. For the first few days, your baby will spend eighteen hours or more a day sleeping, perhaps frustrating for your visitors, but a fabulous and necessary respite for you. (Make the most of it, it doesn't last). Some other facts about your newborn:

He will probably not resemble the peachy stars of TV nappy adverts (although babies born by Caesarean look slightly less squashed, on account of not having being forced into this world like a dollop of Colgate). Many newborns look like cross old tortoises rather than Rubenesque cherubs, with the added attraction of big heads and bandy legs. Understandable, when you consider they've been curled up like pretzels for forty weeks.

In most cases, your baby will be covered in blood and possibly vernix, that mozzarella-textured white coating that protects the skin from amniotic

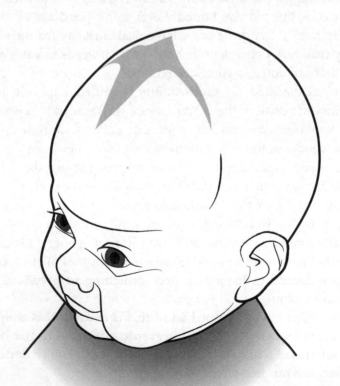

Fontanelles of a newborn

fluid in the womb, although "later" babies generally have less of this. Newborns are also likely to have the following characteristics:

- **A squashed head** – to prepare for her tight exit, your baby is born with skull bones that slide over one another, which can lead to a slightly alarming "cone-shaped" head on arrival. This tends to right itself within a couple of days, although two areas remain soft for longer – one at the front of the head, the other at the back. These kissable fontanelles look vulnerable, but are tougher than they seem – the former will close within eighteen months, the latter within four. Babies born by *ventouse* (vacuum extraction) will have an exaggerated "point", and some develop a raised bruise called a cephalohaematoma that will disappear within the first weeks.

- **Bashed-up eyes** – your baby may look like he's gone five rounds with Audley Harrison, but the bruising and swelling should lessen within a few days. If the birth was particularly rapid, he may also have burst blood vessels in his eyes. Most caucasian babies are born with blue/grey eyes that develop their natural colour within about six months to a year; most black and Asian babies are born with brown eyes.

- **Swollen genitalia** – caused by maternal hormones. If you have a boy, watch for the look of pride on your partner's face at the sight of his newborn's endowment, although he may be less impressed by the swollen breasts, also a by-product of hormones. Some baby girls even briefly have a slight discharge (occasionally bloody) from their vagina.

- **Red skin** – well, you'd be pretty puce if you'd been through what your baby has just been through. However, this pinkness is actually due to the high proportion of red blood cells whizzing around a newborn's body. Quite commonly, the skin turns yellowish in colour, which signifies your child may have jaundice (see p.18). This is rarely serious, and your midwife/health visitor will keep an eye out for it. Some babies also have a light covering of hair called lanugo covering their shoulders, back and forehead and even their ears – more common in babies born a few weeks early.

- **Infantile acne** – to add insult to injury, 25 percent of newborns suffer from this condition (little red and white spots), which tend to reach their peak when you're expecting a visitor you want to impress: this too will vanish within a few weeks. Many infants are often born with "stork marks" or vascular naevi, reddish patches that appear most commonly on the eyelids or nape of the neck, caused by dilated blood vessels. They'll usually disappear gradually at some point in the first year.

- **Umbilical cord** – your baby will also sport the remains of her umbilical cord, plus the little plastic peg, for several days. It starts off shiny silver blue, then turns greeny-yellow, like the inside wiring of a plug. After the midwife removes the peg on about day three, the stump goes black and falls off, usually within ten days.

Initial checks for the baby

Even for the healthiest infant, from the moment they emerge, they will undergo a battery of tests that would make OFSTED proud. If in hospital, until you are discharged, both of you will wear matching bracelets sporting your name, details of the baby's sex, your hospital number and date and time of birth. The baby's surname will be deemed the same as yours, if you are not married or do not use your partner's surname, whatever you subsequently decide to call her.

Other newborn checks

Record of naked weight

Enjoy the spectacle of your newborn being weighed by your midwife like a slab of sausage from the deli counter. Weight can drop by up to 10 percent after delivery, or within the five days it can take for milk to come in if you're breastfeeding, but will be regained when feeding gets in full swing. Breastfed babies can take two to three weeks to return to their birthweight, so don't worry unduly.

Other checks include length and head circumference (so you can tell your friends proudly – "I pushed THAT out", or demonstrate why you couldn't). The average newborn weight is 7.6lbs (3.4kg) with a head circumference of 35cm, and a length of 50cm (2001 figures).

THE APGAR TEST

This test will be performed by the midwife sixty seconds after birth, then again after five minutes. Your baby will receive a score between zero and two for each section (see below); a score of seven or above (out of ten) is deemed to be acceptable. A baby who scores between five and seven may need some help to kickstart breathing, which involves the midwife giving her a vigorous rub, clearing her nose and mouth of mucus and administering oxygen if necessary. Babies who score less than five will be lifted onto a sloping, specially lit and heated trolley in the delivery room, and a paediatrician will be called.

The majority of babies respond well by the time their second APGAR is performed, and turn out perfectly healthy – a low initial APGAR is not indicative of future ill-health. Although a perfect ten is of course indicative of how your baby is already destined for greatness.

APGAR table

Sign	Points		
	0	1	2
Appearance (colour)	pale or blue	body pink, extremities blue	pink
Pulse (heartbeat)	not detectible	below 100	over 100
Grimace (reflex irritability)	no response	grimace	lusty cry
Activity (muscle tone)	flaccid or weak activity	some movement of extremities	good
Respiration (breathing)	none	slow, irregular	good

Vitamin K

You'll also be offered a dose of vitamin K by injection for your baby. Newborns arrive with very little of this essential vitamin which helps their blood to clot and there is only a small amount of it in breastmilk. (If a baby is bottlefed, however, vitamin K is already added to the formula milk). It's made in the baby's bowel by bacteria acquired several weeks after the birth. About 1 in 10,000 babies in the UK suffer from serious bleeding (HDN haemorrhagic disease of the newborn) as a result of vitamin K deficiency. You can still refuse the jab, or ask for a less effective oral version, given in three doses over four weeks.

BCG

Your baby may also be offered the anti-tuberculosis jab but this tends to be restricted to areas where the local population has a high incidence of TB, or if a first-degree relative has the illness.

Hearing test

Some health authorities are now offering this new check at birth – if yours doesn't, you'll receive an appointment at your health clinic within a few weeks. The midwife places a soft-tipped ear-piece in the outer part of the baby's ear, which plays quiet clicking sounds. If your baby can hear okay, a series of lights will flash on a little electronic box, signifying that the ear is producing sounds in response to the clicks. This test usually takes only a few minutes and can be done when the baby is asleep. Don't worry if you get a "false" reading – it's not 100 percent accurate, especially on a tiny baby. The most common reason a baby fails is because of fluid behind the ear-drum which usually resolves spontaneously. You'll be invited for a follow-up examination in a few weeks.

What's next for you?

If you've had a vaginal birth – stitches

Just when you thought the worst was over you may be in for a shock, because just when all you want to do is have a cup of tea, cuddle your baby, and ring your parents with the good news, there is a (rather literal) sting in the tail of this childbirth business.

The vagina was designed to stretch in childbirth, but in about three-quarters of cases, women suffer at least minor tears and abrasions. If you've had an episiotomy (a surgical cut to aid delivery), you'll definitely need stitches.

Your midwife will have a look and decide what needs doing. If you've given birth lying down, any tears will probably start at the back wall of your vagina, heading backwards; if you were upright, they may be more superficial, going forwards. Tears are divided into four categories:

● **1st degree** – superficial tears of the vagina or labia, which often don't need stitching.

● **2nd degree** – tears where the underlying muscle has also torn.

● **3rd degree** – on rare occasions, a tear extends back to the anus. This can happen with an episiotomy, use of forceps or after a long pushing stage with a big baby.

● **4th degree** – extremely rarely, the anal sphincter is torn. Let's not go there.

Sadly, your dignity is about to take a further bashing. For your stitches, your legs will be hoiked to an unnatural angle in a pair of **stirrups**. If your midwife asks whether you can manage without the stirrups, decline – holding your legs up for the time it takes to stitch is more tiring that it looks. Then the midwife (or doctor, if the tears are particularly nasty) will give you an injection of local anaesthetic. Unfortunately, this hurts more than it has any right to at this stage. If you've had an epidural, this can be topped up, or you may be offered gas and air.

Having stitches is also time-consuming. Depending on how bad your tears or cut, it can take up to half an hour, but may often feel much longer than that. The midwife has to repair each layer – the vaginal lining, the muscles, and the external skin – separately. If you can continue to hold your baby while you're being stitched, the time passes more pleasantly. Thankfully, the stitches dissolve on their own within a few weeks.

For care of stitches, bruising, plus all the other after-effects of the extraordinary task of pushing a baby out, see Chapter 2.

If you've had a Caesarean

If you're one of the twenty-odd percent of women who've had a Caesarean birth (up to 25 percent in some urban areas), it goes without saying that you'll have received some nifty needlework of your own. You'll almost certainly be more physically tired than someone who's given birth vaginally, as over half of all Caesarean births are "emergency" deliveries, taking place after you've been in labour for at least 24 hours. However, even if your C-section was planned, you've had a pretty major operation, and recovery usually takes longer than for a vaginal birth. Expect the following:

● Most of those tubes will have to stay in for a while. All women have a catheter for the first 24 hours, plus an intravenous drip for fluids to keep you hydrated and make sure the medics can get to your veins in case of postpartum haemorrhage (emergency bleeding).

● "Best practice" is also to give you an infusion of oxytocin for the first few hours, a hormone which helps your uterus to contract.

● The midwife will check your scar regularly to ensure that no bleeding is taking place and that the loss "per vagina" is minimal.

● The epidural or spinal block will eventually start to wear off – from the toes upwards – and the wound will be sore. Pain is worst for the first couple of days; you'll probably need help even moving up the bed, and positioning your baby for breastfeeding – lying on your side may be easiest. You might be given a shot of morphine or pain-killing Voltarol suppositories.

You probably won't be in a hurry to move anywhere, but as little as six hours after the birth, your midwife will be nagging you to get up and try to walk around – it's important for your circulation, so it's time to join the slow, surgical-stocking-clad shuffle around the ward. Unlike your friends who had vaginal births, it will be standing – not sitting – that's the problem. However, you've got one advantage on the mothers who gave birth through "route one" – a beautifully intact *perineum*, and therefore the edge on placing weight on your bottom without wincing.

As with women who've given birth vaginally, you may have trouble urinating at first – similarly, the anaesthetic may slow your bowels down. For the longer-term recovery from a C-section, see Chapter 2. (*Caesarean Stats: National Statistics 2002.*)

Additional checks

In whatever manner you have given birth, over the first 24 hours a midwife should also screen the following:

- **Temperature** – to monitor any signs of infection, which may require antibiotics.

- **Pulse and blood pressure** – pre-eclampsia (a pregnancy condition involving very high blood pressure) can still occur in the postnatal period. These first two examinations are particularly important if you've had a Caesarean, as are checks on your IV drip and catheter.

- **Breasts** – to ensure there's no nipple damage and to show you how to screen for lumps and blockages of milk, so preventing mastitis (see p.129).

- **Uterus** – to check that it is involuting (returning to the normal non-pregnant size). This can take up to ten days, and is quicker if you breastfeed. If your uterus isn't shrinking as expected, it alerts the midwife to signs of infection or "retained products of placenta", which may require intervention. The midwife will also check that your abdominal muscles haven't separated, which happens in some pregnancies to allow room for the baby to grow. This isn't serious and can usually be treated with physiotherapy and careful exercise.

- **Legs** – to check for swelling and redness which might indicate thrombosis (blood clots) which will be confirmed with an ultrasound scan and be treated with anti-clotting drugs.

- **Emotional state** – while this is obviously a highly charged time for all new mothers, in extraordinarily rare cases, a woman can develop postpartum psychosis, a serious mental illness where a sufferer can experience hallucinations, feel suicidal or try to harm their baby (see p.62).

If you've had a swift discharge from hospital or indeed a home birth, these checks will be carried out by the community midwife in your home.

A note on breastfeeding

In all your time as a new mother, you probably won't come across anything that is as emotive (and emotional) as the decision to breastfeed – or not. Baby experts describe it as a "decision", but sometimes you simply aren't in enough control to make a decision – the situation is taken out of your hands when for one reason or another, you find yourself unable to breastfeed, or the baby just isn't playing ball. (The subject is dealt with fully in Chapter 4.)

However, even at this early stage, if you can give the baby some time at your breast after delivery, it's a positive experience for both of you. For your baby, it will ease her transition to this bright new world and give her comfort – she's born with the reflex to suck, so won't need much persuading at this point. For you, allowing your baby at the breast at least initially will keep your options open while you work out what you want to do. Even if, for whatever reason, you decide not to continue with breastfeeding, it's worth trying to let your baby suck for the first few days to reap the benefit. Don't be alarmed if you think there isn't enough milk coming, your baby won't starve. He won't even be hungry yet. It usually takes three or four days for him to realize he'd quite like something to eat, which coincides with your milk "coming in" – and boy, you'll know about it, when you get those huge, hot, Jordan-sized boulders. Until then, you'll be producing a sugar-and-protein-rich yellow liquid called *colostrum* – it's packed with antibodies and hormones which stimulate digestion.

The feeling of a baby sucking also releases *oxytocin*, the uterus-shrinking hormone which also stimulates milk production. For some mothers, these mini-contractions, or afterpains, can be somewhat painful to say the least (see Chapter 2). Another point about oxytocin is that it's the chemical your brain releases after you've had an orgasm, so that calm, loving feeling you are experiencing is no coincidence.

What happens after you leave the delivery suite

How long you stay in hospital depends on the type of birth you've had, and how the baby is doing. Not so very long ago, new mums spent ten days in hospital and it was considered a "rest". Now it's common to be discharged within 24 hours, and as few as six, if you've had what they call a "straightforward vaginal delivery" (straightforward for whom exactly?) and you and your baby are healthy.

If you've had a Caesarean section, you'll probably have to stay for up to four days, to make sure you are recovering well (see p.16). With a vaginal birth, as soon as you can stand up, you'll be encouraged to take a shower – more hygenic than a bath – most maternity units have "walk-in" units so your birth partner (or midwife, if you don't have a partner with you) can prop up

FIVE THINGS I WISH I'D DONE DIFFERENTLY IN CHILDBIRTH (AND WOULD DO DIFFERENTLY NEXT TIME)

By the mothers

- Begged for an epidural instead of "toughing it out" as my birth plan dictated (*Harriet, 25*)
- Asked my mother to be my birth partner instead of my husband (*Lydia, 34*)
- Listened to that bit in my antenatal class when they told you how to push (*Caroline, 36*)
- Not looked up at the light while they were doing my Caesarean – I could see my intestines in the reflection (*Sam, 39*)
- Had my baby at home (*Viv, 33*)

By the fathers

- Stayed down the "business end" to see my daughter being born (*James, 37*)
- Taken an Ipod, because there were so many hours just hanging around (*Victor, 28*)
- Been more assertive on my wife's behalf when she was in pain and the midwives didn't seem to care (*Ben, 40*)
- Read up a bit more on how to help. Every time I massaged her back, she told me to go away and stop being so "f***ing useless" (*Amit, 30*)
- Worn long sleeves – she kept biting my arm, and it hurt (*Mark, 34*)

your wobbly legs. C-section ladies will be up to shower the next day – as long as the pain relief is working. It's important to keep the scar area clean and dry.

Women who've had vaginal births will need to wash the "exit". Don't spend too much time examining it – you've experienced enough horror for one 24-hour period. Ditto the deflated space-hopper that was once your stomach. It's a good idea to try and wee while you're in the shower, diluting it with warm water so it doesn't sting too much. Don't worry if you can't go to the loo – it's completely normal at this point, either because your bladder and *urethra* (the pipe leading out of it), have taken a bashing, or you're psychologically holding back because you're worried it will hurt. However, it's important that you do pass water within eight hours to avoid a urine infection – a full bladder also stops the uterus contracting, which increases the chance of a postnatal bleed. Speak to a midwife if you're struggling. Moving your bowels is another matter, and may take a few days (see Chapter 2).

You'll then step into the de rigeur paper panties and stick on one of those loaves of bread that masquerade as maternity pads. They need to be that thick because you now have the Mother of all Periods, a bloody discharge known in the trade as *lochia*.

Finally, it's time to hitch a wheelchair taxi ride up to the postnatal ward, babe in arms.

Holding your baby

The first thing is not to be frightened; your newborn is tougher than he looks. However, because a very new baby has only a little head control you will need to make sure that you support his head or he has something to lean on. One way to do this is to scoop him up with both arms, one hand/forearm supporting his bottom and the other against his head. Alternatively, you can lift him up under the arms, gently resting your fingers on the back of his head then turning him so he lies cradled in your arms, head in the crook of your elbow.

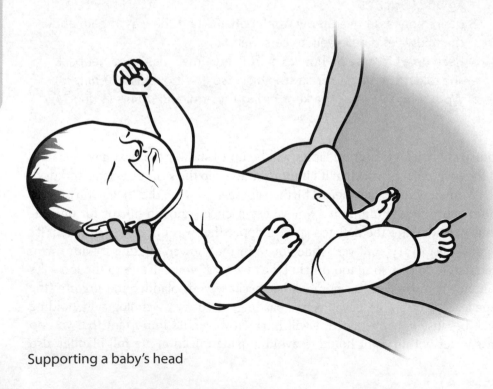

Supporting a baby's head

The maternity ward

In most UK hospitals, your baby will be by your bed with a little plastic box to sleep in – known in the trade as a "fish bowl" – unless there are complications and they need special care.

Depending on how clean, pleasant and friendly the ward, many new mothers enjoy their time here. It's a precious opportunity to suss out how your newborn works. Even on a busy London maternity ward, the midwives should be on hand to help you kickstart breastfeeding if that's what's for you, and show you how to change a nappy and bath your baby. If they seem busy – insist, because once you get home, you're pretty much on your own. For help and advice on attempting baby basics for the first time, see Chapter 2.

MAKING THE BEST OF IT

This is the point you'll realize how you should have thought about the "me" contents of "The Bag", as opposed to the "baby" ones. A quick straw poll of friends resulted in the following "must haves":

- your own pillow
- earplugs
- a pair of dark track-suit pants (anything pale may reveal more than you want)
- some slippers or flip-flops – despite the government's best intentions, hygiene in the hospital wards isn't always up to *Carry on Matron* perfection
- Dettox spray for the loo seat (see above)
- soap and towel
- discman with relaxing music
- camera – this will all seem like a dream one day, so it will be nice to have some concrete proof it really happened
- phone card that works on the ward. Most maternity wards don't allow mobiles because staff maintain they interfere with medical equipment.
- Lots of bottled water, particularly if breastfeeding. Hospital wards are always hot, stuffy places, and even in mid-August, they won't let you open the windows.

Your wedding day apart, this is also the closest you'll come to being treated like a celebrity, as friends and family come to pay homage to the new arrival, bearing gifts of grapes, flowers and little knitted bootees. Or, if you feel like a rest, restricted visiting hours are a huge bonus.

Some hospitals offer "amenity rooms" for around £100 a pop – this basically buys you some privacy and possibly a bathroom, although you won't be soundproofed from the general noise of the ward, and you'll still have plastic under your sheets.

Waiting for discharge

For those women who hate hospitals, you'll probably be itching to get home. However hard it is, you just have to be patient, because even if you've had a good birth, feel fantastic and want to rush home and finish painting the skirting boards in the baby's room, you have to wait for a paediatrician to say it's okay for your baby to leave. Even a six-hour discharge can be more like eight or ten, and when the midwife says the paediatrician will see you in the morning, it'll be more like lunchtime, so more congealed macaroni cheese for you.

While you're waiting, it can be a good idea to ask to see your maternity notes. For the merely curious, it passes the time – you've been a star in your own personal episode of *Holby City*, so why not relish this. On a more serious note, research has shown that women who have had a traumatic birth are more likely to recover quickly and are less likely to fear going though the whole thing again if they understand exactly what happened to them. Ask a midwife to explain what things mean if you don't understand; in the meantime, here's a quick guide to some of the shorthand.

Before your eventual discharge you will see a paediatrician who will perform a swift but intensive top-to-toe checkup on your newborn. This is to screen for any congenital abnormalities and to make sure your baby is well and feeding happily. Ninety-seven percent of babies are born without any problems, so it's more than likely you'll soon be happily heading homeward.

Even so, it can be a bit alarming to see your baby being manhandled,

ABO – May be seen in reference to blood test to check your blood group
AC – Abdominal circumference
AFP – Alpha feto protein (test offered at sixteen weeks to assess risk of problems with baby such as Down syndrome and spina bifida)
APH – Ante partum haemorrhage (bleeding during pregnancy)
BO/BNO – Bowels opened/ Bowels not opened
BPD – Bi parietal diameter. The measurement from one side of the head to the other (ear to ear)
Br – Breech (baby positioned bottom down, head up)
CEPH – Cephalic; means baby is positioned head down – also referred to as vertex
CRL – Crown to rump length (measurement from top of baby's head to his bottom)
C/S – Caesarean section
CTG – Cardiotocograph (the machine used on the delivery suite to measure your contractions and baby's heart rate)
Cx – Cervix
ELSCS – Emergency lower segment Caesarean section
Eng – Engaged (your baby's head has descended into your pelvis)

EPU – Early pregnancy unit

FAU – Fetal assessment unit

FL – Femoral (thigh bone) length

FMF – Fetal movements felt

FHHR – Fetal heart heard regularly (sometimes seen as FHH)

GTT – Glucose tolerance test (for gestational diabetes)

G2 P1 – Gravida 2 (second pregnancy) Para 1 (one child living)

GA – General anaesthetic (one that knocks you out)

Hb – Haemoglobin (iron levels in blood)

HC – Head circumference (measurement of head all around)

IUGR – Intra uterine growth retardation (the baby is small for pregnancy dates)

IV –Intravenous (going into vein)

LA – Local anaesthetic (just numbs a specific area)

LOA – Left occiput anterior (the back of baby's head is to the front left side of your abdomen – a good position)

LOP – Left occiput posterior (the back of baby's head is to the back left side of your abdomen – not such a good position, as the baby has to turn)

Mec – Meconium (baby's first bowel movement)

having his legs spatchcocked like a chicken and tipped backwards to set off his "startle" reflex. But babies are tough.

The notes below are by no means exhaustive; ask the doctor if you want to know more. Checks include examination of:

● **Eyes** – the doctor shines a light into your baby's pupil to look for the "red reflex" – the thing that shines like a werewolf during flash photography. If it's not there, he may have been born with a cataract (opaque lens) which may lead to visual problems. It usually needs correcting with surgery (see Further Resources).

● **Mouth and palate** – around 1 in 800 children in the UK is born with a cleft lip or palate, where the face has not formed properly and there is a split anywhere between the roof of the mouth and the nose. The cleft can be of either the lip, the palate or both, and of varying severity. This condition received a lot of press attention in 2002, when it was revealed that a hospital in Herefordshire offered a late abortion on an affected fetus. Because while a newborn with a severe cleft looks alarming, and may have initial problems feeding or breathing, modern plastic surgery (at ten weeks for cleft lip, around eighteen months for cleft palate) has amazing results (see Further Resources).

- **Back and spine** – spina bifida is a condition where the neural tube fails to close during fetal development and a portion of the spinal cord and nerves fail to develop properly. These days, it's quite rare, due to the widespread encouragement to take folic acid in early pregnancy, and accurate antenatal scanning. If your baby is born with spina bifida, he will have surgery in the first couple of days, although there may still be some permanent disability (see Further Resources).

- **Heart** – many serious heart problems are also picked up in your antenatal scans, but it's still possible for congenital abnormalities to show up after birth. Around ten percent of babies are born with an "innocent" heart murmur which usually disappears within a week (see Further Resources).

- **Hips** – the paediatrician will flex your baby's hips outwards to check for a "click" which, if present, is probably just due to a newborn's unstable ligaments. However, in rare cases, it could suggest a congenital dislocation – where the hip socket has developed incorrectly, meaning the thighbone comes out of the socket. When your baby starts to walk, this will cause a severe limp due to difference in leg length, which in turn can lead to arthritic joint problems in later life. If the condition is mild, you'll be encouraged to dress your baby in double nappies to keep his hips flexed; if severe, he'll have to wear a Velcro harness or plaster cast for six months or so.

N/Eng – Not engaged (your baby's head has not descended into your pelvis)
NNU – Neonatal unit
NICU – Neonatal intensive care unit
NPU – Not passed urine
PIH – Pregnancy induced hypertension (high blood pressure)
PPH – Post partum haemorrhage (bleed after baby is born)
PU – Passed urine
PV – Via vagina
Primip – First pregnancy
Rh – Rhesus (type of blood group)
SCBU – Special care baby unit
SHO – Senior house officer (a junior doctor)
Tr – Transverse (baby is lying sideways in your uterus)
USS – ultrasound scan
VBAC – Vaginal birth after a Caesarean section
VE – Vaginal examination

- **Skin tone** – a yellow tinge often suggests jaundice. It's quite common for newborns to develop jaundice after two days, but worthy of attention if signs appear in less than 24 hours. The doctor will take a blood sample from your baby's heel to measure the level of bilirubin (a chemical formed during the breakdown of red blood cells). If this is high, he'll be given phototherapy – blue light treatment – to help with the excretion of bilirubin, which if ignored, can very rarely cause brain damage.

- **Your baby's nappy** – first passing of urine shows that the kidneys are working okay. A baby's early bowel motions are a scary greeny-black with the texture of tar. To add to the "creature from the black lagoon" effect this is called meconium. You can still be discharged if your baby has not performed, but may be asked to contact the hospital within 24 hours if he still hasn't filled a nappy to check all is working properly.

Your baby's reflexes

All babies are born with amazing, innate reflexes that they "unlearn" as they get used to life outside of the womb. A paediatrician will check all these before you are discharged from hospital.

- **The sucking and rooting reflex** – your baby has been sucking her thumb in the womb, and maintains this automatic response so she can feed on her exit. If you touch her cheek with your finger or breast, she will automatically turn her head towards it in search of food – the urgency to swallow is also inbuilt. If you're breastfeeding, you'll be alarmed at how much strength is in those little jaws.

- **The Moro reflex (startle)** – at any sudden noise, movement or bright camera flash, your baby will throw open his arms and legs and stare in terror. While this looks funny, it's actually an important primitive response to imminent danger.

The Moro reflex

DO ALL BABIES LOOK LIKE THEIR FATHERS?

This is the stuff of urban myth: that to avoid being abandoned by their father, a baby is born with the inbuilt cleverness to look like him. However, geneticists tell a different story: that really small babies resemble each other rather than a specific parent. Several studies have tried to get people to match pictures of infants and their parents, and failed.

(*Robin Dunbar, Professor of Evolutionary Research at Liverpool University*)

- **The grasp reflex** – touch a newborn's palm, and he'll grip on for dear life. Again, this is for survival/security and by four months he'll be able to hold onto things deliberately.

- **The plantar and palmar reflexes** – apply gentle pressure on your baby's toes and they will turn inwards; do the same on the palm of her hand, and her fingers will curl in too.

- **The walking reflex** – hold your newborn upright, with her feet touching the floor, and she will actually "walk" a few steps. This fades completely within a few weeks. And if you stroke the sole of her foot, her big toe will bend backwards while the others spread open. This is called **Babinski's reflex**.

- **The diving reflex** – (aka the Nirvana baby reflex). Remember that underwater infant on the cover of *Nevermind*? Well, babies really can hold their breaths underwater – an instinct makes him close his throat on contact with water. Probably not to be tried at home, though.

The baby with problems

Most babies make their journey from the womb into the world with remarkable ease. However, in a small number of cases, a newborn will need specialist intensive care in a **Special Care Baby Unit** (SCBU) or **Neonatal Intensive Care Unit** (NNU), which may require transfer to another hospital. Such cases include:

- **Prematurity** – babies born before 36 weeks need help because their organs are still maturing, notably their lungs, liver, immune and nervous systems. The earlier the birth, the more intensive the care required.

- **Low weight babies** – those weighing less than 5lb 8oz will need special monitoring.

- **Problems with circulation or breathing** – most of these worries are sorted soon after birth, but your baby may still require the additional help of a respirator, or some intravenous fluids.

- **Birth injuries** – there may be injuries to the neck or shoulders if the baby was large and had a struggle getting out.

For the new parent, already filled with anxiety about their new baby, SCBU can be a frightening place, full of high-tech machines, incubators and alarms. However, with round-the-clock intensive care, a fantastically experienced staff and a wish for you to be intimately involved (washing, feeding and cuddling your newborn) your baby couldn't start his life in better hands (see Further Resources).

The mother with problems

Birth is a very traumatic experience and the most likely emotion you will feel is relief. You are NOT in the least bit abnormal if you don't feel a huge

Having a baby is harrowing enough if you're supported by a loving partner (although, if loving partner isn't coping very well, it might make the whole experience even more stressful). But what about those women who find themselves doing the whole thing on their own? It could be that you went into labour unexpectedly, when your partner was at work. Or, that you don't have a husband or boyfriend at all, but are facing life as a single parent. Many lone parents-to-be have the loving support of a mother, sister or close friend who they invite to be a birth partner, but by no means all. Should you find yourself alone on the maternity ward do make sure the midwives are aware of the fact, so they can make an extra effort to give you attention and advice.

If you are starting life as a single parent, there are several organizations such as **Gingerbread** (see p.253) which can offer help and advice, even in the very early days.

rush of love towards your newborn. "Bonding" can take hours, days or weeks – although there are always the mothers who claim they knew their child intimately before he was born. There aren't many of these. Some honest women will admit not feeling true love for their baby up to six months and beyond – after all, it is quite a one-sided relationship before the heart-melting smiles and gurgles start to happen.

If it makes you feel any better, your child will be feeling quite unconcerned about his/her relationship with you (as long as there are food and cuddles on tap). It can take up to a week before he or she even recognizes who you are. Relax, muddle through, and wait until your inevitable, lifelong infatuation with your baby kicks in.

Before you go home

After you've seen the paediatrician, the midwife will present you with a form detailing the baby's sex, date and time of birth. You'll need to pass

SEVEN THINGS YOU WILL NEED BEFORE LEAVING HOSPITAL

It's easy to get into a tizz about the sheer amount of gear required, but most of it can wait. Below is a list of the basic necessities:

- A car seat
- Nappies (plus wipes or cotton wool, whatever you decide to use to clean baby's bottom), plus padded changing mat
- Somewhere for your baby to sleep (moses basket, carrycot or cot), plus blankets – make sure you have a new mattress if you are using a hand-me-down because second-hand ones apparently increase the risk of cot death
- Something for your baby to wear. Cotton layers are the best: newborn vests and babygros with feet, plus a couple of little hats and "scratch mitts" if the baby has attacked herself with preternaturally sharp nails
- Bottles, formula and sterilizing equipment, if bottlefeeding. There are plenty of flash sterilizers on the market but a pan and boiling water will do the job
- Some way to carry your baby about – many newborns prefer being close to your body, in a "sling"
- For breastfeeding mothers: two or three professionally fitted maternity bras

these to your GP, the community midwife who'll visit you at home, and also to the official when you register the birth (see Chapter 2). You'll probably get a whole other load of bumf, including leaflets on postnatal exercise and baby massage, plus an exciting box of baby products called the "Bounty Pack". Finally, you're given the green light. Yes, you can actually leave. The first job is to strap your baby into the car seat – a remarkably sturdy piece of plastic engineering which you'll only be able

Baby car seat

FIVE THINGS YOU WON'T NEED (YET, OR POSSIBLY EVER)

- A Bugaboo Frog pram or other three-wheeler all-terrain buggy. Many new babies feel overwhelmed in a large vehicle for the first weeks (see below). You'll need a pushchair eventually, but as long as the baby can lay flat, it doesn't need to be state-of-the-art.
- Baby bath. Supported correctly, your newborn will be happy in the washbasin or big bath.
- "Outdoor" clothes à la this season Baby Gap. Excited parents and friends should take care of this for you, at least initially.
- A special nappy bin. If you're that squeamish, nappies can be put in special scented bags before being put out with the rest of the rubbish.
- A special bag with pouches, pockets and zips. Just use an old one of your own: it will only get puked in.

Two things you'll never need again

- An alarm clock
- Dry-clean-only clothes

to carry for five minutes before your arm feels like it's going to fall off even with a baby the weight of a packet of crisps inside. There's more information on baby gear in Chapter 10 but the car seat is initially the most important piece of equipment and you will not be allowed to leave hospital without one. The last thing you need at the moment is scare stories, but the RAC calculates that as many as seven out of ten child car seats are fitted incorrectly, so it's a good idea to make sure you've worked out how to use yours in advance.

Suddenly, the stuffy institution you've been itching to escape turns into a warm, inviting haven. YOU ARE ON YOUR OWN NOW!

Coping at home

How did you cope when your first love dumped you? Or on the first day of that terrifying new job? The answer is – you won't know until you get there, but you'll survive, and it will get easier. Yes, there's a new bundle of responsibility, all this complicated kit to work out, and you can't even sit

THE MIDWIFE

"Last Friday, I spent the evening in the most magical way possible. A woman came in to the hospital, well into established labour. It was her second baby, and her first birth had been long and painful. She was terrified. Still, she hoped to use the birthing pool, and as there was no one else around, I stayed to help, even though I'm head of department.

We quickly developed a bond, and even though she was very anxious, the lady conquered her fear and, most importantly, felt in control. She had no medical intervention and gave birth in the water, just as she'd dreamed of doing. Her husband was in tears, overwhelmed with happiness.

After almost thirty years of midwifery, every birth is extraordinary to me, and I am always honoured to be present. It never ceases to amaze me what a labouring mother can achieve. The physical effort and energy it takes to give birth knocks me for six every time. Whether she's had a Caesarean or a drug-free natural labour, every new mother should walk away feeling like a hero."

Midwife's tips:

- Remember that your baby hasn't read the childcare books. New mums are so worried about getting it right, but in fact there are very few wrong ways of doing it, and lots of right ones. Newborns don't know how or when they are supposed to poo or wee, or that they're meant to eat every three hours, so relax and go with your baby's instinct.
- Take every day at a time, and enjoy your baby. It's a cliché that children grow up so fast, but it's true, so try and make the most of this special time. Babies are pretty good at avoiding drowning or starving, so beyond that, there's nothing serious to worry about.

Maggie Thomson, consultant midwife

down comfortably, let alone take your baby for a walk, but the best thing you can do is surround yourself with people who support you and make you feel happy. Most people look back on the first postpartum days and remember that confusing haze with great affection.

Birth stories

The assisted delivery

"When my daughter was born, my only real feeling was one of relief. I didn't feel like I was her mother, all I wanted to do was go to sleep. Of course I fell madly in love with her eventually, but I'd be lying if I said it was instantaneous.

I went into labour exactly on my due date. At 7pm, I had a show, but no pain. So I went to bed, determined to cram in some sleep, but I was too nervous and excited to drop off. By 11pm, I started experiencing severe period-type pains, but was convinced it was false labour – I didn't want to bother the midwives unnecessarily. My husband, Gavin, on the other hand, was in a complete flap and convinced himself that I was in the third stage of labour. I had to remind him that this was the bit where the placenta was expelled – so where exactly was the baby?

The drive to hospital was the longest in my life with me howling on the back seat as we raced over every speed bump in town. I was still convinced I was in false labour, but the midwife who finally examined me told me I was 9cm dilated. Sadly, she also told me I was too far gone for an epidural and the bleary-eyed anaesthetist who'd been summoned at my request was sent back to bed. Gavin insisted that I be given some gas and air, but the midwife promptly dropped the canister on her foot and had to be sent to casualty.

The relief midwife had the job of getting my baby out, but the baby just didn't want to come. I was told to push but didn't really know how, and an hour of fruitless, exhausting, useless effort followed. By then, my volatile blood pressure was soaring. An epidural can lower bp in this situation, and the anaesthetist was woken up again. It took him three attempts to get in the needle, but because of the pain, I didn't even feel it.

My baby wasn't coming out, my bp was going up, so the midwife started to talk about intervention. When the heartbeat dropped, a young doctor appeared with a ventouse. I thought I'd just be able to lie there, but I still had to push and was given an episiotomy, which I didn't feel because of the epidural. Sienna was finally born at 7.40am. After a quick cuddle with me, I had to be stitched, so I handed her to Gavin and she promptly pooed all over him.

We saw the doctors the next night; Sienna was discharged, but I had to stay in because of my blood pressure. For the first two days I was on the noisy ward without a wink of sleep, but my baby slept beautifully. Finally, I managed to get a private room, and that's when Sienna decided to wake up."

Anna, 32

The elective Caesarean

"I knew exactly how I was going to give birth from around thirteen weeks into my pregnancy: that's when my complete placenta praevia was diagnosed. With the placenta sitting as neatly above the opening to the womb as a saucer balanced on an egg cup, the midwife sympathetically broke the news that I would almost certainly need a Caesarean section. The truth is, I was rather thrilled. I'd never much fancied the idea of birth and pain.

At 37 and a half weeks the day came for my section. It was a long, hungry wait which amplified my nervousness so I asked the doctors to tell me jokes to distract me. The room, though, of course clinical, was not really more so than the normal delivery rooms, and though there were a fair few staff – anaesthetist and assistant, midwives, consultant and assistant and a nurse or two – it didn't feel crowded. The anaesthetist gave me a spinal block, no more than a sting, and then a coldness began to flood my body. Within ten minutes I was sensation-free from my toes to my chest. I suffer slightly from claustrophobia and really dislike the feeling of being unable to move, so I concentrated on pretending I was just doing the relaxation part of a yoga class which did help a great deal.

My husband, Chris, held my hand as they erected a green cloth screen at chest height and my (female) obstetrician, after checking I couldn't feel anything, began the operation. It was staggeringly quick. After just five minutes or so, my beautiful, if rather furious, 8lb 8oz son, Henry, was lifted into the air for me to see. His indignant yells left me in no doubt that he had fully functioning lungs and was extremely cross at being disturbed.

The stitching up afterwards probably took less than half an hour, but to be honest, I couldn't feel a thing, not even the sensation of my baby being lifted out, and time was standing still as I got to know my son. I know I was soon in the recovering room, breastfeeding and with the sensation back in my whole body. It was a fantastic, serene experience. I had no pain, no single second of feeling out of control, and was completely ready to meet my baby."

Leah, 38

After the birth

The emergency Caesarean

"When my waters broke on Christmas Eve without even a sniff of a contraction 24 hours later, my husband Robin and I found ourselves bound for hospital on Christmas morning for an induction. I was hoping for an intervention-free birth, but it now seemed unlikely.

I began the day being hooked up to a syntocinon drip to induce my contractions while listening to the sounds of women's wails from the surrounding delivery rooms. Once things got under way, my labour became a textbook case of *Fawlty Towers* – ineptitude, lack of continuity care, with a never-ending change of midwives, all keen to get off home and start their Christmas; an epidural that only worked down one side of my body. Worst of all, was treatment by a youthful, inexperienced intern who was called to take a fetal blood sample – a particularly uncomfortable procedure where an instrument is inserted (rather like a crochet hook) to get a blood sample from the baby to see if she's breathing enough oxygen during labour. This took eight attempts until the registrar took over with more success.

The results were not good and indicated the baby was in distress, so it was decided for me that the best option would be an emergeny Caesarean. At 9.25, however, my beautiful girl was born – unconventionally, but safe, and my marathon endurance test was over. But not before the surgeon delivered the final insult to my catalogue of inquring after the operation: moaning that she was missing *Only Fools and Horses*."

Shauna, 37

The induction

"At 8.30am on Monday, October 11, twelve days after my due date, I found myself lying spread-eagled in the Day Assessment Unit with a tutting midwife explaining that I was no nearer to giving birth now than I was nine months earlier. With no dilation and no contractions, it looked like we were in for the long haul. The midwife inserted the prostin gel pessary and we prepared ourselves for the inevitable wait.

Fortunately, they let us out for a stroll and we found a footpath meandering away from the hospital. As we headed back up the track my first pain came. By the time we arrived back at the ward at midday I was uncomfortable and my husband ran me a bath. 'Are these proper contractions?' he asked. 'How should I know, I've never had them before,' was all I could reply.

Soon I was attempting to walk downstairs to the delivery suite – not an easy task when your cervix is trying to stretch to fit a baby's head. Before long I was lying flat on my back, strapped up to heart monitors and in some serious pain while my husband was still trying to work out how to use the TENS machine. I was working out how to punch him. Ten minutes later and the doctor delights in informing us that I have progressed to a very exciting 1cm. This seemed a very long way from 10cm. I was told to lie on my left side for the monitoring and to try gas and air.

All at once the contractions came thick and fast. All I could do was squeeze my husband Enzo's hand very hard. Not hard enough … I was gasping for an epidural and feeling pathetic.

A few minutes later the doctor returns to say the baby's heart trace isn't good and they may need to do an emergency C-section. I manage to yelp that I feel pressure which I vaguely remember could be significant.

It was. After 25 minutes of holding my breath and using stomach muscles I'd never previously discovered, I managed to push out my 8lb 10oz bruiser of a baby boy. His Dad cut the cord and my son was whisked off to be checked over before latching on for the first of many feeds. We were both sobbing and the team were in shock – less than an hour from 1cm to birth is a hospital record."

Rebecca, 27

The premature birth

"My eldest son Dylan was born on 21 September, six weeks before his due date. At 8am in the morning my waters broke, but I had no 'show', no contractions and hadn't even thought about packing the 'Bag'. My husband had just left for work near Waterloo (miles away), but luckily my sister was lodging with us at the time. She said it was like 'following a snail around the house'; we promptly called the hospital and were advised to come in straightaway.

When my husband arrived some hours later, there had been no further progress though I was prodded and poked a lot and there was talk of transferring me to another hospital as mine did not have a **Special Care Unit**. The decision in the end was to insert an IV drip with *oxytocin* (chemical induction) and this was carried out just before 4pm. They told my husband to go off and get something to eat as the procedure could take ages. Fortunately, he only went downstairs for a sandwich because within 20 minutes I had dilated to 8cm.

The midwife was astounded at my speedy reaction to the drug and I was carted off to the delivery suite where the 'SWAT' team were waiting. Dylan was born at 4.45 after an emergency *episiotomy* without anaesthetic – the very worst part of the birth. He was completely jaundiced and whisked off to an incubator where he spent the next two weeks.

It was incredibly strange to have delivered a baby and yet take nothing home with us. We visited every day and though I did try to express milk I became completely engorged and developed mastitis (see p.129). The pub lunches and the peaceful nights were a bonus, but sadly they didn't last long!"

Orla, 40

The home birth

"My pre-birth idea of giving birth was mainly informed by TV of the ER type, ie birth being some king of an emergency requiring a big cast and lots of medical assistance. With a child in breech position (head into the ribs) all the NHS advice was to go for a Caesarean in hospital. I felt this wasn't right for me, even more so as I learnt insurance policies had a lot to do with this medical verdict and that only a few brave, independent midwives were happy to support my wish for a home breech birth. (This is not a route for the faint-hearted but I trusted my own instincts.)

When the due date came, I pottered around the house with light contractions, relaxed and not at all scared. By lunchtime, however, the pressure in my pelvis was such that I could not sit in a chair, and I felt it was time to call in the midwives. I had a nice long bath after which the contractions were still regular. Midwife Brenda arrived in the afternoon, helping me find comfortable positions and coaxing me along, whilst my husband kept himself busy filling a birthing pool and cooking dinner. Midwife Jane arrived in the early evening straight from another birth. Contractions then became unbearable and I descended into the pool. Four hour later, I felt extremely exhausted and asked to be examined to find out how dilated I was. 8cm was the answer and that gave me the strength to carry on. Half an hour later, the urge to push became uncontrollable and I left the pool to kneel in front of a bed. Jonas was born within 45 minutes. Brenda only touched him to help the back of his head along. The whole birth happened in natural moonlight (in what was to become my son's bedroom), with Brenda using only a small torch to focus in on the proceedings and it was all wonderfully calm. Of course, the fetal heartbeat was regularly monitored by sonicaid, but so unobtrusively.

When catching up with the other mums from my antenatal class, I found I was the only one to have had a totally positive birth experience.

All the other hospital births had suffered unwanted interventions of various kinds."

Andrea, 37

THE TWENTY MOST POPULAR NAMES IN ENGLAND AND WALES 2004			
	Girls		**Boys**
1.	Emily	1.	Jack
2.	Ellie	2.	Joshua
3.	Jessica	3.	Thomas
4.	Sophie	4.	James
5.	Chloe	5.	Daniel
6.	Lucy	6.	Samuel
7.	Olivia	7.	Oliver
8.	Charlotte	8.	William
9.	Katie	9.	Benjamin
10.	Megan	10.	Joseph

AND THE TOP TWENTY FROM 1974			
	Girls		**Boys**
1.	Sarah	1.	Paul
2.	Claire	2.	Mark
3.	Nicola	3.	David
4.	Emma	4.	Andrew
5.	Lisa	5.	Richard
6.	Joanne	6.	Christopher
7.	Michelle	7.	James
8.	Helen	8.	Simon
9.	Samantha	9.	Michael
10.	Karen	10.	Matthew

Further resources

Books

The Best Friend's Guide to Surviving the First Year of Motherhood by Vicki Iovine (Bloomsbury, £9.99). An entertaining and occasionally laugh-out-loud read where Iovine and her friends give anecdotes about new parenthood. There aren't enough facts for it to be a useful reference book, and it's also very American, set in a world where all babies have their own paediatrician and new "moms" tend to have a private room.

Birth and Beyond by Yehudi Gordon (Vermilion, £17.99). This whopping encyclopaedia by obstetrician-to-the-stars Gordon covers everything from conception and birth to baby development and diet and exercise for the mother. There's also an excellent in-depth 160-page A–Z medical guide. Unusually for a consultant, Gordon is a fan of "holistic healthcare" with emphasis on complementary as well as conventional approaches.

The Contented Little Baby Book by Gina Ford (Vermilion, £9.99). Gina Ford is like marmite. Some women adore her; some women feel queasy at the very mention of her name. But this book has such a cult following, that, mention Gina in a group of new mothers, and everyone knows immediately who and what you are talking about. Her *pièce de résistance* is in the prescriptive daily routines from day one, with the aim of getting a baby to sleep through the nights by six weeks. (See p.69 for more information about babies and routines.)

Secrets of the Baby Whisperer: How to Calm, Connect and Communicate with your Child by Tracy Hogg (Vermilion £10.99). A kind of Gina Ford-lite. Tracy's is more a routine with a soul, based on the acronym EASY (Eating, Activity, Sleeping, You), although some new mothers still find the routines hard to put into practice. There are lots of interesting and insightful sections, such as the "know-your-baby" quiz, and the chapter covering baby body language.

What To Expect, The First Year by Heidi Murkoff, Arlene Eisenberg and Sandee Hathaway (Simon and Schuster £12.99). A comprehensive journey through the first year, organized in monthly instalments (what to expect the first month, second month etc …). Very straight, and, though it's been edited for a UK audience, still rather American in tone. But if there's any other book to have in your baby library, it's this one, for its excellent practical advice.

Your Baby and Child by Penelope Leach (Dorling Kindersley, £18.99). Penelope Leach is one of the world's leading experts in child development. She is also the nemesis of authors like Gina Ford, having spoken openly about her disapproval of *Contented Baby Book*-style routines. Instead, she prefers a more "child-centred" approach. Calm, confident and very thorough.

Your Premature Baby and Child by Amy E. Tracy and Dianne I. Maroney (Berkley, £8.70). An invaluable resource for the parents of premature babies, offering a guide through the complex medical issues, as well as advice and support from parents who have been there.

Websites

www.babycaredirect.com One of the better UK sites specializing in nursery goods, with an extensive range of stock and some good discounts.

www.babycentre.co.uk Excellent website, which covers all areas of parenting, from conception to baby names and toddler tantrums. There are also a vast number of on-line communities, some of which are specific to your baby's birth-month, so you can make "friends" with whom to share concerns for years. Also, the American version, **www.babycenter.com** – much of the content is shared.

www.babynamer.com With 23,000 names on offer, you should find something here. Site offers themed "lists of the day", for example, "British and American female poets".

www.babyworld.co.uk Similar in feel to babycentre, though possibly less comprehensive, and with more of an emphasis on shopping. The health section is highly recommended.

www.homebirth.org.uk Of the greatest use before birth, but still a helpful resource for those who've chosen to have their babies at home.

www.midwivesonline.com With separate sections for both midwives and new parents: a useful resource where health professionals answer a series of frequently asked questions on topics including breastfeeding and new fathers.

www.nctpregnancyandbabycare.com This is the National Childbirth Trust's official website. As well as a wide-ranging (though sketchily detailed) look at baby development, it's a good place to find out about postnatal groups, breastfeeding counsellors and information on the NCT's own books on birth and babies. See p.103 for more on the NCT.

www.salon.com/mwt (mothers who think) A funny, informative and well-written section of the larger salon website, a perfect antidote to the sites and books that talk down to new mothers.

For the baby with problems

The department of child health at Great Ormond Street produce fantastic factsheets for a childhood of common infant illnesses. Visit www.ich.ucl.ac.uk

Other useful resources

BLISS (Baby Life Support Systems) User-friendly site for the parents of sick and premature babies, with message boards, local branches and suggested publications. Tel: 0207 831 9393

Cleft lip and palate: CLAPA (cleft lip and palate association); www.clapa .com Advice, support and social groups for both parents and children. Tel: 0207 833 4883

Congenital heart defects: Children's heart federation; www.childrens-heart-fed.org.uk Informs parents about latest research and childrens' heart units, with the useful "terms parents have asked to be explained". Tel: 0808 808 5000

Foot or hip problems: STEPS; www.steps-charity.org.uk Cutely designed website with helpline, shops, annual events. Tel: 0871 717 0042

Spina bifida: ASBAH (association of spina bifida and hydrocephalus); www.asbah.org Covers research, information and publications, with links to local support groups. Tel: 01733 555998

Tommy's; www.tommys.org A charity supporting parents who have suffered stillbirth or prematurity – the website seems mainly geared around fundraising, but still has important research and information sections. Tel: 08707 707 070

2

The first six weeks

2

The first six weeks*

What you really need after the birth of your baby is a fortnight on the French Riviera. Or at least, one of those lazy weekends where you get up at 11am and lie around watching daytime television. Dream on – those days are over. Although even dreaming might be impossible if you have a baby that stays awake all night. The realization that you won't have any proper recovery time is perhaps the first indication that things won't be "getting back to normal" in a hurry. There's no point in worrying about it now. Welcome to the "new normal", which has its own soft, pink, sweet-smelling consolations. Of course, it's unlikely you've had any time to analyse things yet – more likely you'll be fretting about how to put the sheet on the moses basket, or how to push those stiff little limbs through a newborn vest.

The baby is still quite a passive player, nuzzling away in sweet oblivion on your chest. This is just as well: you're still trying to work out which end eats and which end poos, and it all feels just a bit surreal. But here's a promise – read this chapter again at the end of the

(People often talk about the initial postpartum period as six weeks, but as you'll see, babies – and new parents – don't always stick to prescribed time limits.)

first couple of months, and you'll be changing nappies in the dark, as well as loading the washing machine while feeding the baby and talking on the phone at the same time.

Most new mothers often find themselves going over and over their labour in their heads, either to work out how they managed to get here (small baby; sore private parts), or to convince themselves it really happened. They also frequently suffer from an insatiable desire to tell everyone from their best friend to the window cleaner their birth story. They won't want to hear it, but you'll tell them anyway. The phone hasn't stopped ringing. The flowers haven't stopped arriving. The camera hasn't stopped flashing. And there you are, in a bit of a daze, wondering when you'll wake up and realize it's all been a dream.

Visitors

One thing you can bank on for the first few days is that there will be plenty of people around. Your partner, if you have one, will probably be on paternity leave – it's now a government requirement that, if he satisfies certain conditions, employers give two weeks off with a minimum statutory payment (see box below). If you have family, you'll need to stand there waving a very long stick to

PATERNITY LEAVE

To summarize broadly, the fathers of any babies born after 6 April 2003 are eligible for paternity leave, as long as they have worked for their company for six months ending with the fifteenth week before the baby is due. Fathers may take one or two weeks off within 56 days after the baby is born, and are entitled to £106 a week or 90 percent of their average weekly earnings if this is less than £100. If your partner has a generous company, they may pay him over and above this statutory minimum – he needs to check his employment contract. **Where mothers choose go back to work, men will be entitled to three months' paternity leave, receiving £106 a week. The government is looking to increase this to six months by the end of this parliament.**

keep them away. And even if you are on your own, there will be a community midwife checking up on you and the baby for the first ten days or so.

This busyness is a mixed blessing. On the one hand, this is a happy time and you want to share the excitement with everyone; not without good reason is it sometimes called "the babymoon". But not all women feel up to playing the domestic goddess so soon after giving birth – it's astonishing how many visitors (especially those without children) turn up still expecting a cup of tea and something to eat.

The early whirlwind can also make the loneliness seem worse later, when your partner goes back to work and you're alone in an empty house with a baby to look after. One suggestion is to limit visitors to one "group" a day. Of course, there are women who return to work themselves within weeks of the birth, but it's likely you'll still have some time spent on your own at home.

If you don't feel like entertaining, it's a good idea to record a message on your answerphone saying you'll call people back later. If anyone asks whether they can bring you lunch, take them up on it and ask them to bring dinner as well. And if someone comes in expecting a cup of tea, tell them to make their own.

Midwife and health visitor visits

In the UK, midwives have responsibility for mothers and their new babies for up to 28 days following birth, though in reality they'll look after you until the tenth day postpartum, when you'll be handed over to a health visitor. You will always see a midwife on your first day home, and on day seven for the baby's **Guthrie test** (see below) but other than that, visits are flexible and negotiated depending on how much you or the baby needs extra help, and how busy the midwife is. In some areas, the midwife is unable to confirm an exact time with you, so you may find yourself rather irritatingly confined to the house all day, waiting for her to arrive.

The midwife will continue to check you over physically (see Chapter 1), weigh your baby to make sure she's thriving, and talk to you about contraception (once you've picked yourself off the floor laughing). She will also perform the Guthrie test – or heel prick – where a sample of blood is taken from your baby's heel, and tested for a number of conditions, including:

DON'T FORGET TO REGISTER YOUR BABY'S BIRTH

You have 42 days to do this, and it must be in the borough where your baby was born. The hospital should tell you where to go; or you can visit the website below.

Either parent can register the birth if you are married. If you are not, but would like the father's details on the birth certificate, you'll have to visit the register office together, or obtain a special "statutory declaration".

To provide you with a birth certificate, the registrar needs the baby's name, sex, date and place of birth (plus the time if you have twins), and your details. The registrar will check this information carefully with you – it can be tricky to amend birth certificates later.

You can receive two birth certificates, the free "short" version, which you'll need for child benefit, and a longer, more elaborate version, including your details, which currently costs £3.50. You'll need this for your baby's passport application.

If you have unusual circumstances, most queries are answered on the website www.gro.gov.uk; the website deals with England and Wales but offers links to Scottish and Northern Irish resources.

- **Phenylketonuria (PKU)** – a very rare disease where babies are unable to digest protein, for example milk, meat, fish, cheese and eggs. If it's detected, your baby will be put on a special diet.

- **Congenital hypothyroidism** – lack of the growth hormone thyroxin, which can be supplemented.

Some authorities also test for:

- **Cystic fibrosis** – which affects breathing and digestion.

- **MCAD** (Medium Chain acyl CoA Dehydrogenase) – a condition in which fat metabolism is impaired.

- **Sickle cell disease** – a type of anaemia.

You'll only be contacted in the unlikely event of a positive result.

After around two weeks, a health visitor will visit you at home with the baby's "red book" which contains all records of her birth details, immunizations, plus some interesting developmental information. You may not see your health visitor for a while after that, but she should be available at the local baby clinic, a regular "surgery" which you are encouraged to attend to weigh your baby.

This may well be the last formal contact you have until your "six-week check" where your GP will repeat some of the paediatric examinations, and examine you to make sure you're recovering well from the birth.

How you'll be feeling: physically

There are a very few women – most, it has to be said, on their second or third babies – who can pop one out, come home for a nap, and be shopping at Tesco the next morning. We don't want to hear about these abnormal creatures. Here's a more realistic rundown of the collateral damage:

From a vaginal birth

Who knew what their perineum was, and where, before they went through labour? Well, you certainly know about it now. At best you'll be bruised, stretched and a bit numb; at worst you'll have a nasty set of stitches to negotiate. Even walking to the end of the street can be a slow, laborious expedition.

Rescue plan:

● Take frequent baths, around two a day. The warm water is a blessed relief, and five to ten drops of tea-tree oil – a natural antiseptic available from health shops – can also help.

● Apply some soothing cream. Tea tree and witch-hazel do make things feel better, and you can buy ready-made mixtures in a tube.

● Lean forward when you wee, so that you don't splash any urine onto the stitches.

● Reduce the pressure by lying on your side instead of sitting, or borrowing one of those rubber rings – aka **valley cushions** – that you can buy to relieve haemorrhoids. This is all only temporary, we promise.

- Try some Arnica tablets (see box on homeopathic useful remedies p.57) which are said to reduce swelling.

Constipation

If those maternal hormones didn't get you before you gave birth, you're likely to suffer in this department now. Your bowel may have been "traumatized" by delivery, and therefore unwilling to play ball. Or you'll be so petrified that your delicate stitches will burst that you can't relax enough to perform. They won't, but it can be hard to take this on trust. Three days or more may pass (sorry) before you get back into regular service.

Rescue plan:

- Drink lots of water and fruit juice to keep hydrated, and to replenish fluids lost in labour. Also, try and eat plenty of roughage: bran cereal, dried fruit, nuts etc … Interestingly, chocolate, probably a mainstay of your diet at the moment, can make matters worse.

- Try and get some exercise: even if it's only going up and down the stairs, or do some pelvic floor exercises (see p.215) It may be hard to get out and about if your wound/stitches are particularly nasty.

- If several days have gone by, and you still have no results, you may want to see your GP for a laxative to help you out.

Haemorrhoids

It just keeps on getting better and better, doesn't it? Otherwise known as **piles**, and caused by dilated veins, haemorrhoids are small swellings resembling bunches of grapes which protrude out of your anal passage. If you managed to avoid these in pregnancy, you may find that the stress of pushing, plus constipation after birth, makes them worse.

Rescue plan:

- Try and keep constipation to a minimum (see above).

- When on the toilet, try to avoid straining, and hold a spare maternity pad/wad of loo paper against your perineum to relieve the pressure.

- Pelvic floor exercises can also help.

- If things get really bad, visit your GP who may prescribe some ointment.

Lochia and afterpains

Whatever kind of birth you've had, you'll be experiencing lochia, the flow of blood which will continue like a heavy period for around ten days or so. As time goes on, it will lessen, become brownish and finally, yellowish white. You may find yourself wearing a maternity pad (or even two at once, if necessary – it can be useful at night) for up to six weeks. Usually within a couple of weeks you can swap this for a more discreet "regular" sanitary towel. If your bleeding suddenly gets much heavier, or you start passing large clots, see your doctor – it could be a sign of infection.

At the end of this time, your uterus will have pretty much gone back to its pre-pregnancy size and weight (from 1.2kg to just 50g). For most first-time mothers, this will pass pretty much unnoticed. Second-timers plus may be alarmed to experience afterpains for the first few days – painful contractions that can be almost as bad as those leading up to birth. These are caused by slacker uterine muscles, and are worse during breastfeeding, as the contraction-stimulating hormone **oxytocin** is released.

Rescue plan:

- Keep dosed-up on paracetamol, which is okay even if you're breastfeeding.

- Treat your afterpains as you would a heavy period (remember those?) with warm baths and hot-water bottles. And remember that they will soon subside. With every pain, your womb is getting smaller, and your stomach is getting flatter. In theory.

Pushing injuries

We mentioned the Audley Harrison effect earlier in Chapter 1: it's probably more accurate to cross the strength of a heavyweight boxer with the endurance of Paula Radcliffe when describing the physical effects of pushing a baby out. Other injuries range from aching in the chest and shoulders due to strained muscles, to popped blood vessels in the eyes and broken capillaries in the face. It's not the most attractive moment in your life.

Rescue plan:

- Frozen peas on the eyes; hot baths and massage to the rest of the body.

Your tummy, weight, stretchmarks etc ...

Like many a new mother before you, you probably rushed home hoping to get into your regular jeans now that the baby is out. Sadly, however, despite losing around a stone's worth of baby, placenta and other assorted fluids overnight, you may find those jeans don't go above your knees and that you'll have to stick with your maternity pair for a while longer. Don't despair. Catherine Zeta Jones, Posh Spice and Elizabeth Hurley are NOT NORMAL, unless you have a personal trainer, nutritionist and several 24-hour nannies stashed away upstairs.

Even if your bum and thighs escaped a big weight gain, there's no getting away from the wobble-zone that is your stomach (although, it's often the case that taller women have less damage on account of the baby having more room to grow upwards). This is especially upsetting, because at least when you were pregnant your tummy was taut and magnificent; now it looks like a deflated balloon. Any stretchmarks you gained will also be shouting at you now.

Most women lose around two-thirds of the weight they have gained within a month or so; that last third takes rather longer to shift. Sadly, that little shelf over your trousers may never quite take its leave.

Rescue plan:

- Unfortunately, there is no quick fix. If you are breastfeeding, dieting is out, although this shouldn't be carte blanche to gorge on the Celebrations. Some people find that breastfeeding hastens weight loss; other people find the opposite (see more details in Chapter 4).

- You can start gentle exercise now – for example, walking, if you can manage it, but again, proper work-outs are best left until you are given the "okay" after your six-week check, and beyond if you've had a Caesarean.

- Your stretchmarks may look livid now, and though they will never disappear entirely, they will fade to a pale silver. Vitamin E cream can help your skin remain hydrated. At the end of the day, they're your battle scars. Learn to love them. (For more on weight loss and body image see Chapter 7.)

Pelvic floor exercises

Probably from the minute you found you were pregnant, you'll have found all and sundry banging on at you to do your pelvic floor muscles (aka **Kegels**, or **PC**) exercises, ideally hundreds of them a day. You may not have really bothered – in your pre-pregnancy ignorance, words like stress, incontinence and haemorrhoids related to ladies in old people's homes. Well, no one is going to dare say "I told you so", but now is probably a good time to start, because pelvic floor exercises help with just about every area of recovery, from sorting the above inconveniences to getting you back in shape for sex again (sorry, someone had to mention it sooner or later).

In case you've been wilfully ignoring this information for the past nine months, here's a gentle reminder:

- Clench the muscles that you use to stop yourself weeing.

- Hold these in for as long as you can, up to eight or ten seconds, not forgetting to breathe as you do so.

- Slowly release – in a controlled fashion, don't just let them drop. You can think of it as your muscles being a "lift" going up several floors, stopping at the top and then descending again.

- Relax for a few seconds.

Repeat again. Experts suggest up to 25 repetitions, three or four times a day. See? Hundreds!

Some good news on the body front

Due to the swift fall in levels of progesterone following the birth of your baby, your smooth muscle tone will improve, resolving some of those pregnancy niggles. Heartburn should stop almost immediately, and varicose veins start to improve. You'll also stop having to go to the loo about eighteen times a night, although something called a baby will now be keeping you awake.

I don't think my partner and I have had a conversation since the birth over a month ago. What's going on?

Well hello! Welcome to new parenthood. There's something about babies which gives them a super-special radar that kicks into action every time you want to sit down to eat together, have a bath or dare to risk a conversation. At some point in the next few weeks, your baby will be able to amuse himself long enough for you to say something other than "has he done a poo?" But until then, he'll lie there, crying "meeee meeee meeee" just when you have the audacity to try and think about something else for a change.

Your breasts

For the first two or three days after delivery, it doesn't seem like much is going on in the breast department and they stay pretty much the same size as they were before you had the baby. But, as explained in the previous chapter, your breasts are doing a very important job producing the nutrition-packed **colostrum** for your baby. It's just that there isn't much of it (about half a teaspoon a feed) and you can't really see it coming out. This, as far as you're concerned, is merely the calm before the storm. Because around day three, your milk "comes in" and – oh yes – you'll know about it. Jordan and Pammie have nothing on you.

It'll probably start with a bit of a tingle, a growing sensation of warmth and then, what seems within minutes, they will swell to the size of footballs, as hard as granite and as veiny as marble. This is known in the trade as **engorgement** and is actually rather scary. Not only does this make it difficult to lie down, hold your baby or come within five feet of your partner, it also makes it damn hard to breastfeed because it flattens the nipples out – a cruel irony. Luckily, engorgement is only temporary, and should lessen within 48 hours or so. Even if you are not breastfeeding, you'll experience engorgement; however, if the milk ducts are not stimulated, the white stuff will be reabsorbed into your breast tissue, and they'll return to normal in several days.

If you are feeding the baby yourself, your breasts will soon get used to the miraculous supply-and-demand pattern that characterizes breastfeeding, although you need to watch out for any blocked ducts that could go on to cause **mastitis**, a nasty infection of the breast tissue which is characterized by soreness, a temperature and flu-like symptoms (see p.129).

Many breastfeeding mothers also suffer from sore nipples (see opposite) caused by a baby who is either over-enthusiastic, or not correctly positioned. This may sound a minor inconvenience, but can be really, really painful – and enough to put many women off. A recent report, showed that a third of mothers who started breastfeeding stopped in the first six weeks because of difficulty, and 93 percent of these would have liked to continue (*Office of National Statistics, 2000*).

Rescue plan:

● For engorged breasts feed your baby little and often: the pain may bring you to tears, but she's doing you a big favour.

- Apply an ice-pack (or those frozen peas) after feeding. And make sure your maternity bra is hitched up correctly to provide proper support. One old wives' tale suggests putting a leaf of chilled savoy cabbage in the bra – a matter for personal taste.

- Express a little milk (ie, remove it yourself, not by the baby sucking. This can be done either manually, or with a pump. See p.135.)

For cracked or sore nipples

- Make sure your baby is latched on correctly and encourage him to spend time on both breasts.

- If you're wearing breast pads, make sure that you change them often, as wet skin will stop any cracks from healing. Also make sure your maternity bra is made of cotton.

- While it's true that your nipples do produce natural oils to protect them, sometimes you need a bit of help with lubrication. You just need to take care what you put on them, as it will form part of baby's next meal. Vaseline is not recommended because it can keep the air away from the wound and so interfere with healing but other soothing products including **camomile** or **lanolin** are digestible and can really help. **Kamilosan** (for sore nipples) is available from Boots and health stores. Green Baby also produce a nipple gel (see p.13).
  For more on breasts and breastfeeding see Chapter 4.

What's the lowdown on dummies?

Some people have an almost snobbish aversion to dummies, and feel that they are "giving in" if they give their baby a comforting prop. As with everything, it's a matter of personal choice. Yes, a dummy can definitely

WHEN WILL MY BABY SMILE?

Most babies give their first "meant" smiles by six weeks of age. You may well see your baby show a happy expression in her first two weeks or, but it's actually a reflex action, which often happens during sleep. There's no need to worry if she takes a bit longer – that lovely heart-melting gummy grin is absolutely worth waiting for, and it will simply get bigger and brighter as time goes on.

calm an upset or sucky baby, help send him off to sleep, and give you and your breasts a break at the same time. It's too early for him to become "addicted" but it is a good idea to start weaning him off before three months, when a baby may object to the dummy being taken away. The main thing at this point is to make sure it's sterilized, so there's no risk of infection. An Italian study of 1100 pre-school children also showed that babies who have been given dummies to suck are twice as likely as breastfed children to grow up with badly-spaced teeth.

Things really do get better

"No one told me how long it actually takes to recover from labour or how weird your baby looks in the first few weeks. Or maybe they did and I had selective hearing. Either way I felt totally unprepared.

My labour was pretty quick and I got away with only a few stitches. I did lose copious amounts of blood at first but I still felt pretty fantastic. If only I'd known … the bleeding continued for eight weeks and I hated using pads instead of my usual tampons. I just felt permanently grubby. Then the

HOMEOPATHIC THERAPIES

A growing number of people in this country (half a million at the last count) are turning to complementary or alternative therapies (CAM) including **acupuncture**, **homeopathy** and **reflexology**. And it's certainly true that, in the postnatal period, many women report relief from the post-birth bashing by taking homeopathic remedies.

Homeopathy, from Greek *homeo* (meaning similar) and *pathos* (meaning suffering) was developed by a German doctor, **Samuel Hahnemann**, in the eighteenth century. It's a system of medicine based on treating "like with like", which means that a substance that can cause certain symptoms in a healthy person can cure similar symptoms in an unhealthy person – medicines come from a variety of plants, animal materials and minerals.

It's a controversial area, not least because many practitioners are unregulated, although there are homeopaths with orthodox medical qualifications. Even these, however, struggle to say exactly how homeopathy works – in fact its "placebo" effect is seen as one of its strengths. There is a school of thought that says if something makes you feel better, then it may well be worth a try as long as it's not doing any harm. Below is a list of homeopathic remedies tailored to the days following childbirth. Talk to a homeopath about dosage before you take them.

- **Arnica** – helps with post-birth soreness and bruising – can be taken in tablet form as the cream shouldn't be put on broken skin.
- A mixture of **calendula** and **hypericum** mixed with warm water (20 drops in a quarter of a pint of water) is said to make a soothing bath. Calendula ointment can also help heal cracked nipples.
- **Pulsatilla** tablets are said to help with baby blues.
- Taking **belladonna** can help with the early stages of mastitis.
- **Green Baby perineal gel** – available from health stores, see also www.greenbaby.co.uk
- **Lanes** tea-tree and witch-hazel cream (also to ease a tender perineum) is available from chemists and at www.laneshealth.com

There is disagreement in the medical profession about whether homeopathy is a good idea for babies – hardly any CAM treatments have been tested on children, making it hard to determine what is safe, and what is not. It's always best to check with your doctor first, who can refer you to a homeopath with a medical qualification.

HOMEOPATHIC THERAPIES (contd.)

Some new parents find that an unsettled baby is helped by **cranial osteopathy**, a form of gentle massage that is said to help with excessive crying, feeding and sleeping difficulties. It can also help treat the temporarily misshapen head that affects some babies after a traumatic birth. See Further Resources for additional information.

swelling underneath was like my personal hovercraft cushion. Sitting down was virtually impossible and washing made me positively queasy.

Fortunately, the midwife and health visitor were fantastic. They told me to have tea-tree oil baths, they introduced me to cool gel packs and **valley cushions** – wonderful devices that soothed me down there and allowed me to sit without wincing. They gave me permission to feel knackered for a few more months. They even cooed over my acne-ridden, hairless and flaky-skinned baby. It didn't matter to them that he weed everywhere each time they weighed him or that his skin looked three sizes too big for his body. They reassured me when he lost weight the first week and made appropriate admiring noises when he had piled it all back on and more a couple of weeks later.

Without them, life with a newborn and a post-birth body would have been a lot worse. Thanks to them, I would even consider going through those first few weeks again because they were right – I did get better and James did get better looking."

(Valley cushions can be hired from the NCT. Tel: 0870 444 8707, or check out the website **enquiries@national-childbirth-trust.co.uk**)

Jenny, 31

How you may be feeling emotionally

No one, least of all you, will be able to predict how you will feel in the first few weeks of your baby's life. There are so many factors to throw into the pot – the type of birth you had and the care you had in hospital, the health of your baby, the amount of sleep you are getting, any early problems you are having with feeding. It may also be hard to come to terms with the fact that, for nine months, you were the "special" person that everybody clucked around. Now you've had your baby, the focus has shifted to your offspring and you're in the background folding up the muslin squares, which can take some getting used to. Perhaps it's also hit you that this is a permanent change, the first ever in your life. You can resign from a job, sell a house, end a relationship, but you can't un-birth a baby.

Some women go through great extremes of emotion, detailed below. Some aren't prepared for anything other than unmitigated joy, and feel guilty about that. On the other hand, some feel nothing at all, and they feel guilty about that. Even at this early stage, it's amazing how much unnecessary guilt there is in this mothering business.

"The baby blues": What are they?

A sense of sadness and moodiness, not necessarily linked to a particular event. Or disproportionate anxiety (Will I drop the baby? Will the buggy roll into the street and get crushed by a passing car?) Sufferers may find it hard to sleep, even when the baby is giving them the opportunity.

Are these anxieties common?
Yes. Between 50 and 80 percent of women get a case of the blues.

What causes them?
A number of factors – some "lifestyle", some biological. Tiredness plays a huge role – it's impossible to overestimate the effect of exhaustion on every aspect of your life. So if you had a long labour stretching over several sleepless nights, a disturbed time in hospital and then a baby who won't settle at night, you are bound to feel down. Then there are the physical problems, detailed above. Add to this a baby who's perhaps having trouble feeding or gaining weight, and it's little wonder you are bewildered. In addition, you're experiencing wild hormonal changes as your levels of oestrogen and progesterone fall dramatically after birth, and **prolactin** kicks in, for milk production.

How do I know it's not postnatal depression?
Around ten percent of new mothers are diagnosed with **postnatal depression** (PND). There's no concrete line where the "baby blues" end and serious PND begins. Often it's defined by the length of suffering: the baby blues usually resolve spontaneously after three or four days. Postnatal

depression tends to be characterized by far more dramatic feelings: deep, crushing sadness, hopelessness, panic attacks and low self-esteem. You might be unable to care for your baby or even yourself, and even be plagued by suicidal thoughts.

If you have suffered from depression, or have a family history of the illness, then the postnatal variety may be more likely. See your GP. There's more on postnatal depression below.

How can I beat the blues?

It's your baby, you can cry if you want to. Seriously, getting your emotions out in the open can be a huge help. Surround yourself with people you know will be sympathetic – a friend who has been through it all before, your own mother, perhaps. Get as much rest as you can, but also haul yourself out of the house, see that life is going on as usual, and believe that you will be part of it again, however hard that seems at the moment. LEAVE THE WASHING UP.

"The baby pinks"

Although they're not as well documented – because it's generally a positive experience – many women suffer an almost manic surge after giving birth. For the first three days or so, despite being entirely knackered, they go through a "high", where they feel happy, excited, thrilled with the baby and themselves, and may experience difficulties sleeping. Just keep half an eye on the fact that this energy sadly can't last, and the realities of new motherhood and some tough challenges are waiting just around the corner.

Postnatal depression (PND): What is it?

PND is a depressive illness that follows the birth of a baby. The symptoms are very similar to "ordinary" depression: feeling tearful or sad for no particular reason, finding it hard to sleep even when the baby allows this, eating more or less than usual, being irritable with your partner or baby, and the general feeling of being unable to cope. Sufferers often feel very anxious about the baby, convinced something terrible is about to happen.

PND can take two forms. One type occurs when a patch of postnatal "blues" which started soon after the baby's birth becomes worse and more distressing as time passes. The second develops more slowly and is not noticeable until several weeks after the birth.

Is it common?

Yes. Statistics claim that, ten to fifteen percent of mothers suffer from PND, although the real number is thought to be much higher, as many women refuse help or are too afraid to admit a "weakness". It's not a weakness, it's an illness.

What causes it?

No one really knows, but it's probably a mixture of hormones and a genetic predisposition to depression. Circumstances can also come into play – if you've had a stressful pregnancy or birth or have a lack of support at home. The "usual" stresses of early motherhood – trouble breastfeeding, exhaustion – can be the last straw for a susceptible person. Last year the NCT spoke out about the risk factors for postnatal depression adding that the modern trend for short hospital stays can increase the risk. They also claimed that mothers who'd had IVF, multiple births, or whose own mothers died young, were more vulnerable. On the other hand, having a Caesarean or forceps delivery did not increase the risk.

Will my baby suffer?

Mothers who've had PND talk about wanting to throw their baby out of a window or down the stairs, but it's actually very rare for a woman to harm her baby – in fact, depressed mothers often take care of their baby as well, if not better, than other parents. Such extreme behaviour is more likely in a woman with postpartum psychosis (see p.62). But if you do feel any urge to hurt your baby, call the number below for help.

How can I beat it?

Do speak to a health visitor or GP. There are a number of ways you can get help – through support groups, therapy, antidepressants if need be (a group of antidepressants called SSRIs, including **Seroxat** or **Cipramil** have proven to be very effective). The most important thing is to realize that it's not your fault, you are not a bad mother, and that your baby is oblivious to the whole thing. Depression is a self-limiting illness and it always gets better. See Further Resources.

I was in tears the whole time

"For the first two weeks after Frankie was born, I was on a complete hormonal high. However, when this wore off, I felt oddly detached from him, like he was a stranger's baby. This wasn't helped by the difficulties I had breastfeeding him, and his constant colicky crying. As the weeks passed, I started to feel more and more desperate, like I couldn't cope. My husband worked long hours, and though he really wanted to help, it wasn't fair to keep him from his job. I remember going to my mum's for dinner one night, and Frankie wouldn't stop screaming – no matter what we tried. I ended up in tears myself, and woke up in tears the next morning. To be honest, I can't remember much about those first few weeks, apart from the fact that I was constantly crying. Thank goodness, it never crossed my mind to try and hurt the baby.

My husband and I are reasonably well-off, so we hired a maternity nurse to take some of the strain. But this didn't help me feel better, in fact, it made me feel worse: guilty and spoilt. Eventually, my husband and mum persuaded me to see a GP, who diagnosed postnatal depression. I was put on anti-depressants, and saw a private counsellor, who persuaded me that none of this was my fault and that I would recover. It was a slow process, but within six months, I could feel myself coming out of the shadows, and I was able to look at my little boy with love. When I think back now, it feels like a horrible nightmare that happened to someone else, but it still makes me nervous about having another baby."

Pearl, 34

Postpartum psychosis

Around one in a thousand women suffer a serious mental illness after giving birth. Symptoms are very extreme and may include insomnia, refusal to eat, excessive energy, agitation, hallucinations and bizarre behaviour such as suspicion that someone may be trying to steal your baby. At the extreme end of the spectrum, untreated postpartum psychosis can lead to suicide or infanticide. This illness is a medical emergency and requires hospital admission for intensive psychiatric treatment.

We realized he wouldn't disappear if we blinked

"The first night Rufus was home with us, we didn't have a clue about what to do with this squawking little stranger. It took us an hour to do his first bath – and I cried more during that than throughout my 23 hours of labour. Tony even went to bed wearing his glasses so that he was more ready to cope with any emergency – and I was hanging off the bed with my hand inside the Moses basket so I could feel his breath on my hand. Fortunately, we couldn't sustain such paranoia and slowly realized that Rufus was not going to disappear if we blinked. By week two we ventured out to the park with an overflowing rucksack and an over-dressed baby. By week three, we knew the best position to hold him to get the most satisfying burp. By week four,

I stopped ironing vests. By week five I could tell the difference between a hungry cry and a tired cry. By week six we believed he was here to stay."

Jane, 26

I was determined motherhood wouldn't change me

"Looking back, I placed ridiculous pressure on myself in the weeks following the birth of my daughter, Amanda. It all started during my pregnancy – I was determined that I wouldn't become one of *those* women, who 'let it all go'. I wasn't going to become 'a mother'.

Sure enough, I worked up to 38 weeks, and went into labour within three days of leaving the office. I was extremely fortunate in a fast, relatively straightforward birth that happened in the small hours, so I was back in my hospital bed by 9.30 am. The first thing I did? Whizz through my address book, including my work colleagues who were utterly dumbstruck. The next day I emailed them a photo – they couldn't believe I was back on-line within three hours of getting home.

It can only have been some sort of mania, fuelled by adrenaline and the excitement of actually having 'done it'. I set myself all sorts of ridiculous targets. Every morning, I had to be up, showered and dressed by 8.30. I invited my friends to come and coo at Amanda and made dinner for them. Bonkers!

And then, about a month after she was born, I came to my senses. It's not as if I 'crashed' and subsided into postnatal depression. But I realized I was missing the point a bit. Here was my gorgeous little girl: not just an achievement to rack up, but a marvellous little miracle. She was changing, turning into a person, and I was so busy 'not changing' that I wasn't even taking notice. So I relaxed. I left my emails unread, cancelled a dinner engagement, and increasingly found myself still in my dressing gown at midday, marvelling at the little dimples in her fingers.

Six months later I was back at my desk, on top form. But I'm so glad I woke up and realized the preciousness of those first days with Amanda before they had rushed away for ever."

Diana, 39

Caesarean "guilt"

In the past few years, there's been a lot of media chat about Caesareans, generally complaining about how the UK rates are too high and rising – around 21 percent now (2002 figures), compared with just 5.3 percent in 1973. To accompany this, an increasing number of healthcare professionals are voicing their concern. The most high-profile of these is probably **Dr Michel Odent**, the French obstetrician and natural childbirth pioneer, who recently published a thesis arguing that "industrialized obstetrics" is responsible for all manner of social ills from autism to teenage drug abuse. Then there are the newspaper rants against the celebrities who choose to deliver surgically because they don't fancy the inconvenience of a natural birth.

No wonder that many women who do end up with a C-section find their physical scars healing more quickly than their emotional ones. It's becoming common to find women who feel ashamed, resentful or guilty afterwards, as demonstrated by actress Kate Winslet, who told the world's press that her daughter was born "naturally" and only admitted to a C-section after her son's later vaginal birth because she "felt like a failure".

Of course, nearly all women who end up with a Caesarean do this for a very good reason: not because they are lazy, or "too posh to push", but either because they have a potentially life-threatening condition like *placenta praevia* (the placenta's covering the cervix) or because they or their baby is in distress.

The bottom line is that if a doctor tells you it's time to get the baby out quick, you are not going to argue. So lose the guilt if you can. Some people find that talking helps, and there are a number of support groups set up just for this purpose (see Further Resources). Others find that understanding the reason behind their section helps them to come to terms with it, so ask the medical professionals while you're in hospital, or call them up afterwards if necessary. Also, take comfort in the fact that, as time passes, your attention will move entirely from how your baby was delivered to the excitement of watching him thrive and grow.

I felt I didn't give birth properly

"I was all set for a natural birth but after several hours of labour not progressing and John's heartbeat dropping I had an emergency Caesarean. At the time I was just relieved the pain was about to be over and I would meet my son. On the ward I was pretty smug that I wasn't waddling to the toilet with a crotch full of stitches. I even felt grateful about how well my physical recovery was going in those first couple of weeks at home.

But when John was a month old, I met up with my antenatal class friends. Suddenly I felt very, very envious of their 'normal' deliveries and I am still struggling with a feeling of total failure four months later. Motherhood is such an integral part of being a woman and vaginal birth is a true rite of passage that I didn't have. I really feel like I didn't give birth 'properly' and that has made me overly determined to everything else as naturally as

PHYSICAL RECOVERY FROM A CAESAREAN

It will certainly be a relief to get home again: for one thing, your bed will be so much lower than the hospital one and easier to navigate. Although your pain will certainly have subsided, you might still feel sore twisting your body. Pressing a pillow over the wound can help whenever you stand, sneeze or (God forbid) laugh. Lifting heavy items is out – difficult if you have a young toddler, so you may have to get some extra help. Some insurance companies suggest you may not be covered to drive before six weeks, so check the small print. However, this has recently been reduced to four weeks by some firms, due to the fact that with power steering some cars are a lot lighter and easier to drive.

Some suggestions:

- When lying on your back place a pillow under your thighs, and when on your side, use pillows to support your back, and between your legs.
- When sitting in a chair make sure you are well supported with pillows or cushions. Particularly when breast- or bottlefeeding, use pillows to raise your baby up and protect your stitches.
- Getting in and out of bed – bend your knees up and keep them together, then tighten your tummy muscles and roll onto your side. Push up with your arms and drop your legs over the side, standing up s-l-o-w-l-y. Do the opposite to get into bed.
- To lift – make sure your legs take the strain and not your back or your stomach. Bend your knees and keep your back straight. Pull in your abdominal muscles and pelvic floor before you lift.

(See Further Resources for additional help.)

possible. John sleeps in our bed, I use cloth nappies, I will breastfeed for as long as he wants it … none of that was particularly important to me before John was born.

I know I shouldn't beat myself up about something that was out of my control but I feel sick at the memory of flashing theatre lights and green overalls. I desperately want a vaginal birth next time and will be gutted if it doesn't happen."

Rachel, 30

What your baby will be doing

In the early days, it may still seem that your baby is pretty much asleep 24/7, occasionally surfacing to suck herself back to sleep again, filling a pack of nappies along the way. However, there is a hell of a lot more going on that that. Researchers have identified six different "states of consciousness" that will change dramatically in the first month.

State 1

Deep sleep

Your baby will be lying quietly without moving and won't even wake if a marching band wanders into your living room.

State 2

Light sleep

Your baby will be moving occasionally: you'll see his eyes moving under his lids, and he will startle at sudden noises.

State 3

Drowsiness

Your baby will be in between sleeping and waking, whether dropping off or coming round. He'll stretch, yawn, pull those funny newborn grimaces or kick his arms and legs.

State 4

Quiet alert

Your baby will be pretty chilled out, just watching and listening. There's a lot to take in, after all. The time he spends in this state will increase dramatically throughout the first month.

State 5

Active alert

Your baby will be busy, kicking and looking "happy", though he won't smile properly for a good six weeks or so. Alternatively, he might looking around frantically (often because of hunger) and on the edge of crying.

State 6

Crying

Your baby will be yelling for something – and it's your job to guess what. Is he tired? Hungry? Bored? There are some clues to body language below, and more on deciphering a baby's cries in Chapter 6, but at this stage, a soothing cuddle is the first and best option.

Peter Wolff and Heinz Prechtl

Around day three or four, your baby "wakes up". This, however, is only a relative term, as she will still spend most of the day asleep for long periods of two to four hours. Some babies choose their main sleep chunks to be at night (lucky parents), others prefer daylight hours, and wake up bright-eyed and ready to play around 3am. This often replicates their periods of activity in the womb. Teaching your baby that night time is actually for sleeping can be one of the toughest things to deal with in the early weeks and months (see Chapter 5).

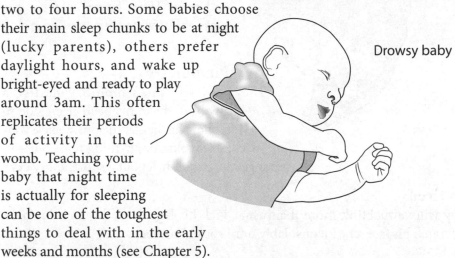

Drowsy baby

Even when your baby is awake, she'll probably be dozing at the breast or bottle, and only be truly alert for just a few minutes at a time.

What will my baby "do" and where should I put her during the day?

As you've no doubt noticed, there's not a huge amount of time left after your newborn has had her fill of sleeping, eating and crying for more of the above. For the rest of the time, when you can bear to put her down, and if she feels happy doing so, she should be kept lying, flat on her back, either in a moses basket or "bouncy chair". Car seats should only be used for car journeys as they don't keep her spine in the best position, although in reality, if your newborn has dropped off on the journey, it's probably okay to leave her to nap for a while

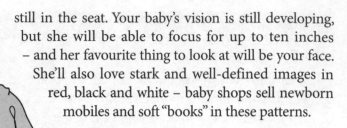

still in the seat. Your baby's vision is still developing, but she will be able to focus for up to ten inches – and her favourite thing to look at will be your face. She'll also love stark and well-defined images in red, black and white – baby shops sell newborn mobiles and soft "books" in these patterns.

What does my baby want?

Babies don't come with a set of instruction manuals, so it's all trial and error. Here, however, are some hints about what they may be trying to say:

I'm hungry
Baby will open mouth wide like a baby bird, shake his head from side to side, chew his hands furiously, suck your neck, shirt collar or anything that comes in range of his mouth, let out a short, angry cry.

I'm tired
Baby will yawn, blink more than usual, kick his legs excitedly, arch his back or scratch his face, cry inconsolably until rocked to sleep.

I've got wind
Baby will let out a high-pitched yelp, draw his knees to his body, tremble slightly, stop eating.

It's all a bit much for me
Baby will turn away, stare, scrunch his fists into his eyes.

I'm cold
Baby will have purplish hands, a quivering bottom lip.

I'm hot
Baby will feel clammy to the touch and "pant" while he's breathing.

I'm doing a poo
Baby will stop sucking if feeding – yep, some decorum even at this age.

Your baby should always be put to sleep on his back. Research shows overwhelmingly that this lowers the risk of **Sudden Infant Death Syndrome** (SIDS, or cot death).
Sleep issues are covered in detail in Chapter 5.

A routine, or not?

Of the many controversial issues in child-rearing, this one often heralds the most heated debate. Do you "go with" your baby, trying to work out when he wants to eat and sleep, or do you try and put him into a strict routine, regardless of what he wants to do?

As with trends about how long your skirt should be, parenting styles come in and out of fashion. Back as far as 1913, a childcare expert called

Truby King was pontificating that "the normal baby should only be fed five times in 24 hours. With eight unbroken hours sleep, the mother has opportunities for … housework, outings, exercise and recreation."

The legendary guru of our parents' generation was **Dr Spock**. His book, *Baby and Child Care*, was first published in 1945, translated into 39 languages and sold fifty million copies worldwide. In the 50s and 60s, it was the bestselling tome after the Bible and though it has fallen out of fashion, look out for a Spock revival because it's just been reissued with a new, modern twist. At the time, Spock was berated for his "liberal, child-centred" approach, although he does suggest nudging a baby towards a routine rather than letting him entirely take charge. All editions have a reassuring opening: "Trust yourself. You know more than you think you do."

If you hadn't heard of **Gina Ford** and *The Contented Little Baby Book* before you went into labour, you are bound to know all about her soon. For the uninitiated, Gina Ford is an old-style Scottish maternity nurse, who maintains that by following her strict routines, your baby will sleep through the night within six weeks. Hers is the top-selling book in the baby market and she has legions of new mothers swearing that she has saved their lives. By equal measure, she has legions of new mothers simply swearing … with frustration.

Only you can decide whether a routine is for you – some babies, and some mothers – fit into a prescribed way of doing things more easily than others. Either way, it's not a decision you need to make immediately, so take the pressure off yourself.

Four good things about a routine

- It gives structure to your day if you are floundering and don't know where to start, with the result that you feel more in control.

- There is a theory that babies are happier and thrive better if they know what's coming next, even when they're this tiny.

- If your baby's in bed early, and at the same time each night, that's valuable and necessary time for you and your partner to spend together.

- It might actually work, and you'll get a night's sleep within six weeks or so.

Four bad things about a routine

- Though the routine enthusiasts insist their plan works with breastfed babies, they often need to eat little and more often than they are "allowed". Plus, midwives often insist that you feed "on demand", ie when the baby tells you they are hungry, which is conflicting advice.

- Routine confines you to the house if you fancy popping out "at sleep time".

- It can be hard to work out complicated schedules when you're so tired, you can barely see the clock, let alone tell the time.

- You might start feeling guilty and "a failure" if you can't stick to it, or your baby rebels.

The Gina Fan

"I wanted Sienna to come with a manual. By the time she was two weeks old, we were floundering, so I bought Gina on a friend's recommendation. It's great: as close to an instruction book as you can get and there's simply no margin for error. You're told what to do and it immediately gives your day some sort of structure. Initially I found it hard to get up at 7am, but the effect was almost instantaneous, and Sienna dropped off to sleep at 7pm from then on."

Anna, 33

BABY SECRETS OF THE ANCIENTS

So we think we know everything about bringing up babies. Here's how people did things in the past:

- Ancient Egyptians breastfed their babies openly for three years. To increase milk flow, they rubbed the mother's back with oil in which the dorsal fin of a Nile perch had been stewed.
- In a tradition that remains evident even today, Chinese babies must not be praised because this may invite the attention of demons and ghosts. Babies who cry are said to be disturbed by evil spirits and a pomelo leaf (type of grapefruit) is placed under their mattress.
- The Amazons fed their babies on formula milk made from almonds.

The Gina Sceptic

"I wasn't sure what to do first: laugh, cry, or throw the book at the wall. In the end, I did all three. Alice simply *would not* go to sleep when I wanted her to, and it just broke my heart to hear her wailing though the door. Then she'd fall asleep at the wrong times: what was I meant to do – wake her with a cattle prod? The book made me feel like a naughty, indisciplined child myself and I just didn't need the extra stress."

Caroline, 36

The practical stuff

Nappy valley

Ask any parent-to-be about their main apprehensions about having a baby, and invariably "I don't know how to change a nappy" will be somewhere in the top five. It's understandable, as gone are the days when everyone mucked in with their enormous families – most of us will never have had cause to go there before we have our own child. But the truth is that changing a nappy soon becomes second nature: it's probably the easiest day-to-day task of them all. The best thing about nappy changing is that it's a job even the most ingenious father is hard-pressed to wriggle out of.

How often should I change a nappy?

The amount of excreta a newborn produces is truly alarming – a sort of one-in, one-out policy after and often during every feed. Over the first few days, the contents of your baby's nappy will gradually lighten in colour from the scary black of **meconium**, to dark green, then paler yellowy-green. The poo of breastfed babies is runny and covers a beautiful colour spectrum from chartreuse to lime green and has the consistency of grainy mustard. Formula-fed babies produce a more "moulded" emission which tends to be darker in colour and more smelly. As you'll come to realize, most shades are normal – just watch out for very loose and watery poos, which may signify diarrhoea, or hard-pellet like clues of constipation, which is rare in breastfed babies.

It's probably a good idea to change as soon as possible after every poo, for the comfort of both you and your baby, although lesser evils can wait a little longer. Unless she is super-sensitive, try to avoid new nappies during the night – the whole changing palaver is likely to send a half-asleep baby into high alert mode, and it could take a while to send her off again. Draw lots for the "first nappy of the day" job.

Disposable or washable?

If you have a conscience about the environment, you may remain immune to the charms of the Pampers marketing departments, and decide to go the old-fashioned route. It's true that disposable nappies are staggeringly un-green: 800 million tons of paper is used annually in making them, which creates huge amounts of waste. Disposables are incredibly resistant to biodegrading – startling when you think that each child uses around 4500 before they are potty-trained. They are also remarkably expensive – around £4 for a pack of newborn nappies (you'll get through at least two of these a week).

However, the latest news is that using washable nappies may not even make that much of a difference. A surprising report from the **Environment Agency** in 2005 concluded that there was "no significant difference between any of the environmental impacts" between reusable and disposable nappies, mainly due to the high-level use of washing machines with reusables. Environmental groups have since questioned these findings, saying the sample surveyed was simply too small.

The bottom line is that you'll need real dedication to use washable nappies. They have to be changed more often than the packaged variety, need to be soaked before you wash them and can end up strewn over every radiator in the house if you don't have a drier. Some councils offer a nappy recycling service, so if reusables appeal, it may be worth checking this out. But for many women, it's all just too much hassle and not really an option.

How to change a nappy

You will need

- A waterproof surface to put your baby on.

- A clean nappy.

- Cotton wool and warm water (for tiny babies who have sensitive bottoms), wipes for later.

- Cream for nappy rash.

- A spare change of clothes in case of "up the back" poos. For the baby, not you, although it does sometimes get that messy.

- A nappy sack, if you choose to use one.

All this should be within reaching distance. You should never leave even a tiny baby unattended.

1. Lay your baby on his back on the mat, and un-pop his vest. If he's wearing socks or booties take them off. Babies take a weird delight in kicking away at their dirty nappies, and the mess is easier to clean off bare feet.

2. Open the old nappy to inspect the damage. To get him clean, you need to lift the baby's legs (ankles together, with one hand, gently). WARNING: Baby boys wee in the air when their penises are exposed, so keep covered with the new nappy or a small towel. Girls do their own, less dramatic stealthy versions.

3. If there's a poo, pull the front part of the nappy down, and use the inside to wipe the worst away from your baby's bottom. Then use damp cotton wool or wipes to clean up. Even wee needs to be wiped away, so baby doesn't get sore. For girls, wipe from front to back, so germs don't go where you don't want them to. Fold the nappy in on itself, and put aside ready to dispose.

4. Apply cream if the baby is sore. Talcum powder is no longer recommended, as babies can inhale the dust and suffer breathing problems.

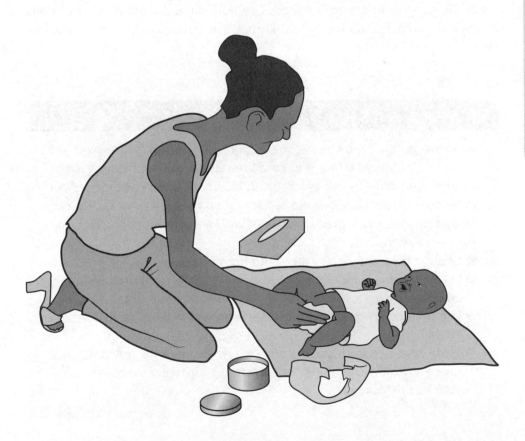

5. Open the new nappy and make sure it's the right way up – velcro tabs at the back, cute design at the front. Slide under the baby's bottom, open the tabs and stick them round the front. If your baby still has her cord clamp attached, try to fasten below her belly button. Newborn nappies are often cut especially low for this reason.
6. Replace baby's clothing.
7. Wash your hands.

If you're using washable nappies much of the process is similar to the above. Reusables probably come ready folded, but for a newborn, you may need to fold them again because they're too big. Position your baby so that the back of the nappy is higher than the front: for boys, tuck the penis down so that wee will be less likely to escape through the top of the nappy. If you're using a nappy wrap, and it's not dirty, you can use it again. Otherwise, put it in the laundry and use a clean one.

Tip the worst of the damage into the toilet, and then put the nappy in your nappy bucket to soak. If you're not using a nappy laundering service, wash the nappies in a separate load. Use hot water, double rinse, and non-biological powder, avoiding anything that can irritate your baby's sensitive skin.

NAPPY RASH

At some point, even the most scrupulously buffed babies will get a touch of nappy rash: a red, sore area around the bottom caused by the ammonia in urine. It's often down to the sensitivity of an individual baby's skin, but old fashioned terry towelling nappies can make things worse, especially if worn with waterproof pants. Here are some treatment tips:

● Change the nappy every time your baby soils it.
● Let him kick around with a bare bottom for several minutes a day and put down a towel to soak up any unexpected fountains.
● Use a barrier cream such as **Sudocrem**, which helps keep bacteria at bay.
● If the rash is not improving after a few days, or has become very raw, your baby may have an infection that needs treatment. Ask your health visitor or GP.

Giving your baby a bath

If there are two things most newborns hate, it's getting naked, and getting wet. So, for the first few weeks, bathtime will be a trial for everyone concerned, with your poor baby startling his way through an aqua-aerobics routine.

The good news at this point is that you don't have to do it every day, although as your baby grows up, the bath can be a helpful part of the "wind-down" towards bedtime. If your baby really gets upset, shelve bathing for a few weeks, and clean his dirtiest bits with a sponge or cotton wool.

Use a baby bath if you have one, but a washbasin can do just as well (though watch drips from the hot tap). The big bath is also okay as long as you are on super-sentry duty.

You will need

- A bath that is warm, but not hot – don't run the water with the baby actually in the bath. (Use the old-fashioned "elbow test" to make sure the temperature is okay.) Your baby won't enjoy the experience if you are over-cautious and use luke-warm water. If you're really worried, dig out a thermometer – ideal temperature is around 25–28°C.

- A flannel and a towel.

- Two cotton wool balls to clean eyes.

- "After bath" clothes, new nappy, nappy cream if you need it.

Undress your baby at the last minute, so he won't be hanging around naked for too long. Covering his body with a towel can help – and remember to watch out for baby-boy golden showers. Gently bring your baby to the bath and kneel down by the side. Gently lower him into the water, supporting his head and neck with one hand, so you can wash with the other. You can buy little floating devices/ towelling "chairs" that support your baby, but should NEVER LEAVE HIM UNATTENDED EVEN FOR A SECOND.

1. The main areas that need cleaning are the head and face, bottom and creases, particularly underneath the neck where all that spare, spit-up milk is busy going sour. If your baby's skin is dry, don't use soap anywhere except his dirtiest bits, it's also too early for bubble baths. On the other hand, it's fine to bathe a baby with the cord stump still on, just go gently around it. When the baby is a little older, you can buy products at most

chemists to help soften dry skin – **aqueous cream** instead of soap, and a liquid paraffin preparation called **Oilatum** which you add to the water.

2. Wet the cotton wool balls with cooled, boiled water and wipe gently, starting at the corner of the eyes between the nose, and working outwards. Use one for each eye.
3. You only need shampoo your baby's hair every week or so. This is highest up on the baby hate list, although it will take a few months for him to twig how much he really hates it. The main thing is to avoid getting suds into your baby's eyes. If your baby has cradle cap (flaky scalp that ranges from mild dandruff to huge yellow scales) you can buy special shampoo.
4. Rinse your baby thoroughly, dry him with a towel, and dress him.

A note on baby's nails: You may have noticed that your newborn arrived complete with razor-sharp nails. The easiest way to keep them short, and therefore stop him scratching himself, is to bite them, or use baby scissors when they are big enough.

Burping your baby

There are few more satisfying sounds than that hearty "beuueurrp" as your baby brings up some wind. Whether breast- or bottlefed – though more likely with the latter – all babies swallow air while they are feeding, which makes them feel prematurely full, and can cause discomfort. A baby with tummy ache will lift his knees up to his stomach, or make a heart-rending little yelp.

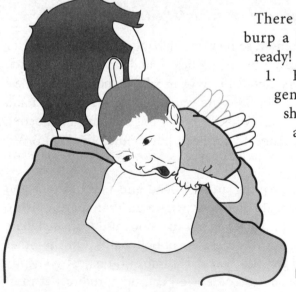

There are three possible ways to burp a baby. Muslin cloths at the ready!

1. Hold him, facing you, and gently place him against one shoulder, arms elevated so the air can move freely from his lungs. Rub or pat gently on the left side of his back.
2. Sit him on your lap, "slumped" forward, holding him under the chin with one hand, and pat with the other.

Burping a baby

3. Let him lie across your lap, face down. Don't forget to support his head with one hand, and pat with the other.

If, after several minutes patting, there's no sound, it's likely your baby doesn't have any wind. If he's still upset, he may be asking for more food. Or he may be struggling to expel the air from the other end, which will happen in due course. Alternatively, you may be one of the unfortunate parents who have to deal with "colic" (a catch-all term for excessive crying in an otherwise healthy baby). See Chapter 6.

Vomiting and possetting

As you (and your carpet) have probably discovered by now, your baby's wind is often accompanied by a little bit of vomited milk, which accounts for the reason most new mothers have the distinctive waffle-textured white muslin cloth hanging over their shoulders and all around their living rooms. Don't worry about it, this is called possetting and is completely normal – it will improve as your baby gets older and her stomach muscles get stronger. Occasionally, a baby will vomit up larger quantities, sometimes in an alarming projectile fashion. This is due to a condition called **gastric reflux**, where the contents of an immature digestive system come back up the gullet and into the mouth. You may want to try giving smaller feeds, and while reflux is rarely serious and almost always goes on its own, if your baby is upset and not feeding happily, it might be worth a quick visit to your GP.

Swaddling your baby

One of the biggest challenges is getting your baby to fall asleep when you want her to (ie roughly between the hours of 11pm and 7am) and to stay there. Many new parents do not achieve this until well into the first year.

In the early days, it makes sense that your newborn, used to feeling snug in the confines of your uterus, might be feeling lost and exposed in the vast confines of a moses basket or cot. Therefore swaddling (wrapping her arms tightly around her body with the use of a cloth) does help some babies to relax. Others hate being confined, and prefer sleeping with their arms above their heads. You just have to see how your baby reacts.

Swaddling was used almost universally before the eighteenth century, but studies over recent years had suggested the practice might lead to breathing problems, or overheating. These have now been disproved: in fact, new American research has shown that babies who are swaddled are more likely to sleep on their back – a position that is universally agreed cuts down on the incidence of Sudden Infant Death Syndrome (or cot death).

How to swaddle

● Fold down one corner of a blanket, and place your baby in the middle of the fold with her head above the edge.

● Pull the left side of the blanket snugly across your baby's chest, making sure her right arm is wrapped close to his body. Then lift your baby's left arm and securely tuck the blanket under her body.

● Bring the bottom of the blanket up and either fold the edge back or tuck it into the first fold. Then pull the last corner of the blanket across your baby's chest, securing her left arm near her body.

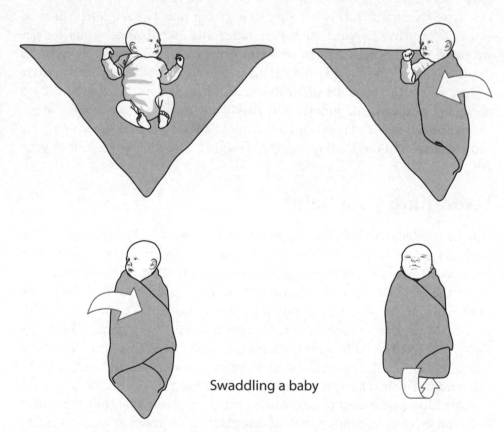

Swaddling a baby

EIGHT THINGS I WOULD HAVE DONE DIFFERENTLY IN THE FIRST SIX WEEKS

- Banned visitors for the first five days, and then asked them to bring a meal instead of flowers. (*Winnie, 27*)
- Said no to being a bridesmaid a month after the baby was due. (*Hermione, 23*)
- Asked for more help – there is no shame in needing it. (*Louisa, 30*)
- Cut a piece of her hair to keep – she was born a redhead but it soon fell out and re-grew mousey-brown. (*Alex, 32*)
- Stuck to my guns and called him Sonny, regardless of my parents' disgust. (*Lorraine, 26*)
- Driven the car with the baby before my husband went back to work. (*Helen, 28*).
- Bought a pack of disposable nappies despite wanting to try cloth – several shooting poos later I ditched the whole earth-mother thing. (*Adelaide, 28*)
- Saved my digital photos of her first few weeks on disc so that they weren't lost when my PC crashed. (*Wendy, 34*)

Further resources

Books

General

Baby and Child Care by Benjamin Spock (Simon and Schuster, £15.99). Our parents' Bible, Dr Spock covers all areas of childcare from birth to school age. Has recently been reissued in a modern format. Classic (or old-fashioned) reading, depending on your standpoint.

The Social Baby by Lynne Murray and Liz Andrews (The Children's Project, £14.99). Fascinating illustrated book which covers your baby's behaviour and body language from the moment of birth. There are also chapters on crying and sleeping.

Postnatal depression

Banish Post Baby Blues by Anne-Marie Sapsted (Thorson's, £2.00 o/p). Out of print, but you may be able to get it on Amazon. The charities recommend it highly for the information and suggestions, but warn the personal accounts are quite harrowing.

Depression After Childbirth by Katharina Dalton (Oxford University Press, £9.79). Dalton's approach is that PND is caused by hormones, and not all doctors agree with this. However, it's a warm, sympathetic and optimistic view of the illness.

Surviving Postnatal Depression: At Home, No one Can Hear You Scream by Cara Aiken (Jessica Langley Press, £15.95). This book is full of positive suggestions and practical tips, based on personal experience (including that of the author) and professional advice from the experts.

Caesarean delivery

The Caesarean Experience by Sarah Clement (Pandora, £7.99). Written by a psychologist, this is a useful look at dealing with post-Caesarean emotions

Caesarean Recovery by Chrissie Gallagher-Mundy (Carroll and Brown, £6.99). A useful book on day-to-day recovery and exercising after a C-section.

Websites

www.aims.co.uk Caesarean support network. Mothers in their own home, who've had Caesareans themselves, give support, advice and point you in the direction of helpful reading matter. Tel: 01624 661 269 (after 6pm).

www.apni.org Association for Postnatal Illness (APNI) – a charity which provides support to mothers suffering from postnatal depression and allied conditions, increases awareness of them, and encourages research into their causes. APNI also publish a number of reasonably priced leaflets, in several languages including Urdu and Bengali. Tel: 0207 386 0868

www.bloomingmarvellous.co.uk Offers a selection of newborn bathing pads and bath slings, as well as a variety of other baby products. Pads and slings are also available in shops like Mothercare and John Lewis.

www.caesarean.org.uk A good, comprehensive site on all aspects of having a C-section, with FAQs, help, advice, birth stories and suggestions of further books and resources.

www.homeopathyhelpline.com The UK's only helpline offers on-line premium-rate homeopathic advice from 9am to midnight; the website is packed with information, tips and resources. Tel: 09065 343 404

www.icmedicine.co.uk The Institute of Complementary Medicine is a charity providing the public with information on all aspects of the safe and best practice of Complementary Medicine, including homeopathy. The ICM administers the British Register of Complementary Practitioners (BRCP), a list of competent professionals. Tel: 0207 237 5165

www.mama.co.uk Meet a Mum Association – a self-help organisation founded by Esther Rantzen, to help the thousands of mothers who become depressed and isolated when their babies are born. MAMA has fifteen nationwide support groups, and an on-line forum where new mothers can "chat".

www.osteopathy.org.uk The General Osteopathic Council website contains links to help you find a practitioner in your area.

3

The new people in your life

3

The new people in your life

I n the early weeks with a new baby, it feels like you've entered a secret fraternity as stacks of new people start to enter your life. To begin with, there are all those buggies – and their owners pushing them up and down the street. Do you honestly remember seeing so many prams before you gave birth? Even if you do, you'll doubtless recall them mainly as obstacles that got in the way of shopping and commuting. But now, as a parent, you're the proud owner of a buggy – and one of the legions of new mothers and fathers who will become, if not friends, people you'll bump into at the baby clinic or postnatal group. At the very least, they'll be sympathetic faces who'll return your knowing smile. Or not, if they are prey to **Competitive Parenting Syndrome** (see below).

Then of course, there are the "baby professionals" – your community midwife, health visitor, GP and the people who write the baby books, to whom you might find yourself turning for advice, or alternatively, find a bit patronizing. If you're lucky, and can afford it, there are also people you can pay to come and help you out: **doulas, maternity nurses** and **nannies**.

Probably the most surprising group – and definitely the most important – is the group of people you thought you knew already: your family and close friends. One frequently neglected phenomenon is the way your relationship with the closest of your friends and relatives can travel through dramatic, exciting, but sometimes difficult, changes when you have a baby.

The last – and least – significant set, but still worthy of mention, are the High Street Busy Bodies. Invariably, old ladies, who take enormous pleasure in sidling up to proclaim that your baby is too hot/too cold/too hungry and should really be wearing scratch mittens. Take some enormous pleasure of your own, by ignoring them entirely.

Your baby's father (formerly known as your partner)

Anyone who tells you they are having a baby to "make their relationship stronger" or "bring them closer together" needs their head examined. Don't doubt for a second that the little person you've just created will bring years of joy and pride – in the long run. But the stresses of the first few months can put intolerable pressure on even the most solid and harmonious relationships.

If you've ever had an argument trying to put together IKEA flat-pack furniture, imagine trying to do that having suffered sleep-deprivation by a platoon of POW guards for a month. It is certainly true that some couples unreservedly adore being new parents, and take to it like a ducky to a baby bath. For others, however, this period really can be the toughest they'll encounter in their whole relationship. It's common for couples to go for days at a time without a proper conversation and to fall into a circle of competitive tiredness ("I'm more exhausted than you are etc"). As for your sex life, well, even if you felt physically up to it, passion squarely takes bottom rank in the new world order. The long-term challenges to your relationship are discussed a little later on in the book. However, in the first few weeks, it's dealing with the immediate fallout that's the main priority. And much of this depends on how your partner, if you have one – husband, boyfriend, girlfriend – is coping with being a parent. (We've used "Dad" for shorthand below.)

Some common reactions

Dad feeling overwhelmed or disappointed

Just as it's taboo for a woman to admit she feels less than thrilled about being a mother, so too is it for a man. In fact, he may be even less prepared for parenthood than you were – at least you could feel your baby growing inside you, and had an active part in his delivery. Some men complain of being ignored by midwives and visitors, feeling like nothing more than a glorified sperm donor. Perhaps your partner had an unrealistically rosy expectation of fatherhood, with visions of footballs being kicked around parks, or a little girl in a fairy outfit sitting on his shoulders. And what's he got? A little red clucking thing that does nothing but cry, sleep and eat, that is so fragile he's terrified witless. Add to this any worries he's got about your physical health, and there's quite a lot to deal with.

It's also worth bearing in mind that your partner will be almost – if not equally – as tired as you are. Even if he's not feeding the baby, he'll have to be a pretty heavy sleeper not to wake up when you do. Sure, from where you're

sitting, skipping off to work every day might seem like a picnic compared with the demands of looking after a newborn, but many offices are still macho places without any special concessions for knackered dads. Although this is *starting* to get better.

Action plan

New parents need to nurture one another, as well as their baby. Which means a concerted effort on your part, as the new arrival is doubtless sucking in every ounce of emotional energy you've got. Rock the baby to sleep, sit down with a cup of tea in the kitchen, and encourage your man to open up. Just talking (him) and listening (you) can clear the air and make him feel better.

It may be difficult to believe this yourself, but reassure him that the day will soon come that your useless baby will start to crawl, smile, play, talk and practise for an eventual place in Arsenal's back four.

Dad feeling jealous of the baby or surplus to requirements

With the 24-hour demands of a newborn, plus your own stress and exhaustion to contend with, it's not surprising that dad gets pushed down into third place. For most men, this probably isn't an issue, but the occasional new father finds he is often grumpy and feels overlooked – and then maybe starts feeling guilty about that. Some men also complain about feeling excluded when their partner is breastfeeding – that this is a cosy little world in which their presence is surplus to requirements.

Action plan

If you suspect your partner's feeling jealous, it's really important to talk about this subject before it festers. But the great news is that there really is no need for him to feel excluded: there's plenty to do! Your partner can "bond" with the baby over a nappy change, in a sling on the way to the shops, or sleeping on his chest at night (some babies really do prefer a big, manly flat surface). Of course, it can be harder to share duties if you are breastfeeding, but after a few weeks, when breastfeeding becomes established, express some milk into a bottle (see p.135) so your partner can attempt to give the baby a feed. He'll love the closeness; you'll welcome the respite. **One tip**: resist the urge to hover over your partner and correct his technique. It's undermining and might undo all the good work.

Dad doesn't "help out"

Some women are lucky enough to find a man who will come home from work, make the dinner, do a 2am bottlefeed, and go to Sainsbury's every Saturday morning while you get a much-needed lie-in. Some aren't. This is a tricky area, because your partner may argue that while you are on maternity leave, the home and baby are your job. But as we all well know, you can't shut down your baby at 5.30pm and re-boot her at 9am, in time for the working day. It's very common for conflicts to emerge over who's doing the most, which eventually become running battles that are never entirely settled.

Action plan

In a sense, our generation is the luckiest yet: our husbands are expected to help out with parenting in a way that our fathers and grandfathers were not (okay, we're expected to work as well, but that's another issue). However, there are plenty of new dads who yearn for the way "it used to be" where the work was divided on strictly gender grounds. You may well be happy with this yourself.

If you aren't, there's a word you are going to have to get used to – **compromise**. And to understand where each of you are coming from, you have to imagine yourself in each other's shoes. Leave him with the baby for a couple of hours; he'll soon see how tough it is, although as he gets more confident, he'll see that it can also be a delight. In the meantime, rather than having stand-up rows about who's doing what, it's far more constructive to sit down and say yes, like it or not, life has changed for both of you. Work out a scheme where you'll both be happy and which gives you both some time off: for example; a lie-in on alternative days. If financial circumstances allow you extra help with babysitting or a cleaner, grab this firmly with both hands.

Dad feeling sexually frustrated

You may be one of those lucky creatures who had fabulous sex during pregnancy: who found that all that whizzing oestrogen turned her into a horny sex goddess, and her burgeoning fertile form was a real turn-on. Or you may be like the rest of us, who found that tiredness, sickness, heartburn and a really grotesque stomach made the idea of sex at best ludicrous, or at worst, a chore. And your partner agreed. Either way, now the baby's out in the open, you'll probably find your man ready to resume normal sexual activity.

It may well take some time for you to be ready. There's no strict medical advice on when you can start doing it again – you don't have to wait for your six-week check, for example – but the mere thought of sex fills many women with horror. Some see it as like losing your virginity all over again. And that's before you even go into the paranoia about the damage you think has been done (your vagina: this big, your baby's head: THIS BIG). Plus the fact that the **prolactin** produced by breastfeeding is also well known to reduce sexual desire (not helped by leaking, overfull breasts).

Action plan

The reassuring news is that many new fathers feel just as libido-drained from exhaustion, and the excitement of a new baby. But the chances are, he'll be up for some action several days, weeks or even months before you are. Don't let yourself be persuaded into something you really aren't ready for. If you're feeling sexual, but not ready for the full Monty, there are plenty of other things you can do. And if you aren't allured by any of these, you'll just have to ask him to bear with you. Things will change – you both just have to believe that and remain patient.

NB: If you're going to have sex, for heaven's sake sort out your contraception. Many people think they can't get pregnant while breastfeeding, and while it is unlikely, it's not impossible (see p.221 for explanation). There's more on sex, parenthood and contraceptive choices in Chapter 7.

The fathers speak!

I missed my wife for the first three months

"No one tells you that the first few weeks after your baby is born are like being a student again. You live on ready-meals and takeaways, you get little or no sleep and you forget to do the washing so none of your clothes match. Many new mothers are often concerned about post-baby sex, but fortunately this happens more often than my mates told me it would. Not that sex is everything, but I did miss that intimacy with my wife. Actually, I missed my wife completely for the first three months. One Saturday my mother-in-law ordered us to go out for dinner and reluctantly we left Alfie with her … along with several bottles of expressed milk, two large packs of nappies, a full pack of wipes, five spare babygros and a new pack of vests. Although we spent the night talking about how lovely Alfie was, it was great to be alone together for a couple of hours.

We now make a point of going out one night a month – it is very nice to have my wife back again, even if we race each other to kiss Alfie first when we get home."

Paul, 30

Freya's changed my attitude to everything

"I was convinced we were having a son and it took me a good few weeks to get my head round the idea of a girl. All my parental fantasies revolved around boys. Once I got over the shock, I have to say I started to like the idea. Apparently only real men have girls – it's something to do with the level of testosterone you produce I think.

Freya has changed my attitude to pretty much everything. It suddenly became very important to reinforce the security on the front door and to fix window locks in each room. We couldn't go out unless she had a hat on – even though she was born in the hottest July on record.

My wife had always earned more than me and that was fine. But I love the fact that my family rely on my salary now. I'd read somewhere that having a child boosts your career and that certainly worked for me – I had this urge to bring home as much money as possible and was promoted within three months."

Jay, 28

Stay-at-home dads

There are now over 155,000 men staying at home to look after the home and family in the UK. Add to this the growing numbers of fathers working

part-time and sharing the childcare, or bringing up children by themselves and it's no longer a novelty to see a man turning up at weigh-day at the baby clinic.

Stay-home dads face all the same challenges as their female counterparts, but these are compounded by the attitudes of people with out-of-date views. Comments like "have you lost your job?" or "so, does she wear the trousers, then?" really don't help a man who may be suffering from low self-esteem just because of silly old-fashioned traditions. The good news is that these attitudes are thankfully becoming more rare and this current generation of fathers is becoming the first to really witness their children growing up, first-hand.

It took time to feel accepted

"I was always more keen to have children than my partner, Rose. So when she finally got pregnant, almost two years ago, I was delighted. As she was the main breadwinner, and because I'm an actor with erratic work, it made sense that I would stay at home to look after the baby while she went back full-time. This was fine with me – I'm not a macho 'gender roles' sort of person.

Looking back, though, I think I can see why Rose was so hesitant. I just hadn't really thought through all the implications of having a baby. The first six months were idyllic with both of us at home with our beautiful daughter, Marina. But when Rose went back to work and I was alone, reality hit home.

The practical stuff was fine: nappies, feeds, sleeping. But I found the endless hours with no real break very difficult. On a bad day, I'd find myself ringing Rose at work to say pathetically: 'she's crying, what shall I do?' This only had the net result of making Rose feel guilty and didn't help anyone.

Rose kept nagging me to get some sort of routine, to get out of the house and go to a local parent-and-baby drop-in. The first time I went was awful – a few women stared at me as if I was some kind of weirdo interloper. The rest simply ignored me. But over the months, it got easier. Rose and I decided that I'd need some sort of help: now my mother takes the baby one day a week, and she goes to a childminder another day. After a busy family weekend, I love my time alone with my daughter. And despite the dodgy start at the drop-in, we all get on famously. I'm 'one of the girls' now."

Steve, 31

Can fathers really get postnatal depression?

You may think: what's he got to complain about? I'm the one doing the night feeds. But even though postnatal illness isn't a formal diagnosis for a man, it's certain that some new fathers have symptoms verging on clinical depression – as many as one in 25, according to a 2005 study in the *Lancet*. And if you step back, it's easy to see why: a huge whirlwind has just arrived, re-defining everything in his life. As well as the issues of jealousy, disappointment and exhaustion detailed above, some men feel crushed by the new weight of financial responsibility, especially if they aren't earning much, or their partner has given up work. Similarly, his relationship with you has undergone a massive transformation, and if you are also suffering with baby-induced stress, home is a difficult place to be right now. You just have to hold on to the fact that things really are temporary and will change for the better. However, if his symptoms of depression are starting to affect your life together, it might be a good idea for him to visit your GP, or consider seeing a counsellor.

The grandparents

Few people would deny that one of the greatest thrills of becoming a parent is introducing your new son or daughter to her grandparents. It's the official stamp on your journey to adulthood, the continuation of the family line, and the knowledge that your child will have a strong source of love and support second only to your own. Mother and daughter relationships, in particular, may get closer in this period; as a new mum yourself, you might understand a bit more where she is "coming from". Don't be surprised if your mother and father seem more relaxed around your baby than you remember them being with you – they've practised on their own children, now they've the luxury of getting it right one generation down the line.

This isn't the case for all families, however, and in some cases couples with new babies might feel a sense of disappointment that their own mothers and fathers are not sharing in their joy as much as they would like, and are not offering any sort of assistance. There can also be difficulties if your parents are divorced and have new partners and there is a "clash" over visiting rights. Or your parents may have moved abroad in a situation likely to become more common as families disperse further – in which case they will largely miss their grandchildren growing up.

When "helping" can actually be the opposite

In the early days, it can be a huge support to have someone who has "been there and done that", with special tips on how to send an overtired baby to sleep. Or simply to come over, do the washing, and make sure the dinner is on the table. On the other hand, many new parents find that what *their* parents see as "helping" is, in fact, interfering. It's tough enough learning to breastfeed a newborn, without your mother (or, worse, mother-in-law) telling you to swap breasts every few minutes when modern advice is to empty one breast completely before offering the other. For an overtired and frazzled new mother, all the advice can be very confusing. The following might help sort the conflicting information:

Four things that have changed since your mother's day

- **Then: Your baby should sleep on his front**

- **Now: Your baby should sleep on his back**
  Doctors used to think that "front sleeping" stopped babies inhaling their own vomit. At the time this seemed reasonable, but it has since been proven to be unfounded and dangerous. Since the "back to sleep" campaign in the 80s, the incidence of **Sudden Infant Death Syndrome** (SIDS, or cot death) has fallen dramatically. See p.174 for more on SIDS.

- **Then: You should breastfeed your baby for "ten minutes each side"**

- **Now: Empty one breast before offering the other.**
  "Ten minutes each side" was a reliable way of making sure your baby had a substantial feed, and that your breasts didn't get too engorged. These days, however, researchers have discovered that breast milk is not uniform. The "**foremilk**" (the first milk to come out in a feed) is good for quenching the baby's thirst, but low in fat. The "**hindmilk**" that follows is rich in fat, calories and protein. If you cut short a feed, the baby may not be receiving the optimum nutrition.

GRANDPARENT GROUNDRULES

In their excitement about the new arrival, or their eagerness to help, your parents might occasionally ride roughshod over your feelings. It can be useful to set out some groundrules at the start, ideally conveyed at a time when you're feeling calm and not too emotional. For example:
- Please ring before you come round – don't just turn up uninvited
- Stop treating me like a child: I'm still learning and need to get this right in my own time
- Ask what you can do to help us, don't just assume you know
- Don't automatically start tidying up without our permission, it feels like an insult
- It's only July; please don't ask which set of parents we are planning on visiting for Christmas

If they won't listen to you, copy this list out and stick it to the front door.

The new people

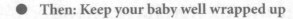
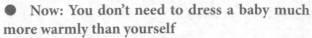

- Then: Keep your baby well wrapped up

- Now: You don't need to dress a baby much more warmly than yourself

Gone are the days when babies were bundled up in babygros, blankets and hats, even in midsummer. A baby's natural thermostat is usually set within the first few days of his life, although it is a good idea to keep his head covered when he's tiny, because that's where he loses the most heat. The most important thing is to avoid overheating while the baby sleeps – this is another factor in SIDS. Try to keep room temperature between 16 and 20°C – the ideal temperature is 18°C.

- Then: Adding baby rice to your baby's bottle at six weeks will make him sleep better

- Now: Current medical advice is that a baby should have no solid food before six months and certainly not before four months

This is because research shows that early-weaned babies are more prone to constipation and diarrhoea, and they have an increased risk of obesity and heart disease later in life. Sadly, there are no "quick fixes" to the sleep solution, but if your baby is getting enough milk, introducing early solids won't necessarily help.

Grandparents on their new family

Life's better for new mothers now

"If I'm honest, I'd have to say that my overwhelming emotion about being a grandparent is envy. I'm not proud to admit it, but it's true. I'm envious of the endless support my daughter has from her boyfriend – the thought of my husband offering to do a night feed was inconceivable. The idea of him changing a nappy was, and is, positively laughable.

I'm envious of the time Lisa has off work and the fact she has a guaranteed job to go back to. I never had the chance to build a career until after my four girls had practically left home and although I loved being a mother, it wasn't the be-all and end-all for me.

I'm envious of the time she has to play with her little girl. We were always encouraged to leave the babies in the cot and not to indulge them. Lisa gets to mess around and cuddle her Katie without any feelings of guilt.

I suppose I'm also envious of the fact that my husband is so much more demonstrative with Katie than he was with our girls. He spent most of his time at work or down the pub when they were young, he barely took time to look inside their cots. I'd kill for the chance to do it all over again – twenty-first century style."

Mary, 57

My feelings of love are indescribable

"I absolutely love being a grandmother – but then I loved every minute of bringing up my children and seeing Eleanor experience the same joy with George is amazing. He has the same rolls of fat around his legs and wrists as she had when she was little and the same look of intense concentration when new people are around. When he gave me his first proper smile at three weeks old, I just couldn't take my eyes off him for a second.

My feelings are almost indescribable. It is definitely different from being a mum. I enjoyed each stage of my own children's development but it all happened so quickly. Seeing George grow brings back such good memories and I can't wait to hear every detail.

Some of the 'rules' of child-rearing have changed, but the basics remain the same. Eleanor asks my advice but I definitely don't feel I have all the answers. I do think it's great that she received such support with breastfeeding; when I was feeding Eleanor myself, I struggled with her big appetite but breastfeeding was frowned upon in the 70s so no one helped out.

I speak to my daughter nearly every day now and we haven't managed that for years. Having George around puts a smile on everybody's face."

Gina, 64

Miriam, Gina, Tracy, Penelope … You'll never meet them, but Ms Stoppard, Ford, Hogg, Leach and their colleagues will become a big influence on your life, by virtue of their books that lay scattered over your front room. When you are at your lowest ebb, the hope that you can find an answer in the pages of a book is tempting, especially if a friend swears by it. And, very often, their advice can be fantastic, with Gina Ford-style routines in particular working well for some people. On the other hand, if you find the advice is making you feel confused, or inadequate, it's time to shut the book away in a dark cupboard. You and your baby will find your own way in time – you don't need "the experts" to make you feel worse.

And a new parent on *her* parents

She teases me about all the books I read

"My mum and dad were much younger than us when they had kids, and they definitely had less money, so their experience of early parenthood was very different to ours. She thinks that there is such a thing as too much knowledge, whereas I like to know exactly where I stand before I do anything.

I had a tough time with Emily's sleeping early on and Mum kept telling me to wean her onto solids at ten weeks. She just couldn't understand why we are now told to wait until six months. She also believes that newborn babies should be fed at four-hourly intervals and would blame any episode of colic, vomiting or screaming on my decision not to feed her that way."

Lucy, 30

Grandparents as carers

Although the days of three generations under one roof are now largely over, grandparents still play a huge part in family life. More than two-thirds of British parents now rely on their mothers and fathers to provide some childcare – an average of six and a half hours a week. And with divorce figures at an all-time high, one in four grandparents is now routinely bringing up children; over one third of grandparents under the age of sixty still have a dependent child of their own living at home. (*Figures from Age Concern.*)

While most grandparents adore having this input, don't automatically assume they'll be thrilled about it – it's quite a different job from coming over for tea once a week to coo over the baby's progress. Your mother and father may feel their child-rearing years are behind them and now desire the freedom to work, travel or go to bridge lessons. Make sure everyone's happy with the arrangement.

As a single parent, I couldn't have coped without them

"My boyfriend left me when I was six months pregnant and I pretty much fell apart. I had to move back home because I couldn't afford my flat on maternity pay and I dreaded it. But my parents were brilliant. My dad

converted his garage into a little studio for us, complete with sink and changing area. They decorated it all and spruced up our old baby furniture whilst I sat on the sofa and cried over my ex.

Once Marco arrived, they could so easily have taken over and become his surrogate parents. But they didn't. They were there whenever I needed them and they couldn't wait to give him kisses and cuddles but they made it absolutely clear that I was his mum.

Actually, it got to the point where I had to beg my mum for her advice – she was so worried about being the overbearing grandmother that she didn't want to interfere. I respect her so much more now that I am a parent. You don't realize how much hard work it is.

I had to go back to work after three months and my parents took on the role of childminders. This can be difficult for a lot of us – I hate the idea of anyone else raising my child and they miss out on the 'dropping-in' element of being grandparents. Having said that, I know Marco is being well looked after and they do respect my instructions so it works pretty well."

Rosie, 29

Other mothers

By the end of your first year with a new baby, you'll have all sorts of new friends in the same boat. Perhaps you've joined an NCT or hospital parentcraft course, and stayed in touch when the babies arrived. Or maybe you've just struck up conversations with other mothers (or fathers) in postnatal groups or at the baby clinic. Before you know it, you've become part of – horror of horrors – a coffee morning circle. It may be called something else, but deep down, you know that's what it is.

In truth, you may well have nothing in common other than children the same age. But, for now, who cares? It can be fantastic to compare notes, anxieties, tips and funny stories with someone who understands entirely. Especially when you are going through exactly the same thing at exactly the same time: it's amazing how quickly you forget the details a few months down the line. In each gathering, however, there will always be a woman suffering from **Competitive Parenting Syndrome**, who will make you feel

THE NCT

To the uninitiated, the NCT can come across as some sinister mixture of the UN and Girl Guides. It stands for the **National Childbirth Trust** (not *Natural* Childbirth Trust, as many people think), although, as an organization the NCT seem firmly in favour of breastfeeding and childbirth without medical intervention: you often see its experts wheeled out to comment on the latest shocking rise in Caesarean statistics.

The NCT, an independent charity, was established in 1957. Without question, its pioneering work over the past fifty years has transformed maternity care – for example, before their campaigning in the 60s, it was virtually unheard of for fathers to attend their children's birth. Largely thanks to the NCT, our generation of mothers is more informed and has more choice than ever before.

Many readers will have come across the NCT during pregnancy, by taking one of their (largely excellent) antenatal classes. But even postnatally, the NCT has a lot to offer. There are nationwide branches which organize weekly get-togethers, nearly-new sales and discussion groups, plus local breastfeeding counsellors. In addition, the NCT publishes useful, practical books and leaflets, and has a comprehensive website.

Most of these services are also available to non-members, but the NCT relies on membership subscriptions (currently £36 a year) to keep going. See also Further Resources for support networks.

NCT enquiry line: 08704 448 707 (9am to 5pm)
www.nctpregnancyandbabycare.com

The new people

that you're child is retarded and you are deeply inadequate. You know, the type: her baby sleeps through the night first, rolls over first, sits up first and can already say "mummy". Work out which one she is, then apologize politely and go find the hobnobs.

Such women are a minor occupational hazard. The most important thing is that getting out of the house and seeing other human beings keeps you on the right side of sanity. Nothing prepares you for the sheer monotony and loneliness of being stuck in the house with a newborn on a cold January day, when it's dark at 3pm and you really can't watch another episode of *Murder She Wrote*. A regular gig with other people who

understand how you feel, whether it's at a church hall "playgroup" or at a special mother-and-baby film screening (see below) can be a real life-saver. As can baby massage, postnatal yoga or exercise classes – the activity is often incidental to the social aspect.

If you live in a rural community or don't fancy the ordeal of face–to-face small-talk with strangers, there are various baby websites that have excellent on-line communities and chatrooms specific to babies of a certain age (see Further Resources).

The "baby professionals"

Your GP

What does a GP do? Family doctors are the first port of call for medical worries as opposed to eating and sleeping problems, which are dealt with by the health visitor. Some GPs also give immunizations.

When you'll see her: Unless you've had a home birth, when your GP comes to your house to do the newborn examination, the first time you'll see your doctor is at your six-week check (unless you and your baby have any medical problems in the early days). Babies under one year old are the most common visitors in a doctor's waiting room.

A GP says:

"A large part of my job is spent reassuring new mothers that their baby is okay. That's fair enough: if you are a first time-mother, how are you meant to know what's normal, and what is not? So I see lots of babies with rashes, which will go on their own, or cradle cap, which can be treated with shampoo or olive oil. Some women are worried that their baby is making funny noises, or breathing loudly at night. Again, that's completely normal. Even if the baby is poorly, it tends to be a viral illness, like a cold, or diarrhoea, which will clear up on its own. So, actually, it's hardly ever anything that needs treatment.

Lots of new mothers think they are wasting my time, and apologize for it, but I don't mind at all. It's true that I see some patients more than others, and often that's to do with how much family support they are getting. Recent research shows that new babies who have a grandmother living close by are far less likely to seek urgent medical help because of the experienced advice they are getting."

Sarah Davey, 33

Sarah's tips:

- Half of all new mothers suffer with haemorrhoids, so don't be embarrassed to ask your doctor or pharmacist for help.

- Expect your baby's crying to peak at six weeks. You'll see a significant improvement by week twelve or thirteen.

Your health visitor

What she does: Although health visitors support community members of all ages, much of their workload is helping families with new children. Your health visitor will be on hand to offer advice on day-to-day baby matters (breastfeeding, sleeping, colic) either at the health clinic, GP surgery or with home visits.

When you'll see her: Some women see their health visitor during pregnancy, but the first visit is usually at your home, ten to fourteen days after the birth, where she hands over the "red book" (personal child health record) and discusses important issues such as immunization. If there are initial problems, you may both decide to arrange another appointment, but the ball is usually left in your court.

A health visitor says:

"Contrary to what people think, we are not checking up on people or 'policing them' – we are guests in your family's home, and if there is any concern, the first thing we will do is discuss it with you. My job is all about sharing information: for example, giving up-to-date information on the latest research on reducing the risk of cot death. We need to be thorough because middle-class mums can mislead you into thinking they are very confident, although they may be struggling like anybody else. It's no shame – there's **no** such thing as the 'perfect parent'.

By chatting to people, we try to find out what's really going on so we can help in the best way we can. For example, a mother may seem obsessed with her baby's growth because she turns up to weigh him every week, but the real issue is that she is lonely and needs some social support. So we might suggest a postnatal drop-in group.

Health visitors have a huge workload, so it can be a challenge giving people as much attention as we'd like. But it's incredibly rewarding to see parents confident with their new baby, especially if they've had a hard time to start with and we've been able to help in any way."

Lynda Skilton, 42

Lynda's tips

● Trust your own gut instinct. If you honestly think there's something wrong with your baby, see it through; call a doctor or even go to A&E if you have to.

I feel like my health visitor doesn't trust me, that she's looking for something to be wrong. Am I a bad mother?

This is a difficult one. It's your health visitor's job to look beneath the surface and make sure that everything is okay (eg to check you don't have postnatal depression and are hiding it well, because you think – wrongly – that it's a sign of weakness). If she's going to continue being your point of contact, perhaps tell her how you feel and ask whether she has any concerns she isn't telling you about. Chances are she will be surprised, and apologetic. Read our mini-interview with a health visitor, above.

● Get to know your baby. Research has shown that newborns don't just "lie there", they are communicating just hours after birth, responding to your voice and bathing in your gaze. Knowing this will make those early days so much more interesting.

If you can afford it, there is also paid help on offer

The maternity nurse

What is a maternity nurse? The maternity nurse is someone who moves in with a family to offer 24-hour help for around six days a week, usually for up to twelve weeks. A maternity nurse offers both practical expertise (bathing, feeding, sterilizing) and emotional support, and she usually sleeps in the baby's room.

How much does she cost? Around £100 a day; most agencies insist on a minimum booking of a fortnight.

Where can I find one?
www.littledarlingsnannyagency.co.uk
www.nannydirectory.co.uk
both nationwide
www.nannyservice.co.uk
(London-based) Tel: 0207 935 3515

A maternity nurse says:

"If, at the end of my stay, I can leave a family feeling happy and assured with their newborn, then I know I've done a good job. For many women these days, having a baby is the first time they're not 100 percent in control of their lives. It can be very traumatic, so I do my very best to ease the relationship between the family and their new arrival.

Take breastfeeding, for example. Few people would doubt it's best for the baby. But some new mothers are very disappointed when they don't pick it up straight away, so I tell them it's a skill that needs to be learnt, like driving, and encourage them to continue. On the other hand, if it's really upsetting the mother or the baby, I'll support the switch to a bottle.

You can't have fixed views in this job – you have to be instinctive and read through the lines about what people want. Many of my clients are high-powered people with strong views. I'd never overrule a mother except in safety issues: the room's too hot, for example, or the baby overdressed. If someone wants a routine, I will support them in it. My personal views are that, yes, a baby needs a routine (bath, bottle, bed, etc.) but you can't be too regimented. Routines are easier for bottlefed babies – the earliest I've got a newborn to sleep through the night is seven and a half weeks (and by through the night I mean 12–6am). The earliest I've had a breastfed baby doing this is at five months old."

Alex Louwther, 37

Alex's tips:

- Don't waste money on fancy gadgets such as baby food blenders or bottle-warmers. Stick to the basics: shops like John Lewis (**www.johnlewis.com**) offer an excellent check list. And the best breast pads are made by Lanisoh (available in Mothercare and Waitrose).

- There is no harm in letting a baby cry for a little while – it's a good workout for their lungs. But keep this to a minimum – twenty minutes of screaming is traumatic for everyone.

The post-birth Doula

What a doula does: Compared with a maternity nurse or nanny, whose job is centred around the baby, a doula's job is to "mother the mother" – whether it's helping her to breastfeed, hold the baby while she has a bath, or have dinner on the table that night. Her only real qualification is that she has children herself.

How much does she cost? Around £10–12 an hour, plus an agency fee. Doulas work an average of four hours a day, for four to six weeks after the birth.

Where can I find one?
British Doulas
www.britishdoulas.co.uk
Tel: 0207 244 6053
Doula UK
http://doula.org.uk
Tel: 0871 433 310 (Both are nationwide)

A doula says:

"My motto is that I will do whatever the mother would like me to do. I've cleaned out a car, carried firewood up six flights of stairs, taken dogs for a walk. Most of the time, however, my day is centred around making sure the mum has had breakfast and has some lunch, doing some shopping and getting dinner prepared if that is what she'd like, filling up and emptying the washing machine, ironing shirts.

Clients have told me that as well as the practical stuff, the main thing is having someone friendly to talk to. I do think that emotional support is vital, especially with breastfeeding. Most mothers sort this out on their own, but I've seen lots of ups and downs while they are getting there. But time after time, new mothers have told me that just having a reassuring, experienced person around makes all the difference.

We also have a lot of laughs with the babies and their funny little ways. I love this job. I've met wonderful mothers and gorgeous babies, and stayed in touch with many of them. In many ways, it's like being an honorary grandmother."

Pru Guthrie, 47

Pru's tips:

- Don't put pressure on yourself to get the baby in a day/night routine early on. If you tell yourself it's a 24-hour cycle, and you are *expected* to be up at night, it can take away some of the stress.

- New motherhood is like climbing a ladder. You start a little way up, then dip down a few rungs from sheer tiredness, but once you start going up again, there's no stopping you.

Further resources

Books

Baby Shock: Your Relationship Survival Guide by Elizabeth Martyn (Vermilion, £7.99). A practical guide to the atom bomb that lands on your relationship with the arrival of a child, with tips on how to manage the demands of work and family, and make time for yourselves.

Fatherhood by Marcus Berkmann (Ebury, £10.99). A jolly (and useful) look at what fathers have to go through from conception to life after birth.

Full-Time Father: How to Succeed as a Stay-at-Home Dad by Richard Hallows (White Ladder Press, £9.99). Hallows gave up work when it became apparent his wife earned far more than he did. His book looks at the issues involved in a man becoming the main carer: self-esteem, friendships, income and the effect on your relationship.

Websites

www.babycentre.co.uk
www.babyworld.co.uk
www.mumsnet.com
Recommended websites with "communities". The baby website community groups offer excellent support: what may start off as an "on-line friendship" with another mother can lead to an enduring "in the flesh" friendship, too, as local parents arrange to meet up.

www.cafamily.org.uk For the parents of children with special needs, the Contact a family website includes medical information, publications and details on campaigns and policy. **Helpline: 0808 808 3555** (open Monday to Friday, 10am–4pm).

www.gingerbread.org.uk Gingerbread is the leading resource for help and support for lone parents. **Helpline: 0800 018 4318** (open Monday to Friday, 10am–4pm)

www.homedad.org.uk Launched in 2000, the HomeDad website is run by a team of stay-home dads with on-line discussions, chatrooms and round-ups of the latest relevant news. Tel: 07752 549 085.

www.nctpregnancyandbabycare.com. To find an NCT postnatal group in your area, call the Enquiry Line on 08704 448 707 or if none exists, consider starting up your own – visit www.growagroup.com

www.parentlineplus.org.uk Parentline Plus is a national charity that works for, and with, parents of children from babyhood to eighteen plus. Has nationwide branches, though not as many – or as widespread – as the NCT. Also runs themed workshops, and has on-line tips and tools. **Helpline: 0808 800 2222** (24 hours, 7 days a week). Tel: 0207 284 5500.

www.picturehouses.co.uk For "mother and baby" screenings nationwide. Other local, independent cinemas may also run them – see your local press.

www.tamba.org.uk The Twins and Multiple Birth Association (TAMBA) is an organization dedicated to parents with twins, triplets and more.

Includes sections with FAQs on eating and sleeping etc, an on-line shop with books and leaflets, details of specialist holidays and local twins clubs. **Helpline: 0800 138 0509** (open daily, 10am–1pm and 7–10pm). Tel: 08707 703 305.

For baby massage and postnatal exercise classes, etc… check your local press or keep an eye out for leaflets in shops and doctors' surgeries. Some websites include:

www.iaim.org.uk The International Association of Infant Massage – includes a map on finding a baby message teacher in your area, and information on courses you can take to learn yourself.

www.postnatalexercise.co.uk Information on when and how to start exercising, and where to find a trainer near you.

The new people

4

Feeding your baby

4

Feeding your baby

The way you feed your baby has repercussions far beyond the main objective: to get some fuel into your newborn so that he can grow and thrive. It starts – bang! – with the "breast vs bottle" debate and continues through the first year with the decision about when to wean and which foods to introduce at which point.

But it is this initial conundrum: "will I breastfeed or give formula milk?" that really preoccupies many mothers. Closely followed by putting your choice into practice while navigating the obstacles along the way.

You may reasonably expect that these issues are tricky enough just between you and your baby, but no – they are also open season for everyone else you know. Ever since that weeny sperm met that teeny egg, you've probably been inundated with advice about everything from maternity jeans to pain relief in labour, but nothing comes close to the busybody interest in whether your baby is breastfed or not. In some circles it reaches a moral fever pitch – the implication you are a "bad mother" who is poisoning her child if you reach for the SMA Gold instead of mother's own. And even if these judgments are not overt, many conscientious mothers who, for whatever reason, find themselves bottlefeeding start to imagine breast-feeding champions whispering viciously about them on street corners.

None of this is made easier by the fact that every week there is a new piece of research about allergies, intelligence and how your baby will be obese unless you breastfeed him exclusively until he's four years old. Okay – that's an exaggeration but you get the point – it's an emotive and difficult area that can lead to an aching head, heart . . . and nipples. Having said all this, once you've overcome the challenges, feeding your baby is one of the most special privileges of motherhood. And this is true, whichever route you take: whether feeling that cute little nibble on your breast, or that fabulous, melting sensation of gazing deep into her eyes while you give her a bottle.

Breast versus bottle

Cards on the table: you'd be hard-pressed to find an expert who would deny the fact that "breast is best" for your baby. Even the manufacturers of formula milk accept this, putting something along the lines of "even closer to breast-milk" on their cartons.

It's simply a question of weighing up the situation you find yourself in, and finding the best answer. If you are ill, or your baby is premature and has to stay in hospital without you, you may find that any "decision" is taken out of your hands. You may want your partner to take on 50 percent of feeding duties; bottlefeeding makes this easier. Or, you may discover that your baby struggles at the breast, that she is not gaining weight and that a healthy, fat child is more important than some ancient "earth-mother" dream.

FEEDING FACT BOX

- In 2000, 69 percent of babies were breastfed initially in the UK – among the lowest rates in Europe. A fifth of their mothers stopped in the first two weeks.
- The top three reasons for stopping between two to six weeks were that the mother had insufficient milk, that breastfeeding was too tiring, and that nipples and breasts had become painful. Other reasons given were that the baby rejected the breast, the mother was ill, or that the baby couldn't be fed by others.
- Women are more likely to breastfeed if: this is their first baby; they are middle class, aged thirty or above, university-educated and have friends who breastfed.
- By the time their babies were four to five months old, 45 percent of breastfeeding mothers were also giving their babies formula milk

(Source: NCT breastfeeding awareness week 2004)

Breastfeeding: the pros and cons

You may have made up your mind what you want to do before the baby comes, or you may "go with it" and see what transpires. Either way, it's good to make a decision with some information at your fingertips. Here are a few pointers.

The big pros

• It's the most nutritious food

"Breastfeeding is an unequalled way of providing ideal food for the healthy growth and development of infants", says the World Health Organization. Indeed, mothers' milk contains exactly the right balance of carbohydrates, protein and fat for your newborn (400 ingredients in all) and it adapts for your baby's changing needs as he grows.

Formula milk, while not being nature's ready-made drink, is *not actively bad* for your baby and newer and better preparations are being produced all the time. Untreated cow's milk, however, is not appropriate as a main drink for the first year (though it can be added to food after six months) because it contains too much sodium and protein and not enough sugar.

(WHO/ UNICEF International Code of Marketing of Breastmilk Substitutes, 1999).

• It's good for the baby

Breastfed babies have fewer illnesses because human milk transfers the mother's antibodies (proteins which fight infection). Various scientific papers have shown that these infants are less likely to catch diseases including bronchitis, pneumonia and ear infections; the make-up of breastmilk also makes diarrhoea and constipation less likely.

It's particularly important to breastfeed your baby if you have a family history of allergies such as asthma, eczema and food allergy. Avoiding formula for a full six months (if possible; not always easy) lowers the risk of these being passed on.

New research shows that later in life, breastfed babies are less likely to become obese, diabetic and less prone to suffer heart attacks.

("Breastfeeding Best for Babies" US Food and Drug Administration Statement by RD Williams, 1995).

("Fecal Secretory Immunoglobulin A in Breastmilk v Formula Feeding in Early Infancy" by A.K. Koutras, Journal of Paediatric Gastro Nutrition, 1989).

• It's good for you

Breastfeeding is accompanied by the release of oxytocin, the formula which helps the uterus return to pre-pregnancy size. These contractions shut off the maternal blood vessels which formerly fed the baby, making it less likely you'll suffer postpartum haemorrhage (substantial bleeding). Sometimes, women who bottlefeed from the start are given oxytocin in hospital to reproduce the same effect.

In the longer term, several studies have shown that breastfeeding is linked with lower rates of pre-menopausal breast cancer, ovarian and endometrial cancer. Osteoporosis (brittle bone disease) is also apparently less common in women who have breastfed.

("Lactation and a Reduced Risk of Premenopausal Breast Cancer" by Newcomb, Storer and Longnecker, New England Journal of Medicine, 1994).
("Influence of breastfeeding and nipple stimulation on postpartum uterine activity" by Chua, Arulkumaran, Lim et al, British Journal of Obstetrics and Gynaecology, 1994).

• It's easy, cheap and you don't need loads of gear

Breastmilk is free, comes at exactly the right temperature, and you don't need to faff around with bottles and sterilizing in the middle of the night. In fact, as you get used to the whole thing, you can bring your baby into bed with you and both drift off to sleep.

The nappies of breastfed babies also smell far more pleasant than the formula variety.

• It's a lovely experience

You can't really get much closer to your baby than feeding her straight from your body. And the oxytocin that's produced by the breastfeeding process can result in a lovely, dreamy feeling, giving the illusion that all is calm and ordered in your world. If it works, who cares if it's just an illusion?

• It smells and tastes nicer than formula

Okay, I don't go round drinking pints of the stuff, but in the interests of research, I have to confess trying a couple of drops of each type. Breast-milk, which looks like thin, greyish skimmed milk, is sweet and smells fresh; formula, which looks whiter and creamier-looking, tastes more sour and has a distinctive smell. On the other hand, if you've been bottlefed from birth, you probably won't know the difference and will glug away perfectly happily.

The debatable pros

• **Your baby will turn out to be cleverer**

One study has shown that the average IQ of seven- and eight-year-old children who had been breastfed as babies was ten points higher than their bottlefed peers. In mitigation, I can safely say that one of the most intelligent people I know – he wrote a master's thesis on James Joyce's *Ulysses* – was exclusively formula-fed.

("Breastfeeding and Later Cognitive and Academic Outcomes" by Horwood and Fergusson, Journal of Paediatrics, 1998).

("The Effect of Exclusive Breastfeeding on Development and Incidence of Infection in Infants" by Wang and Wu, Journal of Human Lactation, 1996).

• **You'll lose weight**

According to some American research, women who breastfeed generally burn 500 extra calories a day, and lose weight faster than bottlefeeding mothers. And while it's certainly true that your uterus shrinks more quickly because of the hormones produced when you are feeding, anecdotal evidence from friends suggests that the unattractive "baby fat" only really started to go once they had stopped. Moreover, because breastfeeding also makes you hungry, it can be very easy to top the 500 calorie "allowance" (500 calories isn't as much as it sounds (it's a ham and cheese toasted sandwich; a tuna mayo baguette or one and a half Twixes).

Another argument in the "breastfeeding keeps you fat" camp is that you can't diet when feeding a baby: rapid weight loss is bad for your baby because it releases toxins into the bloodstream (they're normally stored in your body fat), increasing the amount that end up in your milk.

("Breastfeeding reduces maternal lower body fat" by F. Kramer, Journal of the American Diet Association, 1993).

• **You'll have nice, big breasts**

Depending on how long it's been since your baby has fed, they might border on the alarming. However, speaking as a natural 34A cup, having a (temporary) cleavage was rather a blast. Friends with God-given 36Ds have been less excited.

The cons (and, logically, also the pros of bottlefeeding)

• To begin with, it can take over your life

It's pretty much a universally accepted truth: babies who are breastfed can't last as long between feeds as bottlefed babies because formula milk takes longer to digest. To start with, it feels like many newborns are feeding 24/7, and since each feed can take as long as an hour to begin with, this just about leaves time to go the loo in between. And seeing as small babies can't tell day from night, it follows that you also suffer from …

• Lack of sleep

Even up to three months, some breastfed babies feed every two hours and won't settle without their next milky fix. This is utterly, bone-crushingly, chronically exhausting and rather enough to send you scampering for the bottle (in both senses). The mothers who choose to co-sleep (have their baby in bed with them) suffer less from this, as the little one can snack on and off all night.

• Painful breasts, leaky breasts, cracked nipples etc …

Even when it's going well, breastfeeding holds such delights as hugely engorged breasts which leak through your top for all the world to see. When it's going badly, especially at the start, pain from cracked and bleeding nipples from your baby "latching on" incorrectly (see below) can be so excruciating that, unsurprisingly, it's one of the main reasons women give up.

• Feeding the baby is your job alone

Yes, yes – all the experts say you can express milk into a bottle so your partner can take over, but in reality it's such a pain to do this regularly that you might as well just feed the baby yourself. This also leads to the fact that …

• You are pretty much tied to the baby because she needs feeding so often

Going back to work is pretty difficult for women who are breastfeeding, although it's not impossible (see below). Ditto skipping off for days out shopping alone, or nights on the town. Although these are of limited excitement because …

• You can't get drunk

There's more on breastfeeding and alcohol below (see box) but even if the occasional indulgence is probably okay, getting hammered is strictly out.

• It can nix your sex life

Even if you *wanted* to get back on with it, the hormonal roller coaster of breastfeeding chucks a spanner in the works because the prolactin can squash your libido and progesterone can make you feel dry. Some men are unsurprisingly not keen on sleeping with a milk-cow as a partner and may find your big, leaky breasts a turn-off.

• It's tiring and emotional

Some women complain that they still feel pregnant when they are breastfeeding, and the hormonal cocktail does feel a bit like suffering from permanent PMS – feelings of tiredness, weepiness and irritation are not uncommon.

Despite all this, many women still feel it's still worth persevering because of the long-term benefits for you and the baby. Read on for how to get started.

Breastfeeding

I was determined to breastfeed at all costs

"The only part of my birth-plan I felt really strongly about was that I would breastfeed my daughter, and that the midwives should help me. I had been breastfed as a baby, and most of my friends had chosen to feed their children this way. But it was the health benefits that convinced me the most. Eczema and allergies run in my family, and I wanted to do everything I could to make sure that Alice avoided developing these conditions.

In many ways, I was lucky. Alice took to feeding easily, minutes after birth, so the midwives didn't need to help. I didn't suffer with particularly sore nipples, although regular applications of **camomile cream** probably helped. The engorgement when my milk 'came in', and again when I was cutting back, was very uncomfortable but didn't last too long.

In the first days, the biggest irritations were from everyone telling me that, every time Alice cried, 'she was hungry' – even if she had just had an hour's feed. This made me furious because if they were right (and often they weren't – it was just an easy answer) it was down to me to comfort her. As time went on, she became more efficient at feeding, and so I had more time to myself. The biggest problems were at night, and after eight weeks of every-two-hours feeding, I was shattered and *this* close to giving up and turning to bottle-feeding. But I stuck with it. Things got slowly better, and though I didn't get a decent night's sleep for over six months, I'm so pleased I did breastfeed.

Now she's eighteen months old and a happy, bright little girl. The eczema and allergies have shown no sign of appearing, so I feel it was worth it. And she sleeps through the night perfectly, and those six sleepless months feel like a surreal dream."

Caroline, 36

What breast milk is made of

The first few days

● For two or three days after the birth, your body produces a liquid called **colostrum** – some women leak a bit during the latter stages of pregnancy.

Yellowish in colour, it's much thicker than later breastmilk, and is particularly high in protein, fat-soluble vitamins, minerals and antibodies which pass from mother to baby and provide **passive immunity** for the baby. Passive immunity protects the baby from a wide variety of bacteria and viruses. Don't worry if you can't see the colostrum coming out: your baby only extracts and needs very small quantities.

Days three to fourteen

● Three days or so after the birth, colostrum will be replaced by **transitional milk**, which contains high levels of fat, lactose (the sugar found in milk) and water-soluble vitamins. It is packed with more calories than colostrum.

Two weeks in

● You'll be producing "**mature**" breastmilk. Ninety percent is water, needed to keep your baby hydrated; the other ten percent is made of carbohydrates, proteins and fats which are necessary for both growth and energy. There are two types of mature milk: **foremilk** and **hind-milk**. Foremilk is found during the first ten minutes or so of feeding and is high in water, vitamins and protein. During the latter part of the feed, the baby receives hind-milk, which is richer in fat and necessary for weight gain. A baby needs both fore- and hind-milk to grow and develop properly.

Getting started

Your position:

● To begin with, it's a good idea to set yourself up somewhere quiet and comfortable, with your back well supported with cushions. It can help also to have a special v-shaped cushion on which to rest the baby – especially if you've had a C-section and your scar is still painful (you can buy these cushions at Argos and from the NCT, see Further Resources p.163).

● To help your arms and back, bring the baby to the breast rather than leaning forward and bringing the breast to the baby. And try to drink a glass of water at every feed – it's easy to become dehydrated without realizing it.

Positions for the baby

● The descriptions below look may look complicated, but once you've found the position for you, and done it once or twice, they should become second nature.

• The cradle hold

If you imagine a classic picture of a woman breastfeeding; this is the correct position. Hold your baby against you so that he's lying on his side, directly facing you. His stomach should be against your stomach, and his nose should line up with your nipple. Tuck his lower arm under yours.

If he's feeding on the right breast, rest his head in the crook of your right elbow, with the rest of your arm extending to support his neck and back. You can use your left arm either to cup your breast with a "C"-shaped grip and make it easier for your baby to latch on, to stroke your baby as he's feeding, or to switch on the TV with the remote control (as you get more confident).

Good for: Babies who were delivered vaginally. However, women who've had C-sections may find this position puts pressure on their scar.

The cradle hold

• The clutch hold

Tuck your baby under your arm (on the same side that you're feeding from) like a handbag, head facing forwards, feet threading backwards, through the "hole" made by your arm. Rest your arm on a pillow, and support your baby's shoulders, neck and head with your hand, using your forearm to support her upper back.

Good for: Women who've had C-sections (it stops the baby pressing on your stomach) or who have large breasts.

The clutch hold

Small or premature babies who need extra "guidance" can also benefit. If you have twins, it's the best way to feed both babies at once (two handbags!).

• The cross-over hold

Similar to the cradle hold using opposite arms: you don't support your baby's head in the crook of your arm, but hold it lightly in your hand. So say you're feeding from your left breast, then use your right hand and arm to hold your baby. With your thumb behind one ear, and your fingers behind the other, you should be able to guide her mouth to your breast.

Good for: Babies who find it hard to latch on.

• Lying on your side

Lie on your side with a pillow under your head – it can also help to have one between your knees. Position your baby on her side,

The cross-over hold

facing you, with her head cradled by the hand of your bottom arm. If your baby is too small to be comfortably in line with your nipple, support her on a flat pillow or blanket.

Good for: Mothers who are recovering from a C-section, find themselves feeding a lot at night, or who just fancy a lie-down.

Lying on your side

"Latching on"

Much of the secret to breastfeeding is getting the baby "latched on" correctly, ie stuck onto your breast in the most efficient way to suck down the milk. In short, it's not just your nipple that has to be in her mouth, but a big mouthful of the surrounding breast: if you can see any of the **aureola** (the dark, circular bit around your nipple), it should be at the top.

If it doesn't feel right, don't just pull her off – she'll hang on for dear life and your breast will stretch like a balloon until the nipple leaves her mouth with a resounding and painful "pop". Instead, break the suction by putting your little finger between the baby's gums and your breast.

Feeding your baby

A perfect latch

When your baby is in position, tickle her lips with your nipple: if she turns her head away, gently stroke her cheek on the side nearest to your breast – the "rooting reflex" will ensure she turns towards you. Most babies need no further encouragement to open their mouths to suck – the most important thing is that her mouth is open wide enough to take in not only the nipple, but enough of surrounding the breast (her gums should completely bypass the nipple.) Pull the baby towards you (not vice versa) and off you go. If your baby seems uneasy or frustrated she may not be on properly, so release the suction and start again.

Your "let down"

The "latch", the "let down" – breastfeeding has a whole, arcane language of its own. The "let down" is specialist lingo for the milk-ejection reflex, which normally sets itself off after your baby has been sucking for a few minutes – sometimes earlier, if it's been a while before the last feed. It's the result of a complex biological process where the baby's sucking sends messages to the pituitary gland in your brain, which in turn triggers the release of two hormones: **prolactin** – which stimulates milk production and **oxytocin** – which activates the let-down reflex.

You'll know it's happening because your breasts will go all pins-and-needly (although not all women feel this) and what had been a drip of milk turns into a huge gush, and your other breast might start leaking in sympathy. Your baby will know about it because his steady little drink has turned into a whooshing yard of ale. If he can cope with it, he might start swallowing more

Eight signs your baby is "on" and feeding correctly

● The baby's mouth is wide open.
● His lower lip, if you can see it, is rolled back towards his chin and is further from the nipple than the upper lip.
● If you tug carefully at corner of his lower lip, the baby's tongue is visible cupping your breast.
● His head is slightly tipped back, but not uncomfortably.
● His chin is firmly planted on your breast, but his nose is usually only lightly touching or is free of it.
● While feeding, he makes short, chopping jaw motions to start with, followed by slow, deep, steady jaw motions, about one per second. The muscles in his face will be working so hard, you can even see his ears wiggle.
● He stops sucking and makes a sort of "unnk" sound when he swallows, usually with every one to three jaw strokes.
● He stops every now and then or returns to short sucks, followed by more deep, steady strokes .

Five signs that your baby is not "on", and feeding correctly

● Breastfeeding hurts: either your nipples are sore, or your breasts feel engorged, even after a feed.
● The baby sucks noisily or frantically, without falling into any rhythm.
● He does not seem relaxed .
● He seems hungry, even after a long feed (40 minutes plus) and is reluctant to let your nipple go.
● He is not gaining weight (see below).

The Breastfeeding Supporter

"In the early days, I speak a lot to women who are simply asking 'is this normal?' Sometimes, all they need is reassurance – for example, they may be baffled by how often the baby is feeding, or by the fact he may be 'cluster feeding' – taking several breastfeeds in a row, then nothing for several hours. Other times, they need help with the latch, or with positioning. On the whole, understanding about breastfeeding is improving, although there is still a lot of misinformation out there.

(Contd.)

Because bottlefeeding was more common in the 70s and 80s, a new mother's own mother may not have the information to help out, or may criticize, because perhaps the situation is bringing back memories of a bad experience she had.

In my role, I provide a lot of practical information, but that's not necessarily the most important thing – I'd say that is taking a woman seriously if she is worried. So often, by talking something through, it all becomes clearer. The first days with a new baby are a bit of a daze – there is so much to take in, so much advice coming from so many quarters, and you haven't even had a chance to get to know your baby yet. If I can help a woman to breastfeed as long as she wants to, I think that's a fantastic privilege."

Jane Putsey

Jane's tips:
- Of all the tips you are given about positioning, "nose to nipple" is the most helpful for getting a good latch.
- Before you start to feed, have a good look at your breasts in the mirror. Each side may require a slightly different position as they are not necessarily symmetrical, so if you can work this out in advance, you may save yourself some difficulties.

quickly; if not, he'll probably pull himself off with a bit of a splutter and get a faceful, while anyone within five paces of you will also be showered with a delicate spray. This is particularly embarrassing when it happens in smart restaurants.

Blocked ducts

Every now and then, you might feel a lump develop in one of your breasts after a feed. This is a **blocked duct**, and normally occurs because your baby hasn't entirely emptied the breast. It's worth looking out for these and trying to deal with them straight away, because any lumps might get infected and cause **mastitis** (see below). Most blocked ducts can be cleared with massage: basically, pressing the heal of your hand above the lump and smoothing it towards the nipple. The application of a warm flannel can help release any dry milk, as can expressing after feeds. Keep up your fluid intake, and make sure you rest.

Mastitis

Sometimes, however, it's impossible to prevent mastitis, a common, treatable but nevertheless unpleasant infection. Mastitis is caused by bacteria entering the breast, usually from the baby's mouth, into a milk duct through the cracked skin of a nipple. It's more common in first-time mothers – for whom the rampant jaws of a baby can come as a bit of a shock – usually striking when your baby is between two and six weeks of age.

Mastitis starts off with a sore, hard, hot breast, accompanied by "flu-like symptoms": chills, tiredness and a temperature of around 38.4°C. Mild cases can be treated at home, with rest, lots of fluid and the application of

FEEDING IN PUBLIC

The first time you sit down in a café, baby at your breast, you'll probably feel so self-conscious you might as well be topless dancing on the table, entertaining a group of rugby fans. There are two things to say at this point. First: most people are far too engrossed in their own matters to notice what you are doing, and even if they do, the majority won't bat an eyelid. If you are unlucky to live in an area where a woman breastfeeding is an exotic sight and that people DO stare, tell yourself that you're doing what's best for your baby, and tell them that if it's really bothering them, perhaps they should simply stop gawping. If anyone instructs you to go and use the "breastfeeding facilities", perhaps you should politely point out that they should go and each their lunch in the toilet, too.

The second thing worth mentioning is that as you gain confidence, you'll be able to breastfeed with such aplomb it almost becomes an invisible process – the baby's head tends to cover the "naughty bits" anyway. A few tips from other mothers:

- Wear button-up shirts so you won't have to hoick your t-shirt up to waist level.
- Put a muslin or napkin over the area, although you need to make sure the baby can still breathe.
- If you're still self-conscious, sit with your back to the majority of the crowd.
- Feed your baby before she gets ravenous and starts yelling the place down for her dinner.

BREASTFEEDING AND ALCOHOL

While we're on the subject of guilty pleasures, what about alcohol? There's been a lot of publicity recently about the effects of drinking in pregnancy, with new advice suggesting it's best to avoid alcohol altogether while the baby's brain is still developing. However, the good news is that – with moderation – the *occasional* drink after the baby is "out" and breastfeeding is okay. Alcohol levels peak thirty–ninety minutes after you've had a drink, so it's best to avoid feeding until two or three hours after a glass. You don't have to pump out "contaminated milk", because as alcohol levels dissipate from your blood, they also leave your milk.

None of this is carte blanche for a complete binge, or regular nightly drinking, both of which are still deemed harmful – research shows that chronic exposure to more than two units a day may have an affect on development. In general, however, this is good news for those of us who feel the odd guilt-free glass of merlot keeps us sane. Just be careful about the measures: one unit is calculated as half a pint or a 125ml glass; large pub measures or a full goblet glass in someone's kitchen can easily double this.

(Breastfeeding Network: Wendy Jones PhD)

hot flannels to the affected breast. You can also take **ibuprofen** (nurofen) to bring down the swelling or paracetamol for the pain, but *not aspirin* because it's unsuitable for babies (in extremely rare cases, it's been linked with a rare liver disorder) and the drug can be transmitted through milk. Some people also swear by putting chilled leaves of savoy cabbage inside their bra, an old wives' remedy which seems to actually work.

While it may be agony to continue breastfeeding or expressing, experts recommend you push yourself through the pain barrier to empty the breast. This will keep your milk flowing freely and hence avoid risking more blockages.

See a GP if:

● You don't start feeling better within eight to 24 hours.

● Your temperature continues, or starts to rise.

● Your breast becomes hotter, or more swollen, and red streaks appear.

- You see pus or blood in your milk.

- A cracked nipple looks infected.

More serious cases of mastitis are usually treated with antibiotics and bed-rest. It's important to act swiftly to prevent the tiny risk of an abscess developing, which might need hospital treatment. Most women who've suffered mastitis continue breastfeeding successfully: there's no risk of passing the infection to your baby.

I was surprised how difficult it was

"I always wanted to exclusively breastfeed but I was surprised at how difficult it was at first. Niamh just wouldn't latch on at all. I'd had an emergency Caesarean after a long induced labour so I found it hard to get comfortable initially. We tried lying down at first but that didn't work. Then when I could sit up she still wasn't having any of it. I tried the rugby hold, having her across by chest – but no. It was awful. I was so tired and so sore and I just couldn't work out how to do it.

Niamh was on antibiotics, so we ended up in hospital for ten days. Every time she needed to feed, I would ring the bell and get a midwife to literally shove my

Breastfeeding FAQs

How long should I feed my baby for?

Babies are different; some enjoy a leisurely three-course meal with wine, others gobble down their fast food. An average is twenty minutes or so – although, when you're getting started, it can take up to an hour for a feed. When a baby has had enough, she'll let you know by pulling off or by falling asleep (drinking breastmilk is like mainlining opium). If you don't think she's had enough, try and jiggle her awake, or massage the palm of her hand. You may be fighting a losing battle: it's often impossible to rouse your newborn from a drunken milky slumber.

The latest advice is that a baby should satisfy himself totally on one breast before you offer the other one (compared with the "ten minutes each side" of our mothers' generation). This is so he will get the hind-(or fatty) milk that comes at the end of a feed, not just the foremilk that comes at the start (see "what breast milk is made of" p.122).

And how often?

Most health professionals encourage you to feed "on

demand", ie when the baby wants it. Breastfed newborns feed every two hours or more to begin with, and if yours is one that dawdles over an hour-long lunch, it can feel like you are doing nothing else. If you've got sore breasts, it can feel like infinite torture.

The good news is that as the weeks pass, the baby will become more efficient, and feed less often (every three to four hours), but it's not a good idea to force a routine early on: breastmilk works on a supply-and-demand principle so cutting back artificially will sabotage your supply. In fact, if your baby is sleeping though a feed, you'll need to wake her. Heartbreaking, but necessary.

How do I know she's getting enough?

If your baby is bottlefed, it's easy to see how much is going into her. Sadly no such dice with your breast. However, studies have shown that, for the first twelve weeks, mothers of fully breastfed babies produce about 800ml of milk a day. One way to check she's eating enough is to check her nappy: on average a well-breastfed baby does at least five poos a day for the first two to three months, and has a wet nappy every two hours or so.

nipple in her mouth. To be honest, I would have given up if I'd been at home.

For those first couple of weeks my nipples were cracked but I used camomile ointment and that sorted them out. Gradually we worked out what to do and I breastfed her to five months. To be honest, I don't think I produced enough milk for her anyway and I felt totally liberated when we moved on to bottles."

Gemma, 30

I was saved by a breast-feeding workshop

"If anyone asks me now, I would say that breastfeeding went wonderfully. The truth is that it only started to go well after two weeks of panic, a lifesaving breastfeeding workshop and the help of an Internet forum for mums.

To begin with I didn't know what to do. I thought breastfed babies looked at you in the eye whilst suckling and all mothers produced the right amount of milk. Well neither seemed true. It was a struggle to get her latched on and then she kept popping on and off, spluttering, whilst my milk sprayed the room.

The class was fantastic because I was finally told about correct positioning. They recommended holding baby with one hand on the back of its neck so you can position it sideways, tummy to tummy. Now that might sound simple but it's completely different to how you hold a baby to bottle-feed and that was all I had seen anyone do. That one trick helped me more than anything.

Now our main problem was she was coming off the breast and gagging. I went on an on-line forum and some women suggested I had a very fast flow and to lean back so the milk had to work against gravity and wouldn't choke the baby. Also they helped me relax about the fact that the baby would feed quickly (5–10minutes) and only on one side per feed. With fast flow, that's often the case and she still packed on the weight.

Most of the breastfeeding advice is about too little milk and to be sure to drain each breast so I think the teachers and counsellors should mention that sometimes women produce lots of milk and how to deal with that."

Nell, 34

I had to admit defeat

"I've had it all – cracked bleeding nipples, mastitis, backache and a baby who was having none of it. I was adamant I wanted him to breastfeed, no ifs or buts about it, so I kept trying until at eight weeks I finally had to give up and moved onto formula. It broke my heart.

The urine should be colourless, not yellow, which might suggest dehydration.

Understandably, the fact your baby is gaining weight is an encouraging sign. It's common for newborns to drop a few ounces (up to ten percent of birth weight) the first time they are put on the scales by your midwife or health visitor, but two weeks in, they should be back to birth weight, and increasing. Breastfed babies pack on the pounds more slowly than bottle-fed children – it's worth bearing in mind that the growth curves in your "red book" are aimed at infants who are formula-fed. But as long as your baby continues broadly up the same centile curve, there's no need to worry. See section on "failure to gain weight" p.290 in Chapter 9.

Do I need to give anything else?
Nope, not even water. Breastmilk alone is perfect up to six months of age. After this time, it's important to start introducing solids because your baby starts to need a different set of nutrients.

My baby has suddenly started demanding milk more often. Is this normal?
At around three and six weeks, many babies go through a

"growth spurt" where they feed little and often. Take heart in the fact your baby is thriving, and that this extra activity should only last a day or two.

Breastfeeding is going really well, but is it okay to give my baby an occasional bottle of formula?

Even if your baby is thriving, you still might find the temptation to give yourself a night off. Some women feel that giving heavier formula before bed makes their baby sleep longer, whereas some find it makes no difference whatsoever, or, worse, gives their baby indigestion because he's used to a "lighter" diet.

These considerations aside, you may want to avoid supplementary feeding (as it's called) if you can help it. For starters, if you miss a feed early on, this might mess up the "supply-and-demand" mechanism of breastfeeding, which will end up with you being painfully engorged with a dropping milk supply. When breastfeeding is established, this is less likely to happen. Then there are the health considerations: research has shown that in families

I had a natural birth and my son came out active and a good weight. I tried to get him feeding straight away but he only managed to latch on briefly twice in 45 minutes. That was it for the rest of the day and for the whole of that night. At first the midwives weren't bothered but I was so upset. My breasts were huge too. Everytime I tried, he screamed his head off in such a temper that his face went red-raw like someone was killing him.

By the next day I had a breastfeeding specialist, two paediatricians and various midwives in the cubicle trying to help me whilst someone else stuck my breast in his face to get him to latch on. I just burst into tears. He wouldn't even take my milk from a syringe.

We were discharged three days later and he was just about drinking expressed milk from a bottle. I spent so much money on different nipple shields, breastfeeding aids and paraphernalia that did nothing. Eventually I just had to stop because even the expressing wasn't enough anymore. I hated giving him bottles and I hated seeing my friends sitting there breastfeeding when I knew I had so much milk to give."

Suzanne, 25

What to buy if you're going to breastfeed

Breastfeeding is a good thing for minimalists, because, in theory, all you need is the baby and your breasts. But wherever there is a selling opportunity, you can be sure Avent et al will be happy to fill it with stuff.

Expressing milk

If you've managed to get this far without feeling like a dairy cow, then fear not – the experience of expressing milk is the final descent. In a nutshell, expressing is shorthand for the action of removing milk from your breast (either by hand or with a commercial pump – see below) so you, or someone else, can then put it in a bottle for your baby to drink.

There are several reasons why you might want to express: from the serious – to feed a tiny baby who's in an incubator – to the frivolous – to give you a couple of hours off while you get your hair cut and you want to leave the baby at home. Being able to pump off excess milk when your breasts are engorged is also a blessed relief.

susceptible to milk protein, just one bottle can set off the chain of events leading to allergy or atopic illness such as eczema.

Does it make a difference what I eat?

As in pregnancy, it's good to follow a broadly healthy diet with lots of protein (from meat and eggs), calcium (from dairy) and iron (red meat, green veg) although you no longer have to refrain from pregnancy no-nos such as brie and pâté. Hurray!

There are some arguments that the taste of garlic/curry/chilli goes into breastmilk and gives the baby indigestion, therefore you should ban these foods from your diet. But for every mother with an upset baby, there's another who says it makes no difference whatsoever. See what works for you – after ten months of abstinence, you may resent giving up the joy of a good old chicken tikka masala for no reason.

You can also store breastmilk for future use, in special "freezer bags" available from the usual shops. All equipment must be sterilized – see directions on your pump box, and also our section under "bottle feeding".

STORING BREASTMILK

Where	Temperature	Time
At room temperature	19–22° C	10 hours
In the fridge	0–4° C	8 days
In the freezer compartment inside a normal fridge	Temperature varies	2 weeks
In the freezer compartment with a separate door	Temperature varies	3–4 months
In a separate deep freeze	–19° C	6 months plus

(Source: La Leche League)

Quickie expressing Q & A

How much shall I express at once?
Breastfed babies don't eat that much at once, so put 2–4 ounces in each container to save wasting this precious liquid gold.

Why does my milk look "weird"?
Unlike formula, stored breastmilk separates out into a milk layer and a "cream" layer. It's perfectly normal, just shake it before use.

How do I thaw frozen milk?
Place it under water straight from the tap or immerse in a pan of hot water.

And how do I heat it up?
Again, by immersing in a pan of hot water. Heating up with a microwave is not generally recommended because of "hot spots" that could burn your baby's mouth. But despite this, many time-pressed mothers have caved into the nuclear route so, if this is you, make sure the bottle is properly shaken to equalize the temperature and you should be okay.

Breast pumps

If you are going to express on a regular basis, buying an "expresso machine" is a good idea. It is possible to express by massaging your breasts by hand, but it takes a while and makes an already undignified experience even more, well, undignified. All methods work in largely the same way: stimulating and compressing the **aureola** (area around the nipple) to stimulate the milk ducts, and set off the "let down".

There are broadly three different types of breast pumps you can use:

• Hand-operated pumps

The cheapest variety, they are widely available and easy to use, but generally need to be dismantled and rebuilt every time. The first time we did this in our house set off a panic not seen since the days of Airfix models, but like everything baby-related, it soon becomes second nature. Try not to lose any pieces – the most important component is the smallest, and it tends to fall down the waste-disposal unit when you are washing up.

• Hand-held electric or battery pumps

The next step up, these are faster and more effective than hand-operated pumps and tend to have fewer component pieces.

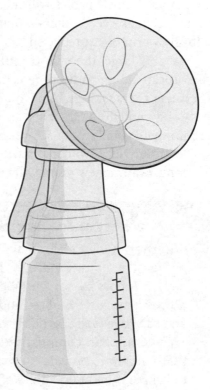

Hand-operated breast pump

• "Hospital grade" pumps

As the name suggests, these are generally kept on maternity wards but are the most effective of all – the action minics a baby's sucking pattern most effectively, and many have a double pump so you can do both breasts at once. This equipment is mainly for women with babies in special care whose mothers want to give them breastmilk, but women who go back to work early and continue breastfeeding also swear by them.

They can be rented from the NCT. For details of your nearest NCT Breastpump Agent contact the NCT Enquiries line. Tel: 0870 444 8707.

The bottle battle: Getting a breastfed baby to take a bottle

Extracting the milk from yourself is all very well; but what about getting your baby to drink it from a new receptacle? Even if you aren't expressing, at some point your baby will need to take milk from a different source, even if it's a year down the line. Some lucky mums have no problems with the switch at all, their babies will merrily suck away and don't mind at all how their meal is served. Others – quite understandably, really – baulk at having a lovely warm breast replaced by a cold piece of silicone.

By and large, the rule on introducing bottles is to wait long enough for breastfeeding to become established, and to avoid "nipple confusion" (because the sucking action on a teat is different from on a nipple) but not long enough for the baby to develop a strong preference. Most experts recommend about five or six weeks for this.

With any luck, your baby will just tuck in straight away. But a word of warning: many a new mum will coo with relief about how their baby accepts

BREASTFEEDING AND WORKING

Whether you've chosen to breastfeed your baby beyond your allocated maternity leave, or have rushed back to work in the early days, it *is* possible to continue. A great deal of conviction is needed, however, because working and feeding is a tiring way of doing things, and can have logistical difficulties.

The European commission has published guidelines suggesting that employers provide a private room to express milk, and a fridge to keep it in, although none of this is legally binding so it depends on your boss.

If you know when you are going back to work, it's a good idea to build up a large supply of milk in the freezer for the baby's carer to offer while you are away. While you're at work, try to express every three hours to keep engorgement (and embarrassing moments during meetings) to a minimum.

Once you've been feeding for a while, it's quite easy to scale down breastfeeding so you just offer night and morning feeds, making expressing for the daytime unnecessary. Just give your boobs enough time to adjust before you go back to work.

a bottle at six weeks, allowing them time to see that film/go shopping and leaving him with a babysitter. By four months, that same baby may resolutely shut his mouth and scream the place down at the thought of anything other than mummy's nice, soft breast. There are no hard-and-fast rules on solving this and often the only resolution is sheer, bloody-minded persistence. Here are some tips anyway:

● Offer the bottle for the first time when the baby is really hungry, so he might not notice. If he's really affronted, try when he's less ravenous. (I know this is a contradiction, but either can work.)

● Warm the teat under hot water so it feels more like a nipple.

Bottlefeeding FAQs

How much milk should I give my baby?

Tiny babies don't eat very much because their stomachs are so small: a newborn will probably only be able to manage a maximum of a couple of ounces per feed, although she will need feeding every couple of hours or so. Within the next four weeks, she'll probably be able to drink three or four ounces, and you can space the feeds more widely. In general, babies naturally fall into a routine of about eight feeds a day (so one every three hours, although hopefully fewer at night) unless you are following a Gina Ford-style routine (see Further Resources).

In contrast with a breastfed baby, you can manage your child's intake. The general rule for how much to give in a 24-hour period is 2.5 to 2.7 ounces per pound of body weight. So if your baby weighs ten pounds, that's 25 to 27 ounces. Look for your baby's clues for how much to give at once – if she consistently leaves an ounce undrunk every time you offer a four-ounce bottle, then reduce the amount offered at each feed.

● Get someone else to feed the baby, so he can't smell your milk.

● Once you've introduced the bottle, give it every two or three days so the baby stays in the swing of it.

● If your baby will take expressed milk, but not formula, have two small bottles ready. Give the expresso first, then try to seamlessly sneak in the new variety.

Bottlefeeding

First things first: don't sweat the white stuff. For whatever reason you find yourself bottlefeeding, rest assured in the knowledge you are giving your baby a form of nutrition that scientists have been slaving over for years and that reaches stringent government standards: formula is packed with proteins, fats, carbohydrates and minerals and although it doesn't contain the natural antibodies of breastmilk, it's a damn fine close second.

Bottlefeeding mothers can revel in the same close contact as their breastfeeding friends. In many ways, you are better placed to give your baby one hundred percent of your relaxed attention without any stresses over sore nipples, latching on or whether the baby is taking in enough milk. Most newborns take readily to sucking from a bottle. You will need:

Six to eight bottles:
You can buy them in two sizes:

- 4oz/120ml which are good for the first few weeks, when your newborn can't eat much in one go

- 8oz/225ml, suitable for thereafter.

Six to eight teats:
These come in latex, and a more hard-wearing silicone. Teats also have varying "flows" which dictate how fast the milk comes out. "Newborn" flow is slower, meaning your baby has to suck harder and is less likely to choke on a flood of liquid. As she grows older and hungrier, you can increase the flow.

I never even considered breastfeeding
"The moment I found out I was pregnant I knew I wanted to formula feed and I have never once regretted my decision, nor felt I was being a bad mum to Holly by not breastfeeding her. I was bottlefed as a baby and I haven't suffered. There were lots

Two- to six-month-olds require anywhere between 23 and 35 ounces a day depending on their appetites; by six months, when solids are introduced, it's about 24 ounces, dropping to 20 ounces when your baby is a year old.

These are rough guidelines: speak to your health visitor if you have any worries.

What's the best way to hold the baby?
Sit comfortably, propped up with cushions if necessary and enjoy the cuddle. Your baby's head should rest in the crook of your arm: don't lay him too flat, or he might get indigestion. Angle the bottle so that the flow of milk is constant, if it comes out in fits and starts, the baby is more likely to get wind. In general, formula-fed babies need winding more often than breastfed ones – often mid-feed, as well as after it, so follow the instructions on p.78. Never leave a baby "propped up" while you do something else.

How do I know when my baby is full?
When breastfed babies have had enough, they pull off – and the same applies for those who are bottlefed. Your baby will have his own way of

telling you, maybe by turning away, or whacking the bottle away with his arm. Don't force your baby to finish the bottle because you might end up with a chubby little tiger: formula-fed babies tend to become more overweight than breastfed ones, and recent studies have shown a higher propensity to obesity later in life.

How warm shall I make the bottle?

Trial and error is the only way to find out what your baby likes best. Breastmilk comes out at blood temperature (when you drip a bit on your wrist, you can't feel it) so it makes sense that many babies enjoy formula milk of a similar warmth. On the other hand, if you can get your newborn used to room temperature milk, or even a chilled shake from the fridge, you're doing yourself a favour. When it comes to midnight feeds, it will be much easier on you if the baby takes his milk "as it comes", without forcing you to faff around with saucepans and bottle-warmers in the small hours.

All the big babycare books and websites have sections on giving formula milk, eg www .babycentre.co.uk

of reasons as to why this was right for me. I wanted the flexibility that someone else could feed her if I needed some sleep. My husband wanted to be involved as much as he could and has always loved giving the night-time bottle. Plus, I am a private person and although I have no problems with seeing other women breastfeed in public I know I couldn't have done it. Of course, I was worried that my decision might affect the way we bonded but I am a great believer in close physical contact and she spent a lot of time sleeping on my chest so she could hear my heartbeat.

I know everyone is told that 'breast is best' but I personally believe that that isn't always the case. I've seen so many friends struggle with breastfeeding. Even during that first night at the hospital the other patients had screaming babies who wouldn't latch on whilst Holly happily tucked into her bottle. It was such a relief after two days of labour not to have to worry about that. Luckily my milk came in and left very quickly with very little discomfort.

To me, if you don't have a burning desire to breastfeed or you are just doing it to do the 'right thing' then don't do it. Bottles are easy, quick and so much less stress and neither of you have to suffer."

Michelle, 32

Choosing a formula

There are few things more baffling than running your eye along the supermarket shelves at the eye-watering array of formulas on offer. Understandably, this can be quite upsetting as you want to give your baby the best you can, but you don't want to be suckered in paying out hugely for something unnecessary. How do you tell if yours is a particularly vomity baby who needs "staydown" milk? If you don't buy organic or macrobiotic, will he grow up damaged? Will he be ostracized by the trendy kids in the nursery?

The bottom line is that all formula milks contain fundamentally the same ingredients – it's the law. The rest is just marketing spin, in the same way that certain brands of tea have different boxes or promise a more refreshing flavour. Sure, you may find your baby likes Cow & Gate more than SMA or vice versa (babies are humans with preferences, too) but the bottom line is, whatever you choose, it's not going to be a disaster.

Note that premature babies are often given special milks, so clearly the choice here is important. Plus, in rare circumstances, infants are allergic or intolerant to cow's milk and might be prescribed soya or specially modified formula. You need to see a GP or dietician before deciding this yourself – there has only been one study on the long-term health implications of feeding a baby soya milk, and it shouldn't be a flippant decision.

Most formula comes in big tins with a scoop, that, if used correctly, picks up exactly the right amount of powder (it's usually one flat scoop for every ounce of water in the bottle). You can also buy ready-made cartons which are handy for travelling or going out but these are more expensive.

Curds, whey and follow-on milk

Concerned parents reading the ingredients on a formula tin may find themselves baffled by "casein"-rich preparations or "milk for hungrier babies". Here's how it works – there are two types of protein in milk: **curds** (casein) and **whey**. Most infant formula has more whey than casein (about a 60:40 ratio, similar to breastmilk). But some milks (often called "second-stage" or "follow-on") have more casein (80 percent, as opposed to 20 percent whey) and these are deemed more filling because they take longer to digest. They also have a higher mineral content.

Generally, milks with a high concentration of casein are not particularly recommended for newborns, because they can cause constipation. Some manufacturers say that "follow-on milk" is needed from six months of age,

143

MAKING UP FEEDS

- Boil the kettle, giving the water enough time to cool down before your baby gets really hungry. If you can help it, don't use reboiled water as this increases sodium content, which isn't good for little kidneys.
- Wash your hands and sterilize the bottles: it can be a good labour-saving tip to have a day's worth of bottles ready to make up one time.
- Fill the bottles with the required amount of boiled water.
- Open the formula. The instructions on the box will tell you how many scoops to add to a certain amount of water. These usually need to be flattened scoops (you can level them off with a clean knife) rather than heaped ones. Never put the powder in before the water as you might get the concentration wrong.
- Replace the teat, put on the lid on and shake.
- Heat the bottle by placing it in a pan of hot water. Microwaves aren't recommended, because they heat unevenly and can cause "hot spots" which burn a baby's mouth. If you DO find yourself using one, make sure you shake the bottle thoroughly.
- If your baby only drinks half the milk, throw it away and don't offer it later. Yes, this is a pain and a waste, but it's better to suffer the inconvenience of making up a new bottle than risk your baby getting ill from a bacterial infection. Made-up bottles last in the fridge for 24 hours.

but health visitors often recommend sticking with the same formula until your baby is a year old, when you can happily switch to normal cow's milk. At six months, your baby will be eating solids and so will get any extra nutrition he needs that way.

Moving onto solids

One of the less well-documented advantages of early motherhood is that the physical state of your home remains pretty much unscathed. Yes, there may be a few plastic rattles kicking about your floorboards, or perhaps a couple of milky-vomit "crop circles" on your carpet, but it's only with the arrival of solid food in all its lurid colours that "The Mess", in earnest, starts to accumulate. From now on, any pretence of Kelly Hoppen-style serenity is history, as your baby meets pureed carrot and mashed banana, and said foodstuffs in turn meet your kitchen floor, your sheepskin rugs and your hair. None of which is helped by the fact that most of a baby's early food tends to be bright orange in colour (eg pureed carrot).

Having said all that, introducing your baby to a more varied, "solid" (though not as we know it) diet is, in general an entertaining experience, not least for the sweet, bemused expressions your baby makes as he expands his gastronomic repertoire.

How do I know my baby is ready for solids?

When your baby is:

- **A good weight**. Ideally double her birth weight (most babies achieve this around six months of age).
- **Can hold her head up, and sit well when supported**. Many babies cannot sit unaided until around seven or eight months old, but she should at least be able to remain upright when propped.
- **Is able to tolerate food in her mouth** without rejecting it automatically. Babies are born with the "tongue thrust" reflex, which causes them to push things out of their mouths automatically – it's a safeguard against choking. If your baby keeps doing this when you try to feed her, wait a while longer.
- **Shows an interest in what you're eating**. Little fat hands reaching out for your toast, and/or knife and fork are a dead giveaway that they're ready for the *prix fixe*.
- **She doesn't seem satisfied with her milk feeds**. This is another confusing one; some experts think that if your baby is getting enough milk, she should remain happy and full for up to six months. But if your has started to wake up, demanding food night after night, you may well decide that this little stomach is ready for something more substantial.

When's the right time to start?

Advice on this can be confusing. In 2003, the **Department of Health** issued the following statement, bringing its policy in line with the **World Health Organization**: "Exclusive breastfeeding is recommended for the first six months of an infant's life, as it provides all the nutrients a baby needs." Before that, the information given for many years was to give the first solid food some time between four and six months.

As with much official advice, the Department of Health's edict is "ideal world" advice, because, as we've seen, for various reasons the six-month breastfeeding thing doesn't work well for everyone. Moreover, some authorities believe that these recommendations are sensible for the developing world, where education and hygiene make exclusive breastfeeding possibly the safest choice for a baby, but not necessary for a country like the UK. However, **HIV** is found in breastmilk, and if you do breastfeed there is a significant chance of passing HIV to your baby. So if you have access to **safe** breastmilk substitutes (formula) then you are advised to not breastfeed. But if you live in a country where safe water isn't available, the risk of life-threatening conditions from formula feeding may be higher than the risk from breastfeeding. Formula can also be too expensive to use regularly in some countries. If you are in this situation it is better to feed your baby breast-milk alone.

In practice, most parents start to introduce solids at some point between four and six months. See box below for clues that your baby is ready for the menu. One thing is clear, however: it is *not* a good idea to start solid feeding before your baby is sixteen weeks old. This is because most younger children find it hard to digest anything apart from breastmilk or formula: moreover, some research has linked the early introduction of solids to eczema and asthma. Most babies this age are not able to sit up properly, meaning that they won't have the correct posture to swallow and digest their food properly, leading to constipation and "colicky" symptoms.

On the other hand, it is also unwise to wait longer than six months before introducing the first solids. When your baby hits the half-year mark, she starts to need more minerals – particularly iron – in her diet because the store she was born with becomes depleted. While some "follow-on" milks have added iron, it's not sufficient. In addition, older babies become set in their ways, and may resist this new experience, refusing foods that a younger baby will eat with relish.

For the first few weeks, solid food is more of a game, an introduction to different tastes and textures rather than a balanced and nutritious meal. Until your baby's first birthday, breast- or formula milk will still be the most important part of her diet.

What to buy for weaning

• Two or three plastic bowls or plates
You can also buy bowls with suckers on the bottom, which stop your baby hurling them off the table.

• Two or three soft-tipped plastic spoons
First spoons are long-handled, with a wide, shallow end, making it easy for the baby to remove the food.

See Chapter 10 for hints on buying high chairs.

Getting started

When? First meals are best offered when your baby is not too tired and in a good mood, probably some time in the middle of the day. "Conventional" mealtimes, or at least the more normal three meals a day can follow later. Give your baby half his breast- or bottlefeed so that he isn't overly ravenous, but not too full to try something new, then finish the milk feed afterwards.

What? Baby rice makes a good opener – you mix it with breastmilk or formula, so it will taste vaguely familiar, even if the texture is a bit different (it's quite like old primary school semolina). It's also gluten-free – gluten is the protein found in many cereals, and some babies have an intolerance to it. You can buy baby rice in chemists or supermarkets; the packet gives instructions on how to make it up.

Where? It's a messy business, so the kitchen is probably a good idea. Use a high chair with towels or cushions for support if your baby flops over. A car seat can also be a good idea – but watch like a hawk if you're putting your baby on the table. If you're fastidious, cover the floor with some plastic sheeting.

How? Put a small amount of food on a soft-tipped spoon, and approach the target. Chances are, your baby will do one of the following:

- Suck the spoon, as if it was a teat.

- Grab it, then wipe the sticky fingers all over himself and all over you.

- Accept the contents, pull a face of intensely comical surprise, then allow said contents to dribble slowly out again.

- Spit the contents violently in your face. Then repeat. Don't worry if she only manages a fraction of two or three teaspoonfuls – that's a triumph.

If your baby really isn't interested, shelve the whole venture for a few days. When he's ready, you'll be amazed how quickly he masters eating, starts to open his mouth wide like a baby bird and becomes excited about new tastes. Or, if there is any intial reticence it could be that he simply doesn't like primary school semolina (let's face it, did *you*?). Finely pureed fruit and veg are just as suitable for early eaters.

What food to give when?

For the first couple of months, runny purees are the way to go – as your baby becomes more confident, you can make them more lumpy. It's funny that, even this early in life, your baby has a preference for sweet foods rather than savoury ones (breastmilk is packed with natural sugars, so she's used to the taste). For this reason, it's important to give vegetables while she hasn't learned to say "no" – this will come soon enough, don't worry. Even so, it's best to stick with the sweeter end of the veggie scale, most members of which come in gorgeous, technicolour – guess what?? – orange!

As you are introducing new foods, do them one at a time so you can see what your baby likes, and if something disagrees with him you can avoid giving it again.

Not before six months

If you decide to give your baby solids before six months, it's still a good idea to avoid certain foods, especially if there is a family history of eczema, asthma or other allergies. These include:

- Wheat products (bread, pasta, rusks)
- Dairy products, including cheese and yoghurt, apart from your baby's usual milk
- Citrus fruits (including orange juice) or berries
- Nuts – avoid nuts, especially peanuts, under six months, in case of peanut allergy (rare, but fatal; see box on anaphylactic shock below)
- Fish
- Eggs
- Honey – not before one year, because in very rare cases it can cause botulism
- Salt and sugar – these should never be added to food

Best foods for four to six months

- Baby rice
- Pureed vegetables: carrots, swede, sweet potato, parsnip, butternut squash
- Pureed fruits: apple, pear and mashed ripe banana (ie with black speckles on the skin)

Best foods for seven to eight months

All the above, plus:
- Pureed lean meats or poultry
- Pureed lentils
- Pureed green vegetables such as broccoli and peas
- Mashed potatoes and rice

Eight months to a year

At around this time, you can institute a breakfast/lunch/dinner routine, although these will probably run earlier than your adult timetable. Your baby is getting ever-closer to a more "adult" diet, and especially if teeth are starting to appear, you can mash rather than puree foods, as well as introduce "finger foods" which he can pick up and experiment with. Even if teeth haven't appeared, most enthusiastic infants can gum their way through almost anything. Always watch your baby carefully so he doesn't choke, and never let him eat "on the run". Try the following:

- Baby breadsticks or rice cakes
- Chopped-up pasta, pieces of bread
- Red meat
- Well-cooked eggs
- Oranges and satsumas
- Fromage frais and yoghurt (show me a baby who doesn't love *Petits Filous*)

To drink:

Babies of six months and up should still be breastfed regularly or drinking around a pint of formula a day. They can also start to drink cooled, boiled water from a soft-spouted beaker. Stay off juice and squash for as long as you can – peer pressure will kick in soon enough – or dilute them right down. You can use normal full-fat cow's milk in cooking and cereals, but not as a main drink until your baby is a year old.

Domestic goddess vs the "jar" alternative

Like many first-time mothers, you'll probably be starting out with the best of intentions – all your baby's food will be organically grown and lovingly hand-prepared. You may even be splashing out on a recipe book of baby and toddler recipes (you've had Delia, Jamie, Nigella – now Annabel (Karmel) is your new culinary Bible). There's no doubting that this is the best and most nutritious way to introduce your little one to solid food, and it's easy for even the least proficient chef: boil the veg or fruit until they are soft, puree them in a blender and freeze for future use. Ice cube trays make perfect storage units as they are in small, ready-made portions which you can defrost at will, increasing the amount you give your baby as she gets bigger.

However, as time goes on and you find yourself travelling with your child, or going back to work, you may well become tempted by the convenience of jars or tins of babyfood. Most mothers feel a twinge of guilt (you don't say!) as they crack open the first jar, but reassure yourself with the fact that all pre-prepared baby food is governed by strict national directives which limit the amount of salt, sugar and other additives. In 2003, there was a national scare about jarred baby food when the European Food Safety Authority reported traces of a potentially harmful chemical called semicarbazide (SEM) in the lids of some jars. As often with news of this type, it was whipped up by the media to hysterical proportions. And while the industry is looking at new ways to package the goods and many manufacturers have stopped using SEM, experts insist that any risk of illness is tiny and that jars continue to be safe.

If you are concerned, one idea is to throw away the top spoonful of baby food, as this would be the only part containing the chemical (if at all). Or, stick to canned, dried or frozen baby foods, all of which are available in supermarkets. The most important thing for your baby's health is that you stick to the storage and preparation instructions on the container.

Can I bring my baby up vegetarian?

In theory, yes, but veggie diets need to be planned carefully so they provide all the ingredients necessary for growth and development. It's important not to fill little stomachs up with high-fibre foods as they may miss out on other nutrients and you must give your baby plenty of milk, cheese, yoghurt and pulses for adequate calcium, vitamins B12 and D. Iron deficiency is common in veggie babies, and though eggs, cereals and green vegetables are not as rich in iron as red meat, they should form a big part of your baby's diet. The vitamin C in a glass of orange juice drunk with the meal will help iron absorption.

A **vegan diet** is even more restricted as it also excludes milk, dairy products and eggs as well as all the other foods already discounted by vegetarians. If you are planning on a strict vegan diet, is it vital that you give your child a variety of vitamin supplements – particularly protein, calcium, vitamins B12 and D, or she could suffer from malnutrition. A quick trip to a GP to help plan your baby's diet regime might not be a bad idea, either.

Food allergies

Sit around any dinner table, and the chances are you will find at least one person with a "food allergy". Often, this is just trendy hypochondriac speak, as true allergy in adults is rare – only 1.5 percent of the population.

By contrast, up to five percent of children are allergic to certain foodstuffs, and the effects can be serious. At the extreme end, there's the risk of **anaphylactic shock**, which can be fatal (see below); other allergic reactions include projectile vomiting, stomach pains and delayed growth. The best way to treat an allergy is to avoid the culprit that causes it and make sure any carers and friends are aware of the problem. The good news is that 90 percent of children grow out of food allergies.

These are the most common foodstuffs which cause them:

● **Milk** – which also means avoiding cheese, butter, yoghurt and even biscuits and cakes. Goat's and soya milk are possible alternatives – but only on a doctor's advice. Young babies can be prescribed special lactose-free or hydrolyzed formulas (milks without a certain sugar, or where the proteins have been treated to lessen the risk of a reaction).

● **Eggs** – the whites are more allergenic than the yolks. Again, biscuits and puddings must be avoided.

● **Nuts** – the most highly publicized and potentially fatal allergy of them all. Whole nuts should be avoided until about five years old because of the danger of choking, and peanuts (or peanut-based foods such as peanut

---

ANAPHYLACTIC SHOCK

In very rare cases people with severe allergies can suffer anaphylactic shock, an instantaneous reaction where their face, lips or tongue swell, they wheeze, have difficulty breathing, or fall unconscious. If you suspect that this is happening, call an ambulance immediately – it's a medical emergency.

Most children with allergies this severe will be given **adrenaline** for them or their carers to carry around with them, in an easy-to-use syringe called an **epi-pen**.

butter) for babies under three years if there are any allergies, asthma or eczema in the family.

If reaction to a certain food is severe, you must go immediately to A&E. In less urgent cases, your GP will refer you to an allergy specialist, although sadly the waiting list is long and you may need to pay privately for a speedy consultation.

Food intolerances

Less dramatic than allergies, because they don't involve the immune system and are not life-threatening, food intolerances causing tummy pain, diarrhoea or vomiting are nevertheless still uncomfortable for a child. It is estimated that around 10–12 percent of the population suffer from intolerances.

The only way to find out if your baby's suffering from a food intolerance is to exclude the culprit – sometimes a detective case of trial and error. Speak to your GP (who may refer you to a nutritionist) before cutting a vital nutrient out of your baby's diet.

Is organic food really better?

Organic food is produced without pesticides, fertilizers or any artificial chemicals and anyone who sets themself up as an organic producer goes through years of strict testing. Many environmentalists – and, of course, the companies that market these products – are convinced that organic food is safer and healthier, but not everyone agrees. The claims fall into two separate sections, the first relating to the potentially harmful effects of pesticides on food. Because they aren't sprayed, organic foods carry fewer pesticide residues, but toxicologists are not convinced that the levels of pesticide residues in conventional food are really worth worrying about anyway.

The second claim is that organic foods are more nutritious. There have been some studies that show them to be higher in vitamin C, essential minerals and cancer-preventing phytonutrients. But the differences tend to be slight – the British Nutrition Foundation (a foundation working with academic and research institutes) maintains there is no evidence that organic crops are nutritionally superior to non-organic foods in terms of vitamin and mineral content. On the downside, there's also a possibility that organic food may even bring risks, such as – according to one study – a higher proportion of certain bacteria in chicken meat.

Of one thing you can be sure, if you buy organically, you'll be paying a good price to match.

ONE WOMAN AND A BABY'S WEANING DIARY

"Weaning Luca onto solid food was, frankly, terrifying. We had been breastfeeding successfully for a few months and I'd just about mastered his daily routine so the thought of facing the 'what to feed him, when to do it and how much to give him' phase made me put off the inevitable for several weeks.

Luca is a big baby who loves to eat so everyone thought he should be weaned early. They'd been saying that since he was born. Of course, the government guidelines now say wait to six months but the food packets still say from four months. I was confused. In the end, he decided for me. At 22 weeks and 17.5lbs, he grabbed my fork and tried to feed himself steak. Time to get the baby rice out. At a loss as to what to do, I relied heavily on the meal plans in Annabel Karmel's food bibles for the taste suggestions, and dipped into Gina Ford's food glossary in her *Weaning Guide*.

A couple of weeks in and I was happy to make it up as I went along. My freezer is now regularly stocked with handy frozen portions and he is starting to have the same food as us which is very exciting and a hell of a lot easier. This is how we began …"

Rebecca, 32

DAY	TIME	FOOD	NOTES
1–2	6.30am	Breastfeed	
	11am	Half milk feed (breast)	
		1 tsp baby rice with expressed breastmilk followed by rest of breastfeed	Grabbed spoon out of my hand and stuffed it in his mouth whilst giggling. Big mess but I think he was ready for this.
	2.30pm	Breastfeed	
	6pm	Breastfeed	

	8pm	Breastfeed	Bedtime
	11pm	Breastfeed	Dreamfeed (while asleep)
3–4	6.30am	Breastfeed	
	11am	Half milk feed (breast)	
		2–3 tsp baby rice with formula milk (to get used to the taste) followed by breastfeed	Gobbles formula rice but it is a lot thicker. Different poos start now.
	2.30pm	Breastfeed	
	6pm	Breastfeed	
	8pm	Breastfeed	Bedtime
	11pm	Breastfeed	Dreamfeed
5–6	6.30am	Breastfeed	
	11am	Half milk feed (breast)	
		2–3 tsp rice with f/m and cooked, pureed pear	Loves pear. More giggles.
	2.30pm	Breastfeed	
	6pm	Breastfeed	
	8pm	Breastfeed	Bedtime
	11pm	Breastfeed	Dreamfeed
7–9	6.30am	Breastfeed	

	11am	Half milk feed (breast)	
		3–4 tsp pureed carrot followed by rest of breastfeed	Slightly shocked but tucked in. Gut didn't approve – seriously bunged him up.
	2.30pm	Breastfeed	
	6pm	Breastfeed	
	8pm	Breastfeed	Bedtime
	11pm	Breastfeed	Dreamfeed
10	6.30am	Breastfeed	
	11am	Half milk feed (breast)	
		Pureed apple, followed by rest of breastfeed	Loved it. Gut did approve – seriously loosened him up.
	2.30pm	Breastfeed	
	6pm	Breastfeed	
	8pm	Breastfeed	Bedtime
	11pm	Breastfeed	Dreamfeed
11	6.30am	Breastfeed	
	11am	Half milk feed (breast)	
		3–4 tsp baby rice with pureed apple followed by rest of breastfeed	Rice + apple = less poo.

	2.30pm	Breastfeed	
	6pm	Breastfeed	
	8pm	Breastfeed	Bedtime
	11pm	Breastfeed	Dreamfeed
12	6.30am	Breastfeed	
	11am	Half milk feed (breast)	
		Mashed banana	Spat out in disgust.
	2.30pm	Breastfeed	
	6pm	Half breastfeed followed by 2 tsp baby rice with pear	Had to make up for earlier disaster.
	8pm	Breastfeed	Bedtime
	11pm	Breastfeed	Dreamfeed
13–14	6.30am	Breastfeed	
	11am	Half milk feed (breast)	
		Pureed butternut squash followed by rest of breastfeed	Immediate hit. To be repeated. Day 2 successfully add potato.
	2.30pm	Breastfeed	
	6pm	Half breastfeed followed by 3–4 tsp baby rice with pear or apple	
	8pm	Half breastfeed	Bedtime

	11pm	Breastfeed	Was hoping dinner would get rid of this feed. Not yet.
15–16	6.30am	Breastfeed	
	11am	Half milk feed (breast)	
		Pureed sweet potato followed by rest of breastfeed	Another success. Harder poos. Bigger mess.
	2.30pm	Breastfeed	
	6pm	Half breastfeed followed by 3–4 tsp baby rice with pear or apple	
	8pm	Half breastfeed	Bedtime
			Turned down dreamfeed. Progress…
17–18	6.30am	Breastfeed	
	11am	Half milk feed (breast)	
		Pureed mango followed by rest of breastfeed	Eyes crossed in shock day 1. Better day 2. Poos smell horribly sweet.
	2.30pm	Breastfeed	
	6pm	Half breastfeed followed by 3–4 tsp baby rice with pear or apple	Getting bored of pear and apple (me, not him).

	8pm	Half breastfeed	Bedtime
	4am	Breastfeed	Hmmm, something not working.
19–20	6.30am	Breastfeed	
	11am	Half milk feed (breast)	
		Pureed acorn squash and parsnip	Wanting much bigger portions now.
	2.30pm	Breastfeed	Fussing.
	6pm	Half breastfeed followed by baby rice with mango	Much more fun.
	8pm	Half breastfeed	Bedtime
	4am	Half breastfeed	Ok, getting better.
21–22	6.30am	Breastfeed	
	11am	Half milk feed (breast)	Fussing – time for formula?
	11.30am	Mashed avocado	Refused to swallow. Had green smile. Added banana and all is well.
	2.30pm	Breastfeed	
	6pm	Half breastfeed followed by baby rice with papaya	Wow, couldn't get the spoon in fast enough.
	8pm	Half breastfeed	Bedtime
	11pm	Half breastfeed	Trial and error

23–24	6.30am	Breastfeed	
	11am	Half milk feed (formula)	Gobbled up his bottle. Oh well.
	11.30am	Courgette	Favourite vegetable so far.
	2.30pm	Breastfeed	
	6pm	Half breastfeed followed by baby rice with papaya	Papaya + courgette = baby heaven.
	7.30pm	Half breastfeed	Bedtime
25–26	6.30am	Breastfeed	
	8am	Creamy porridge with grated pear	First attempt at breakfast – devoured with a smile.
	11.30am	Half milk feed (formula)	
	12pm	Courgette, potato and sweet potato Yoghurt	Surprised with the cold texture but grabs with both hands.
	2.30pm	Formula feed	Offer breast first but not interested.
	6pm	Baby rice with apple, pear and banana	
	7.30pm	Breastfeed	Bedtime
27–28 (6 months)	6.30am	Breastfeed	
	8am	Weetabix with grated apple	Happily takes grated raw fruit and eats a whole weetabix.

11.30am	Half milk feed (formula)	
12pm	Broccoli Yoghurt	Total horror. Absolute refusal unless mixed with carrot and banana yoghurt. Yuck.
2.30pm	Formula feed	Offer breast first but not interested.
6pm	Baby rice with mango and papaya	
7.15pm	Formula feed	Weaning himself off breast and to earlier nights.

Further resources

Books

Annabel Karmel's New Complete Baby and Toddler Meal Planner (Ebury, £8.99). Karmel is the Jamie Oliver of the under-threes, and this is the first in a series of several child cookbooks. From basic purees to more complicated dinners, there's something here for even the most kitchen-averse mother, as well as those devoted to introducing their child to the joys of gastronomy.

Breastfeeding for Beginners (NCT) by Caroline Deacon (Harpercollins, £5.99). Detailed, practical advice from parents and NCT counsellors, written in the easily accessible style of all the NCT books. As well as covering all the basics for first-timers, has sections on premature babies and twins.

Caring for your child with severe food allergies by Lisa Cipriano Collins (John Wiley and Sons, £6.80). Written by a marriage therapist with a child allergic to nuts, this book separates the myths of allergy from the reality, as well as tackling the emotional traumas involved.

The Complete Guide to Food Allergy and Intolerance by Professor Jonathan Brostoff and Linda Gamlin (Bloomsbury, £5.99). Brostoff is a leading expert in the subject of food allergy and intolerance, and this book is considered a leading resource for parents with affected children.

The Contented Little Baby Book by Gina Ford (Vermilion, £9.99). Some mothers argue that Gina's routines work better with bottlefed babies, so they may be worth a look.

The Contented Little Baby Book of Weaning by Gina Ford (Vermilion, £6.99). The next in the series for Gina fans, with an easy-to-follow "programme" and advice. Even those who disregarded her routines for tiny babies may find some useful suggestions here.

First Foods and Weaning (NCT) by Ravinder Lilly (Thorsons, £6.99). A good basic guide, this book has tips on when your baby's ready for solids, what foods to give when, and some straightforward early recipes.

Rose Elliot's Mother, Baby and Toddler Book: A Unique Guide to Raising a Baby on a Healthy Vegetarian Diet (Hochland Communications, £8.95). Highly recommended by vegetarian parents, this book is split into two parts. The first explains how to give your baby all the nutrition he needs while avoiding meat products, and the second has a selection of recipes.

Secrets of the Baby Whisperer by Tracy Hogg (Vermilion, £10.99). There tend to be few "dedicated" books and websites on formula feeding, simply because it doesn't arouse the same emotional fervour as breastfeeding. But all the main baby reference books have sections on how to get started. Chapter 4 of this book pronounces: "*Stand up for your right to give baby formula.*" She's realistic about the fact that many women do not breastfeed, and the book is written with that in mind.

Successful Breastfeeding (Royal College of Midwives, £12.99). This is actually written with midwives in mind, but is an interesting read for those who want more than the basics, and are keen to see what the professionals are told.

What to Expect, The First Year by Murkoff, Eisenberg and Hathaway (Simon and Schuster, £12.99). Chapter 4 has good, comprehensive advice on the early days.

What to Expect When Breastfeeding and What to Expect If You Can't by Clare Byam-Cook (Vermilion, £7.99). A realistic (some say defeatist) look at the difficulties some women find in breastfeeding. Byam-Cook is a breastfeeding counsellor, and her experienced advice aims to remove the guilt for those who are struggling.

Websites

www.actionagainstallergy.co.uk Useful site covering all allergies, not just food-related ones, with newsletters, links to scientific papers, and advice on finding an appropriate doctor.

www.anaphylaxis.org.uk A campaigning group to support those with a severe allergies leading to anaphylactic shock. This site includes information for young adults, schools, and "outs" products that may contain nuts.

www.babycentre.co.uk Has a dedicated "formula-feeding" section, plus an on-line community where mothers can share experiences, thoughts and concerns.

www.breastfeedingnetwork.org.uk Founded as an offshoot of the NCT in 1997, the Breastfeeding Network is positively evangelical about the benefits of breastfeeding. They have an excellent resource of "advisers"(see helpline below) and the website if packed with information. Helpline: 0870 444 8708 (open 9.30am–9.30pm, every day).

www.kellymom.com A fantastically thorough site, set up by an American breastfeeding counsellor. You've got a question? This site will answer it somewhere – from how to get your baby to take a bottle of expressed milk, to the latest on all the scientific papers.

www.laleche.org.uk The La Leche League is a worldwide organization with an "international mission" to promote breastfeeding. While this is highly laudable, the site is possibly less user-friendly for those who want help with personal problems, rather than a mere interest in the bigger picture. Helpline: 0845 120 2918 (24 hours)

www.nctpregnancyandbaby.com This site has a good, detailed "feeding your baby" section. While the NCT are clearly of the "breast is best" school, they do at least countenance the fact that some women may bottlefeed, whereas some of the more purist sites do not. Helpline: 0870 900 8787 (open 8am–10pm, every day).

www.nutrition.org.uk And now the science: the British Nutrition Foundation site has a useful "maternal and infant nutrition" section for those who want to see the reasons babies are advised to eat what they do.

www.planorganic.com "The heart of organic food and farming": this site is for dedicated organic fans, with farming news, scientific references and suggestions on where to shop.

www.smanutrition.co.uk Obviously – and unashamedly – sponsored by the formula manufacturers SMA, this nevertheless has some useful sections on feeding and weaning tips, and the nutritional value of formula milk.

www.soilassociation.org A comprehensive guide to the organic lifestyle, with sections on why organic food is recommended, and the best places to find it.

www.vegetarianbaby.com International website for those who've decided to bring up their baby vegetarian or vegan, with recipes, book reviews and a community to meet other like-minded parents.

Other helplines

The Breastfeeding Network SupportLine Tel: 08704 448 708
NCT Breastfeeding Helpline Tel: 08709 008 787

5

Sleeping

5

Sleeping

It's impossible to overestimate the effects of **sleep deprivation** on the new parent. The word "tired" is simply inadequate and doesn't even begin to cover the confusion, bewilderment, frustration, failing sense of humour and the inability to do easy tasks, like put the bread in the toaster, find the butter, take it out of the fridge and muster the coordination skills to spread it on the toast. The person who coined the phrase "sleeping like a baby" deserves to be subjected to six months' sleep deprivation at the hands of a snorting, grunting, ravenous, stomach-the-size-of-a-walnut, 24-hour-partying newborn. And even when the baby does finally drop off, do you take the opportunity to do so yourself? No! There you are, hanging onto the end of the moses basket checking that she is still breathing.

If you're thinking that the author's personal experience is colouring the introduction to this chapter, well, yes, you're right. Not all new babies are so energetic, and many people have three- or four-hour periods of uninterrupted sleep from the word go, which is just about enough to get by on and stay sane. Some lucky parents have babies who sleep through from the early days – if this is you, keep it to yourself or you may find your deranged fellow parents quietly avoiding you.

The good news is that every single baby learns to sleep for several consecutive hours of darkness eventually and most people have a reasonable night by the time their child is about six months old. That, however, is scant consolation to the frantic mother, eight weeks in, who doesn't think she can survive another night, let along wait four more months. You just have to take it on trust: it does get better, you will survive, and you will even one day stay up late enough to catch the end of *EASTENDERS*.

How a new baby sleeps

For adults, as well as babies, sleep is not a constant process. We "cycle" through different levels of consciousness, from light sleep, to dream sleep (also known as **REM** sleep), to deep sleep, and back again, often waking in between, though we don't remember this in the morning. Adults spend about six hours in deep sleep and two hours in REM sleep. Newborns have twice as many light sleep cycles as adults and spend about half their time in REM sleep, which is very important for growth and development. You can tell a baby is in REM sleep because you can see her eyes moving under the lids, and her body is motionless apart from the occasional twitch. A baby in deep sleep is almost motionless, impossible to rouse and makes little sucking movements. Every now and then, she will "startle" in the same way adults occasionally do, as they are dropping off.

The main problem for new parents is that babies' overall sleep cycles are very short – about fifty or sixty minutes. This means they come to the surface every hour or so: your baby will squirm, pull remarkable faces, breathe unevenly and wave his arms and legs about. Some newborns can bypass this period and get themselves back to sleep on their own, like adults do. Some can go for five or six hours without waking – occasionally more, which is okay as long as the baby is healthy and gaining weight.

The vast majority of babies, however, need a bit of rocking and "shushing" to go back to sleep; others need a breast- or bottlefeed. And then there are the rest, for whom the only thing that works is hours pounding the landing on their daddy's shoulder. Take solace in the fact that, as a baby gets older, the sleep cycle lengthens.

When a new baby sleeps

Unfortunately for us, newborns don't come out understanding about day/night patterns – known in the trade as **circadian rhythms** – and they sleep for about eighteen scattered hours a day. To begin with, half of this will be at night, and half during the day. Somewhere between three and six months, your baby should start to mimic adult patterns – again, some babies learn this more naturally than others, and others need direction. From around three months, the plan is that your baby will be having a longer chunk of sleep at night, and several short "naps" during the day. If you're following a book like Gina Ford, you'll have been trying to institute this routine from day one. Details on sleep "training" are in the table below.

How long should my baby sleep for, and when?
The table below is a rough guide:

Age	Total sleep	Hours at night	Hours in day
1 month	15 hours	8½	7 (3 naps)
3 months	15 hours	10	5 (3 naps)
6 months	14 hours	11	3¼ (2 naps)
9 months	14 hours	11	3 (2 naps)
12 months	13 hours	11¼	2 (1 nap)
18 months	13 hours	11¼	2 (1 nap)

(Source: babycentre.co.uk)

A boost for sleep-deprived parents – three reassuring things about frequent waking

- **It's a survival mechanism.** With such tiny stomachs and milk that is quickly digested (especially breastmilk) a baby needs to eat frequently to thrive. You've got evolution to thank for this. If a stone-age baby could sleep through other threatening circumstances, like getting too cold, or not being able to breathe because of a stuffy nose, his life could have been in danger.
- **It's good for development.** Experts say that during the frequent cycles of REM sleep, a baby's body increases the manufacture of certain nerve proteins which help the brain develop. During the REM stage a baby's "learning" is at its height, as your newborn processes information he picked up during the day.
- **It's not your fault.** Babies have different temperaments. The fact that you are up half the night is not because you're a useless parent. Your smug friends with well-settled babies are merely lucky – nothing more.

My baby slept too much

"People complain that their babies keep them up at night, but our problem was completely the opposite. Freddie slept so deeply and for so long, that he didn't feed properly, and for many months his weight was a source of great concern to us. From day one, he would easily go for seven hours without a breastfeed and when he did wake up, he'd drop off again half way through.

By the time he was weighed a week after his birth he was quite a long way below his birth weight, and he continued to lose more. The health visitor kept asking me if I was feeding on demand. I was, but Freddie just didn't demand very much. When friends told me I looked "well rested", it made me feel terrible. After a couple more weeks of this, I realized that I needed to do something, so I set my alarm clock after six hours at night (he'd be too sleepy to eat any earlier). During the day, I'd try and feed him every three hours, and woke him up after five. We continued doing this until he went onto solid food, when the situation got a bit better.

Freddie's weight gain has always been slow and it has been upsetting – I'd choose a baby who eats but doesn't sleep over a baby who sleeps but doesn't eat any day."

Mel, 35

My first baby kept me awake all night, my second slept beautifully

"When Henry was born he turned out to be a dreadful sleeper. At night he would keep me on my toes by either waking every twenty minutes for five minutes, or opening his eyes at 2am and staying wide awake for three hours. I'd call my husband to declare that I was doing something very wrong, what could it be? I bought shares in under-eye concealer. I also turned to the dreaded Baby Books. In my despair I read them all – Gina, *Baby Whisperer*, the *NCT Sleep book*, Ferber – and drove myself into a frenzy trying to understand their routines and trying to make my baby fit into them. What I failed to realize was that as Henry was only a few months old and thus unable to read, he had no idea what he was meant to do. Looking back, he was just a baby who needed a lot of physical support in the form of a dummy and being held. The nightmare ended at around eight months when he finally slept through. He was just ready to do it.

My daughter, Cecily, is now twelve weeks old. She knew the difference between day and night within a fortnight and without any intervention from me or any imposed routines. She now sleeps from 8pm to 6am, has a five-minute feed and then crashes out for another two hours. How did I do it? I didn't. I simply fed her when she woke and she went back to sleep instantly, something that was impossible for Henry. Different children, different experiences. So my advice to anyone with a Henry is to stop blaming yourself. And you might have a Cecily next time."

Leah, 41

Where should my baby sleep?

Though at times it sounds as though you are sharing a room with the inhabitants of a farmyard, official advice is that your baby should sleep in your room for the first six months. A large cot is not necessary at this stage – babies can feel vulnerable and swamped with so much space around them. Many parents invest in a temporary bed such as a moses basket or carrycot, which will last you for the first three months or so, depending on the size of your baby. Understandably, it takes some newborns time to get used to sleeping alone, even in a snug little cradle – they've been carried around inside you, hearing your heartbeat for nine months, and a creaky wicker basket simply will not do. Swaddling can help an infant feel more secure (see p.79) but many babies find it hard to settle at first unless they are sleeping in bed next to their mother, skin to skin.

My baby wouldn't settle anywhere but in bed with us
"Before Alice was born, I adored the moses basket – all pristine white, lacy and innocent. But after several weeks, I was ready to burn the damn thing. From the very first evening, Alice *hated* it. She would fall fast asleep at my breast, and I would gently, ever-so-slowly lower her into the basket, holding my breath for fear she'd wake up. Just as I turned to tip-toe away, her eyes would spring open, she'd start clucking and I'd have to start the whole process again. One night, when she was nine weeks old, this happened every twenty minutes, until I was pounding the floor with exhausted frustration.

The only place Alice was happy was in bed with us. But I had this nagging voice in my head telling me that we were 'getting her into bad habits' and felt guilty about co-sleeping even though, actually, it suited us all very well as I was breastfeeding her. So, night after night, we tearfully tried different combinations – moses basket on legs, moses basket on floor, moses basket inside cot, baby inside cot – none of them worked.

In the end, sheer desperation forced me to give up and let her sleep with us. Finally, a reasonable night's sleep for everyone. At about four months, Alice went into her own cot in her own room. It took a few nights to make the transition, and she still spent several hours each night in bed with us, but we gradually reduced the amount until she was happily sleeping in there full-time."

Caroline, 36

Sharing a bed with your baby

In nine out of ten homes the world over, a baby shares a bed with his parents. However, **co-sleeping**, as it is called, has a mixed press in countries like America and the UK, where some experts talk of "teaching bad habits" and "encouraging dependence". There have also been a very few cases of parents rolling over and squashing their babies, but these are incredibly rare – especially if you follow the advice in the box opposite. Yet because of these

Three good things about co-sleeping

- It makes breastfeeding easier and warmer for both of you.
- There is evidence that co-sleeping decreases the incidence of cot death (see p.174) as it stimulates the baby's breathing and regulates their temperature.
- Your baby will feel calm and loved.

Three not-so-good things about co-sleeping

- Your baby may disturb you.
- You might be so worried about squashing your baby that you don't sleep properly. In reality, this rarely happens unless you've been drinking or taken drugs – mothers who breastfeed tend to sleep in a position that stops the baby going under the covers or pillow.
- You don't have any "time off" and having a baby in bed isn't exactly great for your sex life (the perfect contraception, really).

Before you co-sleep, make sure

- The baby cannot fall out of bed or get stuck between the mattress and the wall.
- Your partner is aware of the baby – if, for example, he comes to bed after you.
- The baby is not overdressed. He should wear the same amount of layers as you, and should not wear a baby sleeping bag as well as being under the covers. Sheets and blankets are best to lower the risk of overheating, but if the baby is sleeping under a duvet, a nappy and vest is enough clothing.
- Your room is well ventilated, and not too warm: ideally 16–18° C.

You should not share a bed with your baby if...

You smoke, have been drinking or taking drugs, or are ill. Confusingly, official advice also warns against co-sleeping if you are "unusually tired", which is surely the default position for most new parents. You should never fall asleep on a sofa with your baby because of the risk of them slipping between the cushions.

cases, the Foundation for the Study of Infant Death maintains: "the safest place for a baby to sleep is in a cot in the parents' bedroom".

Ultimately, you need to do what works for you. If your baby is happy in the moses basket, then great. But some newborns are not – bedsharing, for the first few weeks at least, can often lead to the best and happiest nights' sleep for all of you.

Don't feel guilty about your decision. While few people would want a hairy teenage son in their beds, it seems churlish to talk of fostering independence in a baby who is merely days old. Relax. He'll move into his own bed soon enough, though it can make the transition easier if he's less than a year old.

Anyone would think co-sleeping was a cardinal sin

"Every book and leaflet I've read, and every health visitor I talk to seems to think I am committing the absolute cardinal sin by sharing a bed with my eight-month-old son. But the trouble is, we love having Dylan in bed with us and it is the only way to guarantee he will sleep through. We don't smoke or drink, we only use sheets and thin blankets and we have a large bed so he has plenty of space. He loves sleeping on his side but struggles to do that in his cot whereas it is very easy when he has us curled around him.

When Dylan was first born, the midwife tucked him up in bed with me and showed us how to breastfeed lying down – she said it was the most natural thing in the world and the easiest transition from womb to world. I agree. He is still breastfeeding and now just crawls over to me, has a suck and then turns to cuddle his Daddy for the night. I don't have to get up, or work out if he is actually hungry – he just helps himself and then snuggles down. I'm not thinking ahead too much about settling Dylan in his own bed, it will happen when the time is right, although I am starting to put him in his cot for daytime naps so it becomes a familiar and comfortable place to be."

Sara, 28

Sudden Infant Death Syndrome (SIDS, or cot death)

It's every parent's worst fear, but cot death – the sudden and unexpected death of a baby for no apparent reason – is very unusual. It affects fewer than one in two thousand babies, and this statistic is falling every year.

No one is sure what causes an apparently healthy baby to die, but as more research is completed on the subject, it seems likely that many SIDS babies may have been born with underlying defects either of the heart, or their breathing mechanism. SIDS is most common between two and four months, and is uncommon after six. Boys, premature and low-birth-weight babies seem to be slightly more at risk.

Since the launch of the **Reduce the Risk campaign** in England and Wales in 1991, the number of babies dying of cot death has fallen by 75 percent. These are the recommendations:

● **Place your baby on their back to sleep** from the very beginning. This is the most important advice of all – one Australian study suggested that a baby sleeping on her stomach may inadvertently compress arteries in her neck, which can cut off blood flow to the brain; another that such babies inhale too much carbon dioxide. If yours is one of the babies that seems happier on his front, it can cause a real headache – dare you take a risk and allow him to sleep that way, giving everyone a better night (but racking yourself with guilt at the thought that something terrible might happen)? Few health visitors will compromise on the official advice, but, when pressed, one had this to say:

"If a parent decides to place babies on their front to sleep, despite research and recommendations by professionals, then it would be better for that baby to sleep in the parents' bedroom with the parents not under the influence of any drugs or medicines, for them **not to smoke**, and the room temperature to be correct."

● **Side sleeping** is not as safe as back sleeping. When the baby is strong enough to roll over onto her front (at around six months), it's fine to leave her in that position.

● Some parents find that **cranial osteopathy** can help a baby settle on his back more comfortably. See p.197 and Further Resources for more information.

● **Don't let your baby get too hot or too cold** – a room temperature of 18°C is about right. Her head must remain uncovered, and she mustn't be too near a radiator.

● **Place your baby in the "feet to foot" position,** ie with her feet at the bottom end of the cot, so she can't wriggle under the blanket.

● **Use a firm mattress and tightly fitting sheets** – baby "sleeping bags" are probably best of all. Don't have any cuddly toys or pillows in bed with a tiny baby.

Sleeping

Surviving sleep deprivation

It's quite easy to become obsessed with the amount of sleep you haven't had. This compounds an already stressful situation, particularly if you get so wound up about it you can't switch off when the opportunity arises, and suffer self-induced insomnia on top of it all. The most important thing here is not to lose perspective: quite tricky really, as loss of perspective is a well-documented symptom of sleep deprivation. In the meantime, a few things can help you cope:

- **Ask someone to babysit, so you can get a bit of sleep in the day.** Lots of people tell you to "sleep when the baby sleeps" which in practice is quite difficult, as new babies have unpredictable sleep patterns and a habit of waking up just as you're dropping off. If someone else is in the house, you'll know that even if your baby wakes, they are in good hands, so you can take a power nap.

- **Don't stuff yourself with junk food.** There's nothing more tempting than trying to boost your energy with doughnuts, chocolate croissants and whole packets of digestives but in reality, eating this much sugar is counter-productive: after a sharp spike in energy, you'll be feeling more sluggish than before. Better to stick to slow-release carbohydrates like wholemeal bread and pasta if you can, although downing the odd life-saving jaffa cake can only be good for the morale.

- **Do some exercise.** Probably the last thing you'll feel like doing, but even a brisk walk to the park will get fresh air into your lungs and your **endorphins** (feel-good chemicals released by exercise) pumping. Force yourself out of the front door every day, even if it's raining.

- **Make life easy for yourself.** Don't take on any extra demands, like entertaining friends, work commitments or reading hard novels.

    NB:) Extreme exhaustion – especially when you aren't able to fall asleep when your baby allows – might be a symptom of **postnatal depression**. However, if you are depressed, this tiredness is also accompanied by other symptoms including tearfulness and an inability or lack of desire to look after yourself or your newborn. A good night's sleep alone won't put these right. See Chapter 2 for more details.

Sleeping

If a baby is ill, teething or upset by a change in circumstances, it's likely that she'll take several steps back and start waking up again. This is normal. The situation may right itself spontaneously, or you may need to temporarily reapply whichever methods you chose first time round.

Introducing "sleep habits" for your baby

Whether you've been attempting a routine from day one, or are happy to go with your baby's flow, by around three months in, even the most selfless parent will be praying for a better night's sleep. There have been reams written about the best way of achieving this, and there are two main American theorists who occupy opposite ends of the parenting spectrum, **William Sears** and **Richard Ferber** (see below), though there is a continuum that runs between them.

The Sears approach

Dr Sears is a Californian paediatrician. Broadly speaking, he maintains that it is normal for a baby to wake at night and she should be cuddled and comforted until she's ready to learn to fall asleep on her own. Sears is also in favour of babies sharing the family bed. His catchphrase is "attachment parenting".

The Ferber approach

In stark contrast is the approach suggested by Dr Richard Ferber, director of the Center for Paediatric Sleep Disorders at Boston's Children's Hospital. He thinks that bad sleep habits are learned, and can therefore be unlearned. Ferber's advice is that you should let your baby cry for a predetermined number of minutes before going in to check on her, comfort her briefly with a pat or a verbal reassurance, but not pick her up. The parents should then repeat the pattern at increasing intervals of time until the baby falls asleep – for example, after five minutes, then ten, then fifteen. Ferber warns: "if you cave in, your efforts will be for naught. This is also known as 'controlled crying'".

Some of the bestselling babycare writers have adapted their routines with modified versions of the Ferber approach.

So, what's best for you?

Both of these approaches provoke passionate reactions – both for and against – so it's clear that neither is right nor wrong for everyone. As with so many baby issues, you'll probably find your own middle ground sooner or later. There's another important observation here: many a parent has picked up the latest "miracle" sleep solution, only for it to fail, and for them to have another terrible night. Most of the babycare gurus concede that results aren't instant and take a week or two to work, yet a parent desperate for sleep may not have the patience to appreciate this. Any disappointment is compounded by exhaustion, making you feel like a bad parent who has failed yet again. Easy to say once you are out the other side, but don't be too hard on yourself and be assured you are in good company.

We lay there hand in hand in the dark while our baby screamed his head off

"Until Liam was about six months old, I'd been going to him whenever he woke in the night and given him a feed. Steve and I now decided we wanted to get a proper night's sleep back, so we thought we'd give controlled crying a go. It is such a difficult and stressful process. We followed the advice in one of the baby books, going back after five minutes, then ten ... gradually

> ### OUT-OF-CONTROLLED CRYING?
>
> At the end of 2004, there was a lot of coverage about controlled crying in the papers – with helpful headlines such as: "Does crying damage babies' brains?" The dramatic conclusion was that leaving a baby to cry for twenty minutes can lead to emotional disorders later in life. Other well-regarded scientists disputed this evidence. Wherever the truth lies, such stories do not make comfortable reading. One consensus, however, is that controlled crying is inappropriate before a baby is six months old – for very small infants, crying is a genuine plea for help, rather than a way of grabbing attention. If it's used judiciously, anecdotal evidence does show that controlled crying after the half-year mark can help parents to a better night. And twenty minutes is much longer than it sounds when you're listening to a baby yelling in the other room – even the most iron-willed parents would be hard-pushed to cope with the noise and heartache for any longer.

increasing the gap between visits. We didn't pick Liam up, just spoke to him softly, saying things like: 'mummy's asleep, daddy's asleep, Agnes and Lauren (our next door neighbours) are asleep – it's time for Liam to go to sleep, too.' In between, we'd go back to bed, lying wide awake in the dark, holding hands, listening to our baby scream his head off.

For that first night, the process went on for about an hour and a half, and by the end of it, I was in tears. We stood firm for the first two nights. But on the third we were especially tired, so I caved in and gave Liam a feed. Steve got annoyed – this is meant to 'undo' your good work, and show your baby that continued crying pays off. In the following week, Steve had a busy period at work where he needed to feel alert, so we shelved the whole plan and went back to our old ways. What we did, however, was agree a date to try again when Liam was older and less vulnerable. This time we stuck to the plan, and within a week it worked – he started going from 8pm to 7am without disturbing us."

Juliette, 34

179

THE EARLY-WAKING BABY

You may be patting your back about the fact your newborn is no longer waking up at 2am – but the flipside is that he's awake at five and ready to rock. This is no fun – and it can be worse in summer months because it gets light so early. If a too-light bedroom is the problem, it might be worth investing in "black-out blinds". Otherwise, you may want to start reducing the number and length of naps during the day (but don't phase them out altogether), putting your baby to bed later (but ideally not after 9pm) and investing in a cot-side diversion, for example, a musical battery-operated mobile, that you can switch on then blearily go back to bed for another thirty minutes or so.

Small steps to help your child (and you) get a better night's sleep

Most authors across the parenting spectrum agree on a few broad, commonsense "strategies" to coax your baby to sleep for longer. Just bear in mind that they might not necessarily work straight away.

• Start to establish a "bedtime"

In all probability, for the first few weeks, your baby "went to bed" when you did. For most new parents, this works pretty well – you can still have some sort of a social life, take your baby to restaurants, friends' houses etc … Plus, there's the bonus of any longer chunks of sleep coinciding with your own. However, when your baby reaches around the twelve-week mark, it's a good moment to start thinking about instituting bedtime. Some time between 7 and 8.30pm is probably appropriate – any later, and babies become "overtired" and too wired to fall asleep. Don't worry if it takes a while for this to work: most babies don't operate like clockwork. One tip is to start at your usual bedtime and work backwards, putting your baby down fifteen minutes earlier each night.

Some experts also suggest waking your baby up at the same time every morning to keep their "sleep clock" in order – a challenge for even the toughest-minded parent desperate for a lie-in.

• Arrange consistent nap times

Your baby also needs regular snatches of sleep during the day – it's not generally true that keeping your infant up all day will make them sleep longer at night – they'll get overtired and often hysterical. You may notice your baby falling into a pattern of naps, eg one in the morning – about an hour after waking – one around lunchtime – and another in the late afternoon. Either follow your baby's lead or institute your own timetable based on his "mummy-I'm-tired" clues (see p.66), although it's a good idea to avoid naps within two hours of bedtime. As he gets older, he'll probably drop the late afternoon nap, and then the morning one. Many babies need a middle-of-the-day sleep up to their second birthdays. It's a sad day for parents when this one is finally dropped.

• Devise a bedtime routine, and stick to it

Although the concept of a strict routine is a controversial one, even the most "child-centred" experts agree that small children feel comforted by the same things happening in the same order, every day. This is especially relevant around bedtime, because it helps them relax. So, an example could be a bath, then a feed, followed by a cuddle while you read a story or watch the news, then bed. (Closely followed by a quick dash to the kitchen for a glass of wine for you.) It doesn't matter which routine you choose, as long as you stick to it as much as possible.

Again, cosy bedtime routines don't usually fall into place overnight, but they do eventually produce results.

• Make sure your baby's room is the right environment for sleep

If your child has trouble falling asleep, or continues waking during the night, you might want to check:

Room temperature: That it's not too hot or too cold.

Noise: It's not a good idea to tiptoe around a newborn; you want to get them used to a certain amount of household noise. However, there may be a specific sound, eg consistently slamming doors, that wakes your baby up. On the other hand, some babies are soothed by "white noise", eg a fan, or the sound of a washing machine. Although putting the washing machine in your baby's room is a rather extreme solution.

Light: Some babies love pitch darkness, others like the door slightly ajar, or a nightlight. Trial and error is the only way to find out what works for you and your baby.

• Encourage your baby to fall asleep on his own

A really tricky one. Most newborns need a "prop" to fall asleep – a breast- or bottlefeed, a dummy, a car journey etc ... Experts call these "sleep

WEANING YOUR OLDER BABY OFF A NIGHT-TIME FEED

Breastfed babies tend to need feeding at night for longer than the bottlefed variety – at least once or twice (if you're lucky) until they are three months old; they still may need an early-hours snack up to six months. Beyond that, your baby is physically capable of getting through 'til dawn without eating – the sucking has simply become a comforting custom.

Around the middle of the first year, you may want to pass on the message that the midnight bar is permanently shut. Some suggestions:

- **Increase the size of the bedtime feed**. If your baby drops off before he's had enough, be ruthless – tickle his feet, massage the palms of his hand, blow on him to wake him up.

- **Be ruthless, and go "cold turkey"**. If you can bear it, you might want to decide to withdraw the feed permanently, this instant. Your baby will be furious, and won't hold back in letting you know. It's damned uncomfortable for all concerned if you just leave him to scream – controlled crying is a kinder approach. Despite what the purists say, even if you eventually "cave in" and give the feed a few minutes later than the previous night, that's progress.

- **Start reducing the amount you offer**. Keep offering the feed for now – but in smaller quantities. So, if you are breastfeeding, call "time" after five minutes instead of ten. If you usually give four ounces of formula, drop it to three, then to two a week later. Keep reducing until your baby realizes it's just not worth waking up for a dribble of milk.

Of course, some parents may enjoy their 3am cuddle so much, they don't mind being disturbed when their baby wakes up to feed, even as far in as the first year. As with everything in this book, it's a matter of personal choice, and nothing to be ashamed of.

associations". At some point, however, your baby will have to learn to fall asleep without these associations, because when she wakes in the small hours (as all babies do) she will need to drop off again without your assistance. This can be the toughest nut to crack. A parent desperate for sleep will often search for the quickest solution and it doesn't take a genius to work out that this will prolong the problem.

Some books talk about putting your baby down "sleepy but awake" which conjures images of a fluffy, dopey baby who will just turn over and nod off. In reality, this doesn't always happen – some infants scream and refuse to fall asleep at the allotted time: others fall asleep easily but wake up later and stay awake until they've had a bottle or a cuddle.

There are no easy answers to this: a consistent bedtime routine can help, as can introducing a "security object" such as a special teddy, or an item of clothing that smells of you. The only certainty is that you will need patience – the controlled crying process, described on p.177, may help here. Other parents are happy to bide their time and wait for the baby to outgrow the need for sleep associations in his own time.

If lack of sleep becomes an intractable problem, the last resort might entail contacting a **sleep counsellor** to see if they can coax your baby into a better night. There are a few NHS sleep clinics out there, usually run by health visitors, but it may come as no surprise that most sleep clinics and counsellors are private. Don't expect a miracle cure, although just having moral support from an "expert" might give you the impetus you need to follow through your chosen sleep plan, whether it's controlled crying or otherwise. Ask your health visitor or GP for more details.

The sleep counsellor

"What constitutes a 'sleep problem' is highly subjective – what's acceptable for one household is not for another, and people's tolerances vary widely. The main problem is not with the baby; it's when parents find themselves unable to cope through sheer exhaustion. If a family came to me with a two-week-old baby who was up every two hours, I would tell them it was normal. However, if this was still the case by six weeks, it might be different. At that stage, a baby should be able to do a six- or seven-hour stretch at night, and there might be ways I can help guide the parents to help their child achieve this.

I tend to focus on two main things. First, getting the child into some sort of bedtime routine – this provides cues that bedtime is approaching and prepares him for sleep. The other is teaching the baby to settle by themselves without sleep associations. I'm firmly of the school that you can teach your baby to sleep through the night – it's not a question of whether the child can do it, but rather whether the parents have the stamina. Take controlled crying, for example: it's fantastic if done properly, but if not, it creates unnecessary tension for everybody. I tend not to recommend it until the baby is six months old, when the baby physically does not need to eat so much at night, and the parents feel more confident about how robust their child has become."

Tracey Marshall

Tracey's tips

● The most important thing is to teach your baby to settle without your **sleep associations**. Encourage him to a) settle without props and b) settle without your presence. There is a temporary place for dummies if they are used wisely for a sucky baby, but always bear in mind that babies – and parents – can become dependent. (See our section on sleep associations above.)

● **Make your bedtime routine relaxing, consistent, but also short.** A three-month-old can act on "sleep cues" for about thirty minutes. If you make your routine any longer than that, they might get overtired or excited if their daddy walks through the door, and unable to settle. Babies aged six months and up should have a 30–45 minute routine.

Further resources

Books

The NCT Book of Sleep by Penny Hames (HarperCollins, price varies on Amazon). It doesn't claim to have the miracle cure, but this is a good, in-depth explanation of how a baby sleeps, with a discussion of sleep theories. There are lots of personal experiences from other parents, and places to go for help.

The No-Cry Sleep Solution: Gentle Ways to Help Your Baby Sleep Through the Night by Elizabeth Pantley (Contemporary Books, £6.99).

Pantley is a mother of four who had two children who slept perfectly, and two who didn't. Her book is a reassuring, realistic and gentle guide to help red-eyed parents get through the nightmare without resorting to tough "crying-it-out" methods.

The Science of Parenting by Margot Sunderland (Dorling Kindersley, £16.99). Sunderland is an experienced child psychologist and has based the book on over seven hundred research studies. Her theory is that some parenting techniques involving strict routines can cause permanent damage to a baby's developing brain and personality, and offers kinder solutions to common problems including sleeping, crying and "naughty" behaviour.

Sleeping and Night-time Parenting by William Sears (La Leche International) – it's an American book but you can order it on Amazon. Sears is of the "attachment parenting" school, meaning he's in favour of co-sleeping and breastfeeding. But his book also provides practical advice on night-waking, SIDS and babies with special needs.

Solving Your Child's Sleep Problems by Richard Ferber (Dorling Kindersley, £7.99). The father of "controlled crying" – thousands of parents report great success with Ferber's methods. Even if they are not for you, the book is still fascinating on understanding a baby's sleep rhythms.

Three in a Bed by Deborah Jackson (Bloomsbury, £7.99). The co-sleeper's Bible. Jackson begs parents to trust their own instincts if they want to be close to their children at night, though her arguments are also backed up by scientific research.

For a baby buying guide to cots see Chapter 10.

Websites

www.cranial.org.uk The website of the Sutherland Society, the largest UK organization for cranial osteopaths, with over 300 members in the UK and overseas.

www.sids.org.uk Dedicated to SIDS/cot death, this site reports on research, runs campaigns, and has a "support" section for bereaved parents.

6

Crying

6

Crying

I magine a pneumatic drill going off in your head. A football team scratching their nails down a blackboard. A whole concert arena cracking their knuckles at once – none of this comes close to the distress of hearing your own baby screaming inconsolably. It's an evolutionary fact: we are hard-wired to react to a baby's cry to ensure the survival of our species.

Don't be fooled by the pathetic bleating lamb you brought home from the hospital. In the space of a week or so, most infants realize what their lungs are for, find their voices and hey – they'll let you know about it. Crying is what babies do; fair enough really, considering the lack of communication tools at their disposal. Quite simply, they don't have any other way of letting you know that they are hungry, tired, cold – even bored. Some clever people tell you that there are ways of deciphering cries and working out what they mean (you can even buy a machine that purports to interpret them for you) but for the first few weeks, until your baby has learned to smile and make eye contact to give you some clue of success, it's an endless programme of trial, error, praying and driving round the block at 4am. The only person who can really tell you the reason a baby is crying is the baby itself, and that's not a huge amount of help.

Hot on the heels of sleep-deprivation (and the two often come as a buy-one-get-one-free package), excessive crying is one of the hardest things to cope with as a new parent. First of all, there's physical noise, which can reach as loud as 115 decibels – just five decibels short of the pain threshold. At vulnerable times, such as the small hours, or in the early evening when you're exhausted – a favourite of "colicky" babies – it will sound louder than ever. You'll be even more aware of this if you live in a block of flats, or in a terrace with thin walls, and have the neighbours to think of. Then there's the incessant yanking at your heartstrings, as if the baby is accusing you of being such a useless mother that you might as well find her a new home. You won't be the first – or the last – parent to think like this.

Why is my baby crying?

Until you become more familiar with your baby's likes, dislikes and daily patterns, it's worth running through a check list of potential reasons/ solutions to see if any of them works. Here are a few suggestions: (see also section on p.68, "What does my baby want?")

"I'm hungry"

It's always logical to consider this first, as hunger is the most common reason new babies cry. Even if it feels like minutes since you last offered the breast or the bottle, weeny stomachs empty very quickly, and a baby without a full belly is *not* happy. Some newborns become positively frantic, which can lead to other problems, because by the time they do get their milk they may gulp down air, leading to further upset.

"I've got wind"

Try burping your baby using the advice on p.78. Some windy newborns need burping before and during feeds, as well as after them.

"I'm tired"

Before launching into a sleepless screechfest, most babies give earlier cues, such as rubbing their eyes or yawning, but you'd be forgiven for missing them. The problem is that a frazzled, overtired baby finds it hard to fall asleep on her own, especially if she's had people around her all day. Take her into a quiet room away from any stimulation, try rocking and singing. If all else fails, putting your baby into a sling, against your body, or in the car, usually has instant results.

"I've done a poo"

While many babies are totally unconcerned about the idea of lying around in their own mess and some even rather like the vague warm feeling, others hate it. It's always worth seeing if a nappy change does the trick. If your baby seems sore down below, follow our advice for treating nappy rash (p.76).

"I'm too hot/cold"

An ideal temperature for your baby's room is about 18°C, but if she is upset, it's a good idea to worm your way under the babygro and feel her stomach to gauge whether she's overheated, or cool. Feeling her hands or feet is misleading, as babies' extremities are always cold. Add or remove an extra layer as necessary. If your baby is one of the varieties that hates nappies or bathtime, complete these chores with the minimum of fuss, and speed through "naked" moments.

"I need to suck"

All babies are born with the instinct to suck, and some find it incredibly reassuring, as well as a way of getting their lunch – research has shown that sucking can lower their heart rates. If you are sure your baby has had enough to eat, a clean finger or dummy can help ease the situation. As these babies get older, they usually find their way to their own fists or thumbs.

"I'm not very well"

As you become more experienced, you'll be able to tell your baby's "normal" cry from one that signifies there's something more seriously wrong. Even from the early days, however, your instinct is a really powerful tool – if you have a nagging worry at the back of your mind, it's always worth visiting your GP, especially if the crying is accompanied by vomiting, diarrhoea or a high temperature. Ill babies often cry in a higher-pitched, more urgent way than those who are merely upset, or they may moan weakly. On the contrary, if your newborn is often vocal and appears unusually quiet, it might be worth checking that out, too.

"I'm feeling alone and vulnerable"

If you've ruled out all the above, a cuddle with mummy or daddy might be all that your baby needs. Some newborns are perfectly happy in the moses basket or, when they're old enough, under the baby gym, as long as they can hear or see you in the background. Others, however, love to be held close. Enjoy this period, because it won't last. And if you need to empty the washing machine or make lunch, put your baby into a sling.

Swaddling your tiny baby (see p.79) can also help them relax, as it replicates the closeness of being in the uterus. You can't spoil a newborn with too much cuddling.

"Something's wrong and I don't know what it is but I'm so overcome I'm just going to scream until you guess what it is and put it right"

Speaks for itself really. It's not uncommon for your baby to work herself into such a tizz that she's forgotten the reason that set her off in the first place. This often happens at certain times of the day – early evening is a particular favourite – and it ranges from a few minutes of broken-hearted sobbing, to several hours of uncontrollable screeching. The good news is that these hours of woe peak at around six weeks, and usually tail off after three months. See section on "colic" below.

(Note) It's also worth bearing in mind that some perfectly happy babies cry themselves to sleep: it's just part of their wind-down routine.

THE CUDDLE CURE

American paediatrician **Harvey Karp** has his own theory as to what makes new babies particularly sensitive. He explains the first twelve weeks of life as the "fourth trimester" – that human babies are actually born three months too soon. A newborn horse or cow can run around moments after birth, but a baby person is useless. However, Karp's argument continues, if she were born three months later, the baby's brain would be so developed and her head so big that she wouldn't be able to fit through the mother's birth canal. Hence, for the first twelve weeks, she needs to feel hugged and secure, as if still in the uterus. Karp has a system called the five "S's" which he claims can help calm an upset newborn. In brief, they are:

- **Swaddling**: Keeping a baby wrapped up tight immediately transports her back to the uterus.
- **Side/stomach**: Laying a crying baby (or holding her in your arms) in this position during the day *but not to sleep* can help quell the startle reflex which can be upsetting.
- **Shushing**: Loud white noise, either made by you, or by the sound of a hairdryer/vacuum cleaner is supposed to mimic the whoosh of blood flowing though your arteries in the womb.
- **Swinging**: A motionless bed feels weird to a baby who was used to being on the move when you were pregnant. Rhythmic, monotonous, jiggling movement can help calm a baby.
- **Sucking**: Whether it's on a breast, bottle or a dummy, this guides your baby to a deeper sense of relaxation.

All five of these combined are called "the cuddle cure".

Is it ever okay to leave my baby to cry?

You've finally lowered yourself into that inviting bath that you've been waiting for all day, and the yowling begins. Should you get out immediately and run to your baby? The truth is that, once every so often, letting your baby cry for a few minutes won't do any damage – the love you give for the rest of the day easily makes up for it. Whether you will enjoy your bath is another matter … In general, however, it's not a good idea to leave a baby to cry. Newborns cry because they need something – even if it's just a cuddle – not because they are naughty or manipulative. You can't spoil a tiny baby, so don't tell yourself you are setting bad precedents for the future.

What is a normal amount of daily crying?

The peak of the "crying season" is between three and six weeks of age. Research carried out in the 80s showed that the average baby cries about two hours a day in total at six weeks, although 25 percent of babies wailed for more than three hours. By the time they were three months old, however, hardly any of these babies cried for more than an hour a day. Although your baby will no doubt confound all these stats – it's what babies do best, after all.

(Source: T Berry Brazelton, 1982)

Colic

Ask a frazzled new mother why her baby's so upset, go to the health visitor for a diagnosis, and you'll probably get rolled eyes, a resigned sigh, and the word "colic". Colic, as a medical diagnosis, doesn't actually exist, which is of little comfort to the twenty to thirty percent of parents that have a newborn who wails inconsolably for hours on end, pull his knees up to his chest and appears generally uncomfortable.

Instead, colic has become a catch-all term for babies who cry for more than three hours a day, for more than three days in one week. It comes from the Greek word *kolikos* which means "large intestine" – in ancient Greece, parents believed that tummy ache started off their babies' screaming fits and, looking at a "colicky" baby, it's easy to see why. However, research over the years has largely discounted the idea that colic is caused by a major stomach upset. Different studies have shown that a) x-rays of colicky babies revealed no more gas trapped in their intestines than their calmer friends b) colicky babies happily burp and fart for the rest of the day without any fuss and c) it's a normal response for any upset baby to pull their knees up to their chests.

To be on the safe side, it is worth visiting a doctor to rule out gastric illness – constipation or diarrhoea can give symptoms that look like colic but they can and need to be treated by a doctor.

Here are some modern theories about colic:

• Your oversensitive baby is merely reacting to the bewildering spectacle of being alive

The most accepted explanation. At the end of the day – when the crying often really gets going – these babies are overtired from a day of new sights, sounds and smells, and unable to rewind. Edgy infants may also be hyper-sensitive about the normal workings of their digestive systems, and overreact to sensations that other babies take in their strides. To paraphrase one parenting expert: they act like a smoke alarm going off, when all you've done is burn a piece of toast.

• Your baby is reacting to something in his diet

This is pretty rare – fewer than one in ten bottlefed babies are intolerant to dairy. If you suspect this might be the case with your baby, see your GP – soya formulas are not generally recommended without consultation. If your baby is being breastfed, it's worth talking to a health visitor or breastfeeding counsellor to make sure he's getting enough hind-milk (see p.97).

• Your baby is reacting to something in his environment

A study in 2000 showed that breastfed babies of mothers who smoked were more likely to suffer with colicky symptoms, as were those who lived in a house where other relatives smoked. The more smokers in the household, the more likely (and worse) the colic.

- **Your baby has reflux** (see box below)

If you have a colicky baby, the ponderings of scientists really aren't that impressive and certainly don't bring you any closer to solving the problem. Here are a few pointers to get through the early days with a screeching banshee:

● Some experts feel that examining the make-up of **your baby's feed** can make a difference.

  If you are breastfeeding the lactose-rich foremilk (released at the start of feeds) can cause discomfort to some babies: try to feed longer on the same breast or, if your baby is feeding every hour or more, on the same side for the next feed.

  If you are formula feeding, stick with "first" rather than "follow-on" or "hungrier baby" milks. The latter are heavier in a milk protein called **casein** which is harder to digest than formulas rich in whey.

● Make sure your baby has **burped** during and after feeds because trapped wind can be painful.

● Some people swear by **antispasmodic drops** you can buy from the chemist, such as Infacol or gripe water, which you give your baby before a feed. Some say they don't make any difference. Either way, they won't do any harm. You'll need to give drops at every feed and continue for a few days to see results.

Crying

REFLUX

Reflux (a shortened version of Gastro-oesophageal reflux or GOR) is a common condition for newborns. In short, it happens because the baby's digestive system is not fully mature, and the contents of the stomach (including stomach acid) are splashed back up the baby's throat, causing heartburn or vomiting. Though it sounds alarming, reflux is very common in babies a few weeks old, and most usually grow out of it by four months. Many infants happily vomit their way through this stage without any feelings of discomfort, or have mildly unpleasant bouts that are easily soothed. Others, however, are very upset by it, and they may benefit from a visit to the doctor. For more on reflux, see p.297.

The crying game: Five things that worked for us

● The Baby Mozart video, from Baby Einstein. James was transfixed. I don't know why, but Bach just didn't cut it. *(Rachel, 33)*
● Putting Henry in his buggy and getting out of the door – even if it was just to post a letter. *(Leah, 41)*
● Taking Anna into bed, stripping off both our top halves, and letting her lie on my chest. *(Gina, 36)*
● Not rocking Freddie – for some reason, it overstimulated him and he preferred to be still. *(Mel, 35)*
● Singing "Jake-a-lake" repeatedly (Jake is my son's name), to the tune of Brahm's Lullaby while holding him close and walking round the room. *(Caroline, 37)*

● Try the "cuddle cure" or any of the separate elements to see if they help your baby (see above). Holding your baby upright rather than horizontal may also help.

● Distractions such as singing, music or taking your baby out of the house often work.

● There is also a theory that cranial osteopathy can help calm colicky infants. See opposite for more details.

● Take a step back. Being anxious or stressed doesn't make your baby colicky, but it won't help either of you calm down. See if you can enlist your partner and take "time out", even if it's just a walk to the shops to buy a newspaper. It's amazing how the tiniest break can put things back into perspective.

Three reassuring things about having a colicky baby

● It doesn't affect your baby's sense of well-being at all, (although his parents have become alcoholics from the stress of it all).

● Colicky babies gain weight at the same rate or more quickly than those who don't scream and shout for hours.

● There is a theory that demanding babies are likely to be cleverer and better at solving problems when they're toddlers than those who are more chilled-out.

She cried for five hours every night

"From the time Phoebe was three weeks old, to when she was about three months, my husband and I didn't eat an evening meal together: one of us was always walking about with her on their shoulder. Basically, she would start crying from about 6pm, and not stop until we all collapsed, exhausted, at around 11pm. The pitch would vary – from mild grizzling to full-on screaming, and she'd pull her knees up to her tummy as if something was hurting. The only thing that seemed to work was constant breastfeeding, but it seemed a rather boring and painful way to spend the evening, and I was worried about her little tummy exploding from too much milk. A dummy helped, but only as a last resort because we always had to hold it in her mouth – she never took to sucking it properly itself. We also tried gripe water a couple of times, but the effects were rather alarming: Phoebe shuddered, let out a violent burp, yet it didn't ultimately stop her crying.

When she was about three months old, the colic went away on its own. Yes, it was tiring and a bit exasperating, but compared to friends who had terrible problems with feeding and sleeping, I felt we'd got off quite lightly."

Hermione, 34

CRANIAL OSTEOPATHY

Some parents suffering with a sleepless or irritable baby, do find that visiting a cranial osteopath can have amazing results. The theory is that birth is a very stressful event. As the baby makes its way through the birth canal, its skull bones bend and overlap (see Chapter 1), moulding to an unusual shape. With most babies, the bones "unmould", but for a few, it is either incomplete, or a painful process. Cranial osteopaths aim to ease abnormal tension by gently applying pressure on the baby's head, neck and spine, to relieve stress and encourage the body to "re-balance itself".

Conditions that can be helped:

Feeding problems: Caused by irritated nerves to the tongue and face muscles, which make sucking difficult.

Crying: Caused by pressure on the head, especially when lying down.

Sleep disturbances: Caused by tension on the bony casing of the skull, which keeps the baby's nervous system alert.

Using a dummy saved us

"Before Luca was born, I promised myself that we would never 'stoop' to using a dummy. But a dummy was the only thing that helped us through a short, but very painful, colicky patch. From about two to four weeks he would suddenly start to scream at about 6pm and carry on crying or moaning whilst wriggling around until at least midnight.

He was a very 'sucky' baby and the only way to calm him down was to put him on the breast. All very well, but he'd get full, and I would need a break occasionally. Finally, the health visitor recommended a dummy – but said to treat it the American way, as a 'pacifier' not a dummy – we just gave it to Luca when he was upset, rather than letting him have it all day. For some warped reason that took away some of the guilt and I sent my husband off to buy a pack.

This seemed to work. Luca even seemed to find it easier to pass wind at the bottom end. And when he didn't need to suck anymore, he spat it out straight away. Dummies are added to my 'never say never' list and I would definitely recommend them."

Rebecca, 32

When crying gets too much: The Cry-sis helpline volunteer

"People ring us either because they are concerned something is wrong with the baby, or because they are worried that they can't cope with the crying. In the first instance, I will always ask if they have seen a doctor or a health visitor. Then, we'll chat through any of the other things that could upset a healthy baby – their eating and sleeping habits, whether there have been any upsets in the family, whether they had a traumatic birth that might benefit from cranial osteopathy. Often it's a matter of trial and error – babies can be upset by all sorts of things, from the pattern on the curtains to the shadow a tree makes outside their bedroom window. I always listen to the background noise on the phone – sometimes excessive sound from the TV or radio can upset a nervy baby.

Whether a crying baby becomes a problem or not, depends on how much the parent can take. To one mother, a baby could be grizzling

Sometimes, my baby's crying upsets me so much, I'm petrified I'm going to crack up and hurt him

First things first: there is an almighty difference between thinking it and actually doing it – the former doesn't make you a violent child abuser. Because while you won't be the first distraught parent who thinks about throwing your baby out of the window, the number of people who actually do harm their children is very small. If you feel yourself being overcome by negative feelings, put your baby down somewhere safe (cot, moses basket or buggy) and leave the room immediately. Take some deep breaths, and do something to relax – put on some music, the TV, pick up the phone. If you can, ask a friend or relative to come round. The moment will soon pass and you'll be grateful for your actions.

If you find yourself feeling continually angry or hostile towards your baby, you may want to see your GP – these could be symptoms of postnatal depression.

for a couple of hours; to another, that same baby could be hysterical all afternoon and driving her to distraction. It's not abnormal for sleep-deprived parents at the end of their tether to feel they are going to 'snap' and we reassure them that they aren't alone. Cry-sis volunteers are not psychologists, but our approach is to help put things into perspective: we tell them to put the baby safely in the cot, make a cup of tea, then calm down before going back upstairs again. Sometimes, all a distraught parent needs is for someone to be listening at the end of the phone. We've had people thank us profusely after thirty minutes where we've done nothing but sit there, and let them unload, without the judgements they may get from a mother or a friend."

Janet Bullen, chair of Cry-sis

Janet's tips

For the baby: Try baby massage, a warm bath, swaddling. One colleague swears by laying on the floor with the baby, face to face, for an instant calming result.

For the parent: Take the pressure off yourself. You might be able to control a demanding job, a newborn is another matter. Expect your baby to cry and that you'll find it tough at times.

Cry-sis is a charity which was formed by a small group of parents who experienced problems with crying or sleepless babies. Volunteers are fully trained, but do not offer medical advice.

www.cry-sis.org.uk

Seven days a week 9am–10pm

Tel: 08451 228 669; (08451 ACT NOW)

Crying and the older baby

Teething

For many babies, teething is a painless process. Others become very upset by the emergence of their first chompers and don't have any restraint when it comes to letting you know. On average, the first teeth appear between four and seven months, starting with the two front bottom teeth (central incisors) and then the top two. However, to the expectant parent waiting for those promising white ridges to break through the gums, it feels like the process has been going on forever, as your baby drools, chews on his fists, your fingers, table legs and any object that comes within his reach. As a rule (and contrary to old wives' tales) teething should not cause diarrhoea or a high temperature, so see your doctor if either of these occur.

Some babies, upset by their emerging teeth, are grumpy on and off for weeks, some let out short squeals when they are eating because it's painful, others have disturbed sleep. Here are some things that can help:

- Give your baby something cold to chew on: a plastic spoon that you've kept in the fridge, or a shop-bought rubber teething ring.

- Wipe your baby's face often so he doesn't get a rash from all that slobber – this can also cause discomfort.

- Teething gels or a kiddy-friendly paracetamol liquid such as Calpol can help, but consult your doctor first.

For more on teething as part of baby development, see Chapter 9.

Separation anxiety

For the first half-year of your baby's life, you could probably have left him with anyone and he'd be happy as long as they cuddled him, fed him and kept him warm. Perhaps you've been telling yourself proudly how well adjusted your newborn is, but don't kid yourself – it's merely because your baby is like an amnesiac goldfish. If he can't see you, you don't exist. However, from about six or seven months – and more usually when your baby approaches his first birthday – all this can change. He might suddenly start to get nervous when you leave him, even if it's to go to the loo or make a cup of tea. "Separation anxiety", as it's called, comes in waves, and is normally resolved by the end of the second year.

As a general explanation: babies of this age learn a concept called "object permanence", just because they can't see something, they know it now does exist – as when they drop a piece of toast off the table, and bend over to look for it. Because they now understand that you've gone away, but don't yet have a concept of time, they get can get quite panicky if you aren't in the room. Even a baby who was previously happy with a babysitter, grandparents or even your

partner (and babies can be more attached to their dads than their mums) will get weepy and clingy. Some babies even get upset when they are taken to bed because you're leaving them to an uncertain fate in a nasty, dark room.

The good news about separation anxiety is that it's a normal and reassuring part of development. This isn't particularly helpful when you're wringing your hands with guilt on the nursery doorstep, or dragging a child clamped around your knees down the street, but here are some pointers to help ease the trauma:

● Playing a game such as "peek-a-boo'" (hiding your face with your hands, and taking them away again) teaches your baby that things disappear, and come back again.

● If you, say, are planning to go back to work, try practice separations. Tell your baby that you are going into another room, tell them you will be back soon and come back in smiling and saying "hello". Your baby won't understand the words yet, but she'll get used to the fact that you do always come back.

● When you really do leave, don't agonize over your departure. Instead, get into a predictable routine. Give him a kiss, tell him that you will be back, then leave. If you are dropping your baby at someone else's house or a nursery, it can be reassuring if you spend a few minutes together while they get acclimatized.

Some babies also cry when their parents come back. It's not because he is having so much fun and doesn't want to leave. It's because your return has left him overcome with relief, and a few tears will ensure a big kiss and a cuddle.

Fears and phobias

The flipside of separation anxiety is that your baby will no longer welcome all things and people with a big gummy smile, and may even start crying when strangers approach. Sometimes, he might even "take against" a previously loved relative or friend, such as a grandfather, which can be very upsetting. Again, this is a normal part of growing up, and it will resolve itself by the time the baby is a year old or soon after.

Equally common is a growing fear of everyday objects which were hitherto accepted or even ignored: the vacuum cleaner, the loo flushing, the family dog. A couple of suggestions to combat this:

- Don't force your baby to sit on grandpa's lap or to pat the family dog. It won't help the situation and might even make it worse, as your baby will only have his negative associations reinforced. And don't make fun of the situation either – your baby won't understand what there is to laugh at.

- Build confidence slowly, by helping your baby become familiar with the feared object or person. Sometimes, just having them in the same room, but without any close interaction can help improve things.

Frustration

As your baby gets older, he'll learn to do loads of new things – and will simultaneously realize that there are a million and one other things he can't do. Whether it's standing up or putting a star-shaped brick into a star-shaped hole or pulling your boiling cup of tea all over him, if he is thwarted he'll probably go red in the face and start howling hot tears. It's heartbreaking to see your angry little baby getting so upset, but psychologists recommend helping and guiding – showing how to put the brick into the hole and letting him actually do it – rather than taking over and doing it for him. Trial and error is all part of the learning process.

Further resources

Sleeping solutions

Babycalming by Caroline Deacon (Harpercollins, £8.99). Deacon is an NCT breastfeeding counsellor, and this is a sane, realistic view of problems with sleeping, feeding and crying, with a substantial section on colic.

Crying Baby, Sleepless Nights by Sandy Jones (Harvard Common Press, available on Amazon). Helps parents discover the causes of their baby's distress, and covers the myths and realities of life with colic.

The Happiest Baby by Dr Harvey Karp (Penguin, £6.99). Karp has his own theories on colicky babies and the best way to calm them – with his easy-to-follow five-step "cuddle cure".

Websites

www.cry-sis.com Website allied to the charity (see p.198) which has suggestions on how to calm a crying or sleepless baby. Also contains a booklist and helpline number.

www.infantreflux.org American site dedicated to this problem, offering medical explanations, suggestions for treatment and further reading.

www.colichelp.com Useful, supportive and humorous site with research, tips and chatrooms.

NSPCC helpline Tel: 08088 005 000

7

Remember me?

7

Remember me?

One of the biggest misconceptions about new parenthood is the way that becoming a mother will *change* you. The idea seems to be this: that you'll come home after a few hours of panting and pushing or surgery a completely different person to the one who entered the labour ward the day before. Yes, life around you has changed. No more spontaneous nights out, no more lie-ins. You even wish you'd listened to those people who told you to pack in the cinema trips before the imminent arrival. And the reason for all this? The marvellous creation snuffling away next to you, the joy of which will increasingly hit home as time passes. But just because you've given birth does not mean that everything you held dear or fascinated you beforehand suddenly ceases to exist.

There are some women who instantaneously see their new role in life as a mother to the exclusion of all else, but for most people, this just isn't the case any more. So, at some point in the first year after you've had your baby, you may sit up and realize that you want to reclaim the person formerly known as "you". To every woman, this means something different. It could mean going back to work. It could mean losing enough weight to fit back into your Seven jeans. It could mean buying the latest Booker winner, and actually finishing a chapter, or having an evening out with your friends and talking about something other than your baby.

The weird world of maternity leave

You probably spent the entire run of your pregnancy "counting down" to the moment you could kick off your work shoes and stop squeezing your huge bulk onto public transport or behind the wheel of your car. It was a beautiful fantasy – no more deadlines, computer screens or demanding managers. And for many new parents, the reality does indeed live up to the dream – hours snuggled up with a new baby, cooing with well-meaning relatives – all the while knowing that someone else is dealing with the difficult clients at work. For others, however, life is now about getting to grips with the most difficult client of all. And if you are having the usual troubles encouraging your baby to eat, sleep and stop crying, you may even find yourself pining nostalgically for the good old days of the evil boss who at least didn't lie in wait in your bedroom complaining at two o'clock in the morning.

There's another truth about babycare which is barely whispered in the hallowed aisles of Mothercare. It's relentless, and it can be incredibly *boring*. Nappy, feed, nappy, nappy, feed, nappy – and so it goes on, interminably, until you see the first glimmer the day your baby suddenly looks you in the eye and rewards you with a gummy grin of recognition. Even after that, the endless days at home with a newborn can be gruelling and isolating – especially if your only conversation is with (or about) your baby. This can be more difficult if you're taking a break from an interesting career – suddenly, you've gone from someone with status and identity to – well – someone's mother. No one's doubting it's the most important job in the world but it can take a while to get used to this change in "status". Many women feel guilty for thinking this, and even more guilty for telling others how they feel – in many (often older) circles, it just isn't the acceptable face of motherhood and is derided as cold and unnatural.

Yet the fact you find aspects of being a parent boring or unenjoyable does not mean you don't love your baby, and anyone who makes this implication has a severe lack of imagination and is obviously missing the point.

I was literally banging my head against the wall

"I was too frightened to admit it for ages, but I found the first four months with Amy unrewarding and mind-numbingly dull. I had come from a busy job where I was head of department – now, I was stuck at home with my sweet but rather unresponsive little girl. I didn't find the day-to-day babycare difficult, but in the long hours while Amy slept or lay under her babygym, I was bored. It was winter, it rained and got dark at 3pm, so going out wasn't that attractive an option. I was too tired to read, but couldn't bring myself to turn on the TV – watching daytime telly made me feel guilty, like I was somehow sciving off work. At 28, I was the first of my circle to have a baby, so none of my friends were on maternity leave, and though they did come and visit, we weren't really on the same planet. Worst of all was the fact that my husband worked long hours and often wasn't home before 8pm. Come 5pm, I'd literally be banging my head against the wall, and ringing him up, begging him to come home.

Maternity leave survival guide: Seven suggestions to stop yourself going insane

- I made sure I had one thing that got me out of the house every day – a baby massage class, a visit to a friend's house, or even a walk down the road to the post office constituted a triumph. *(Helen, 35)*
- Meeting with my NCT group religiously once a week – it was like a support network. Two of the girls I really got on with, the rest weren't really "me" but we still all kept each other going. *(Marianne, 40)*
- We hired a cleaner – that meant I wasn't always staring at the washing in despair and could use any leftover time to catch up on all the books I was desperate to read. *(Shauna, 36)*
- Don't take on any work – even if you think you'll be up to it. I'm self-employed, and was sure I could finish a project in the first three months. I couldn't and it piled on unnecessary stress. *(Lesley, 37)*
- I made a big effort to do activities that weren't just baby-centred: going to a gallery, or a pub with a garden – young babies don't care where they are, and will just sleep in the buggy. *(Gina, 28)*
- We accepted babysitting help whenever it was offered, to give my husband and me some time together. The first time we went out, I left my parents a 'manual' which cracked them up. *(Amanda, 31)*
- By sorting out my childcare early. I'd put my son's name on our nursery waiting list before he was born, so I didn't have the stress of finding a place in the last precious months before going back to work. *(Winnie, 33)*

Things got better as spring arrived, Amy started doing more, and I made friends in the local 'baby fraternity' with women in a very similar situation to me. At six months I went back to work part-time and found the balance perfect. Amy is two and a half now – I find every day utterly fascinating. Perhaps I'm just not a 'baby' type of person."

India, 30

I felt special and irreplaceable
"I loved both my maternity leaves – I took six months off first time round, and then a year, after the law changed to allow this. Yes, it can be boring looking after a small baby, but as I was comparing it to my stressful job as a solicitor, it was fantastic. My baby really needed *me* – whereas at work, someone else could cover. So that made me feel special and irreplaceable. And I knew my employers had to keep a job open for me, so I always felt secure that I wasn't going to be a stay-at-home mum for ever – this really helped me enjoy and cherish my time with my sons. I always felt (with some dread) that I was going to work until I was sixty, so this time at home was just a brief period to enjoy. Also, I didn't want to look back and feel I had short-changed my sons or myself by rushing back to work before I was ready to."

Justine, 35

Getting back: your body

Take a look at the most widespread images of new motherhood: various actresses and models back in skinny jeans and slinky eveningwear within weeks of giving birth – the speed with which celebrities snap back into shape is truly alarming. The "normality" of this is one of the biggest myths perpetrated by the media and the pressure shakes down to the rest of us. It's hardly surprising, that, when they return from hospital, many women imagine they'll be back in their jeans within six weeks – a recent magazine* survey revealed that 93 percent of women are unhappy with their post-baby body. None of this is made any easier by the way people look at a woman after she's given birth, when their eyes dart straight to your belly to, quite literally, size you up.

It might be helpful to point out that celebrities do not inhabit the same world as we do. They have nutritionists, trainers, round-the-clock maternity care and less inhibition about consulting cosmetic surgeons. Normal people crave carbohydrate from lack of sleep and don't have a personal chef in the kitchen whipping up steamed fish and broccoli. As for going to the gym or taking a punishing pilates class – when and how, exactly? If it makes you feel any better, famous women are forced to these extremes because if they don't, life won't be worth living from the hounding they'll get in the press – it's their job to look good, one of the things for which they are paid such vast amounts of money. You can hardly imagine Liz Hurley smacking her lips with glee at the "72-bites-a-day" diet she followed to lose her baby weight when she really would have preferred sampling the fare at her friends' children's birthday parties.

Mother and Baby magazine

Pregnancy weight gain

Most women put on an average of 22 to 32lbs during pregnancy, so it doesn't take a genius to work out that if your baby weighs, say, eight pounds, the remainder of this is not going to disappear overnight. Here's a breakdown of what weighs what:

Baby	6–9lbs
Placenta	1lb
Amniotic fluid	2lbs
Breast enlargement	1–3lbs
Uterus enlargement	2lbs
Increased blood volume	3–4lbs
Increased fluid volume	2–3lbs
*Fat stores	4–8lb
Total	22–32lbs

* The bit that's really hard to shift

Two-thirds of weight disappears within the first month as your body expels fluids through lochia (the post-birth discharge) and sweating. If you are breastfeeding, you'll obviously keep on the extra pounds of milk-producing udders.

However, dealing with a post-baby body is not just about the numbers on the scales. For many women, it's the slack muscle tone of their stomach, the stretched skin, or the "muffin top" – that squidgy bit that appears over the top of their low-cut jeans – that causes feelings of gloom. If you're breastfeeding, the damage takes longer to become apparent – and there seems to be some odd law of physics that takes the bounce and fullness out of your breasts, redistributes it nice and evenly around your middle, leaving your sad little bosom looking like a pair of used teabags.

How to lose the baby weight – a realistic approach

It's a truism of postnatal literature that it takes around nine months to lose your extra pounds – ie, forty weeks to put them on, and forty weeks to get rid of them. But so much depends on individual factors: your genetic predisposition; how many cakes you ate during pregnancy; your postnatal lifestyle; whether you are breastfeeding and whether this sucks away your fat or dramatically increases your appetite. It's maddening and unfair, but there are no quick fixes. It can take a concerted effort, and a big dose of good humour before you start to feel happy with the way your body looks again. Crash dieting and insane work-outs are not the answer, and can be really harmful for both you (and the baby, if you are breastfeeding). It sounds dull, dull, dull, but sensible eating, and regular exercise – babysitters permitting – really is the way to go. A realistic goal is no more than a pound (half a kilogram) a week.

The dietician

"Pregnancy and birth make enormous changes to a woman's body shape and her metabolism, and there is a period of readjustment that takes months. It's important not to rush into a huge weight loss straight away – the chances are that it won't be fat you are losing, but water or muscle. This is even more important if you are breastfeeding as your energy needs are higher, and you need extra calcium (from dairy products, broccoli and calcium-fortified soya products) and protein (from meat, eggs and cheese or tofu beans and legumes).

On the other hand, it's never too early to get into good eating habits and being active with your new baby. The first step in losing weight is being committed that you want to do it. Even if you are sleeping at odd times, try to eat regularly – sitting down for breakfast with your partner is a good start, then having a good lunch and dinner, allowing for healthy snacks and the odd biscuit throughout the day (see below for recommended foods). I would not suggest cutting out whole food groups *a la* Atkins or going on the cabbage soup diet: yes, you will lose weight quickly, but the long-term effects are still unclear. It's also impossible to follow a complicated food regime when

GI – A DIET THAT WORKS?

Finally, there is a diet that nutritionists and dieticians do actually like. The **GI (Glycaemic Index) diet** is based on research from the 1980s which revealed that while some starchy foods raised blood sugar levels quite dramatically, others had little effect. This led to a scale called the **Glycaemic Index**, which ranked foods based on the effect they had on blood sugar levels. The Index runs from 0–100 and uses glucose – which has a GI value of 100 – as the benchmark. In simple terms, the GI Index reveals whether certain foods raise blood sugar levels substantially, moderately or marginally. Foods that have only a slow, small effect on blood sugar have a low GI value, and are encouraged, as they stay in your system and stop you getting hungry. Those causing a large, rapid rise in blood sugar have a high GI value and are best avoided.

Low GI foods include porridge, wholemeal spaghetti, cherries and fettucini.

High GI foods include white rice, jacket potatoes and – surprisingly – watermelon.

you are exhausted from looking after a newborn. There's nothing wrong with having a few ready meals in the fridge for those nights when you can't put the baby down, as long as they are low-fat, low-salt, and you supplement them with a big helping of vegetables on the side. Frozen or tinned veg are just as good as fresh ones. When you go shopping, fill the fridge with quick, healthy food, so there's always a good option when you get hungry. And don't pick on the baby's leftovers."

Frankie Phillips, registered dietician

Frankie's weight-loss tips

● Cut down on portion size, rather than changing the components of a meal, or serve up smaller helpings of starch (potatoes, pasta) and protein but fill the rest of the plate up with vegetables.

● Swap full-fat cheese and milk for the lower fat variety.

Some ideas for balanced meals

● **For breakfast**: Granary toast and low-fat spread; breakfast cereal or porridge with milk and dried fruit; poached or scrambled eggs; yoghurt and banana. Serve with orange juice rather than tea, as this aids iron absorption.

● **For lunch**: Pitta with low-fat hummus; jacket potato and beans; ham and tomato toasted sandwich, followed by fruit or a yoghurt.

● **For dinner**: Pasta with chicken and vegetables; lean steak, jacket potato and vegetables; fish, boiled potatoes and broccoli.

Exercising: What happened to your body in pregnancy

Before you start hunting high and low for your trainers, there is one important thing to bear in mind. Even if you had a quick vaginal birth and feel fantastic, there have been subtle and essential changes to your body during the past nine months:

- **Your joints** – In the lead up to birth, your body releases a group of hormones called *relaxin* that increase the suppleness and elasticity of your ligaments. It's the effect of relaxin that allows your abdominal muscles to stretch, and your pelvis to open to push the baby out. After birth, the production of relaxin stops, but the legacy remains for about five months. For this reason, you run the risk of back and joint problems if you resume high-impact exercise too early.

- **Your stomach muscles** – It goes without saying that these will have been stretched alarmingly, but in two-thirds of women, certain stomach muscles (the *rectus abdominus* muscles) actually separate to accommodate the baby. This isn't a problem in itself, but does mean that if you twist too much, backache can occur, especially if you have a subsequent pregnancy. Here's a quick way to check whether it's happened to you:

- Lie flat on your back with your feet flat on the floor and your knees bent.

- Put the fingers of your left hand, palm inwards, just above your belly button.

- Breathe in, lift your head and shoulders off the floor, and slide your right hand up your thigh, away from your body. This makes your stomach muscles tighten.

- You should be able to feel a gap between them. If it's greater than three "finger-widths" you'll need to wait a while before you start sit-ups (until the gap lessens to two finger-widths or fewer).

Getting started: The first six weeks or so

If you've had a Caesarean, it's essential to wait for your six-week check before starting to do anything but the gentlest exercise, and possibly as long as eight to ten weeks, so you allow your incision to heal correctly. However, whether you've had a Caesarean or a natural birth, you can start exercising the pelvic floor and abdominal muscles while you are still in hospital. These exercises are crucial because they encourage blood supply to the muscles, helping them to heal, and make it less likely that you'll suffer from stress incontinence in the future (leaking small amounts of urine when you sneeze or jump).

Pelvic floor exercises: Start gently and aim to build up to ten sets of "long" holds, lasting ten seconds each, and ten groups of ten "fast" holds, where you lift, hold and release. It's like training for a marathon: don't attempt the maximum at first, but increase slowly over eight weeks or so.

Navel pull-ins: Keeping your spine in its "neutral" position, pull your tummy button into your spine, as if you are zipping up a pair of jeans, and hold it for two breaths. For best results, do these alongside pelvic floor exercises.

Go for a good walk: Either with the buggy, or with the baby in a sling (get your partner to push or carry if you've had a C-section). Wear the sling high, so you won't hurt your back. If you feel unwell, or are in any pain, stop exercising immediately. Too much exercise in the early weeks can also increase the flow of lochia, make it redder, or cause it to start again. Take notice of your body, and slow down.

Six weeks to five months

Start gentle, low-impact exercise to music: Such movement is perfect for rejoining your neuromuscular pathways, – in other words, helping you become coordinated again after the strains of pregnancy. It also helps to realign your posture, reopening the front of the shoulder and hip. Some maternity units offer special exercise classes, or see the postnatal exercise website below to find an instructor near you. If joining a "regular" group, make sure the instructor knows you have just had a baby, so they can tailor exercises accordingly.

Try swimming: A great exercise for general toning and cardiovascular fitness. It's important to check that your scar tissue (from a Caesarean or any vaginal/perineal tears) has healed – ask your GP at your six-week check.

Pilates and yoga: Offer excellent, dedicated exercises to strengthen pelvic muscles and realign posture (see Further Resources).

A good old push with a buggy: Make sure you work up a sweat.

WHEN YOUR WEIGHT-GAIN BECOMES A PSYCHOLOGICAL PROBLEM

Even the most mentally robust woman would agree she'd like to look her best after giving birth. And while most of us do no more than sigh wistfully at the tight little tops on the high street, there are some new mothers who become preoccupied with their size to a worrying and unhealthy degree. "Postnatal anorexia" as a condition is very rare, although women who have suffered from eating disorders in the past can have specific difficulties during pregnancy and afterwards. This needs proper psychiatric help. Severe weight loss often goes hand in hand with postnatal depression (see p.62).

Five months and upwards

You can now join in a regular aerobic class: As long as you are completely healed from a difficult birth. It still might be a good idea to hold off from badminton, tennis or any sports that require a lot of twisting – this can still damage the rectus muscles.

The latest research recommends half an hour of aerobic activity three times a week, or a low-level exercise for twenty minutes (ie going to the shops with the buggy) every day. Consistency is the key.

If you're breastfeeding,

- Try to feed before exercise. Unless you enjoy running with a couple of boulders in your bra and like the "leaky" sensation. Also, recent research has shown that some babies don't like the taste of breastmilk within an hour of exercise so you might want to wait a while.

- Wear a well-fitting exercise bra for support.

- Drink plenty of fluids before you exercise to keep hydrated, and try not to work out on an empty stomach.

The psychotherapist

"In the first few months at home with a baby, new mothers are vulnerable to feeling down about the way they look. When you are pregnant, you have a purpose – a prize – you are making a baby. But after the baby is born, you go from the person being nurtured, the centre of attention, to the person doing the nurturing, while the baby is the star of the show. On top of being exhausted, this can lead to feelings of being overwhelmed, and difficulty in losing weight compounds the problem. For many of us, who we are has a lot to do with what we look like, and of all the changes in pregnancy, one of the biggest shocks is that your body doesn't go 'back to normal' after the birth. It's common to go through an identity crisis – this new 'mum' doesn't resemble the 'old you'. The ultimate goal is to work towards accepting the way you now look – it's far from easy, and it takes time."

Holli Rubin, counselling psychologist

Holli's tips:

- **Incorporate the baby into the things you love doing.** To start with, babies are very portable – so simply take them with you.

- **Be honest about how you feel you look.** Acknowledge that your body has changed – you'll always have an excuse if you never entirely get your figure back. Besides, what's more important, a beautiful son or daughter, or a flat stomach and a six-pack?

Getting back: Your sex life

Of all the things designed to make you feel inadequate during the first year of motherhood, the very best of them all is the six-week "deadline" after which many books and leaflets deem you can now have sex. As if, on the way home from your GP check, you'll undergo a *Thriller*-type metamorphosis to the super-sexy you of your honeymoon night. If you're not ready, this can add to the oppressive "to do" list that already exists in the fog of your brain.

According to **Relate** (the relationship counselling service), around eighty percent of people feel a loss of sexual desire after having a baby (the other twenty percent are probably the ones who also lie in women's magazine quizzes). Of course, there are always exceptions – and if that's you, well please keep quiet about it for the sake of the rest of us and don't forget to use a condom.

For the vast majority of women, however, the resumption of "normal" sexual relations takes rather longer than six weeks. Even a couple of months in, the thought of anything "up there" following on from what has come out from "down there" fills many women with speechless horror, especially if you've had an assisted delivery and/or stitches. Despite the whispered rumour, having a Caesarean does not make for a more gleeful sex life – you may be intact in one exit hole, but the alternative escape hatch in your stomach can remain painful for months.

All this is just for starters. The breastfeeding hormone **prolactin** can also have the effect of crushing your libido, as can leaky breasts (for both of you). Night after night of broken sleep hardly sets you up for an evening of chandelier-swinging, nor does having a newborn sleeping peacefully in the bed beside you. Even as your child gets older, finding small pieces of plastic toy vegetable under the duvet is not conducive to a roaring orgasm-fest.

The first and most important step to coming to terms with this state of affairs is that it's pretty much the same for everyone. The second step is to realize that the majority of people with a child eventually go on to have at least one more. Go figure out the rest.

Will my private parts ever be the same again?

Myth: Your vagina is now the size of a canyon, and will remain so forever more.

  Reality: Yes, of course you have stretched to let your baby out, but the vagina is incredibly elastic, and will return close to pre-pregnancy size. How close depends on how many children you've had and the luck of the genetic draw – but pelvic floor exercises (see p.215) can make a huge difference.

The sex psychologist

Waiting anything up to a year is normal

"The main problem with sex these days is that we are simply not allowed to 'fail'. And some people see any diminution in their sex lives after having their baby as failure. There's no doubting the arrival of a baby makes a huge difference, with many women feeling under pressure to have the 'aspirational' love life as portrayed in the movies when they couldn't feel less like it.

There is no consensus, however, about what's 'normal' when it comes to postnatal sex – women who've recently given birth tend not to join sex surveys because they assume they don't apply to them, meaning we have less information. Yes, there are some new mothers who have incredibly strong sexual feelings after a baby, but these are generally a minority. But I would say that waiting anything up to a year to resume full sex lies within the normal range – if, beyond that, you find sex painful or the thought of doing it frightening, you should speak to a doctor.

Another rarely discussed thing is how people feel embarrassed about having sex again with a long-term partner. The longer you leave it, the harder it can be to start again but it's important to realize that this is incredibly common (see tips on how to kick-start your sex life below).

Many women rush back into full sex 'to keep their partner happy'. A surprising finding from research is that many men don't crave penetrative sex as much as you'd think – they are often happy with physical comfort, or cuddles. Some men suffer from erection problems the first few times they have sex again, but it's often because they're worried about hurting you, or getting you pregnant again, rather than because they have lost interest in you as a sexual being after watching you give birth."

Dr Petra Boynton, sex psychologist

Tips on "getting back in the saddle"

- **Take things at your own pace:** Some women find having sex after birth a bit like losing their virginity again. Hard as it may seem, talk to your partner, share how you are feeling and have the confidence to say "I'm nervous." Chances are, he will be, too.

- **Build up slowly:** Kissing, touching, masturbating, using fingers. It's okay *not* to have an orgasm – it still counts.

- **Use lubricant:** A water-based lubricant like KY jelly can make a huge difference to the first few times of full penetration, where you might be feeling nervous, tense or dry. Don't use oil-based lubricants like Vaseline – they can weaken the latex of a condom.

- **Try different positions:** "Woman on top", or "side by side" is actually good after a vaginal birth, as you can control penetration, if going in too deep makes you sore. After a C-section, "doggy style" can hurt, but you may find that if you lay on your back and he stays raised above you (as if he's doing press-ups) this could ease the pressure on your scar. Use pillows

How long did you wait, and how was it for you?

"We did it just before my six-week check. I felt I needed to make sure everything still 'worked' although I can't say I enjoyed it much. We used KY jelly the first few times to ease the soreness, and things did get better quite quickly after that."

Caroline, 37

"Nine months. I had a very traumatic delivery (the baby didn't want to come out, they had to use ventouse and I had an episiotomy) and 'the first time' felt like a huge barrier, almost a phobia. But my husband was fantastic, we went slowly and it was actually really nice to get connected on that level again."

Gina, 29

"About two months after my first baby, and three weeks after my next one. Second time around, the damage wasn't nearly so bad, and I felt much more confident and happy about it."

Andrea, 39

to support you and move slowly at first. Stop if you feel any pain – it's probably better to wait until any scar tissue has healed.

- **Don't feel pressure to be a sex goddess:** It's okay to feel self-conscious about your stretch marks or stomach. If you want to have sex with the lights off, or half-dressed, then go ahead. No one's watching or judging.

- **It's quality, not quantity that matters now:** Repeated academic surveys have shown that people who have sex twice a week aren't necessarily happier than those who do it once a month or less.

Contraception

Though the thought of contraception may now seem as important and relevant as a course of flying lessons, it is worth considering, as your libido (or your partner) may creep up on you unexpected. And as many shocked parents with a short gap between children will testify, your fertility can come back equally unexpectedly after a birth: on average five to eight weeks if you're bottlefeeding, and, despite what's widely touted, even while you are breastfeeding.

You do not need to have had a period to be fertile again: a woman ovulates two weeks before she starts bleeding, so you could be ready to conceive without knowing it. After a baby, many women decide to use a different form of contraception than they did antenatally, either because they know they are going to have another child in the near future, or because they're sure the "baby shop" is permanently closed. Here are the contraceptive options:

Short-term solutions

Thinking of adding to your family within the next couple of years? The following are recommended:

The pill
99 percent effective (if used correctly – this applies to all other methods).

If you are breastfeeding, you can't take the combined pill (Femodene, Marvelon, Microgynon etc ...) because oestrogen is secreted in the

THE MORNING-AFTER PILL

If you've had an "accident" and can't cope with the possible consequences, emergency contraception is available from your GP and now over the counter from your chemist (for about £24). The current form of morning-after pill is **Levonelle**, which has to be taken within 72 hours. It consists of two tablets which you take immediately, and is 90 percent effective – the sooner you take it after sex, the better.

breastmilk and therefore passed to the baby. Instead, you'll be prescribed the progesterone-only (or mini) pill (eg Micronor).

Pros: Easy and effective – allowing for spontaneity in your love life. Repeated studies have shown that most women can safely take the pill until menopause, and it can decrease your risk of ovarian and uterine cancer.

Cons: Not suitable for everyone – you can't take the pill with heart disease, for example. Some studies have reported a small increased risk of breast cancer.

Condoms

Pros: 97 percent effective. If you have a new partner, condoms provide protection against HIV and STD.

Cons: It's tempting to get carried away and take "a risk" which may not (or perhaps will, depending on how you look at it) pay off. Condoms can also occasionally break.

Diaphragm or cap

94 percent effective. Before using any device you used before getting pregnant, you'll need to check with your GP or clinic to make sure that it still fits, as your cervix and vagina change shape during pregnancy and birth. The same applies if you have lost or gained more than half a stone.

Pros and cons: Similar to condoms.

Natural family planning

85 percent effective. This method helps a woman recognize the fertile period of her menstrual cycle by noting changes in temperature and the consistency of cervical mucus. It must be taught by a specialist teacher to be effective. NFP dictates abstinence from sex during your fertile periods.

Pros: For women who don't want to take hormones, use physical devices or have religious beliefs which preclude contraception.

Cons: You need to get it spot-on – it can take up to six cycles to understand your menstrual pattern correctly. Illness, stress or travel can change your cycle, and – obviously – there are certain times of the month when you can't have sex.

Long-term solutions

Contraceptive injections

99 percent effective. More likely to be offered at Family Planning Clinics than by your GP.

Pros: A single injection of a drug called **Depo-Provera** in the upper arm or buttocks can provide contraception for up to three months.

Cons: Fertility can take a few months to return to normal afterwards, and your menstrual cycle can become irregular, with heavier periods. Health considerations are similar to the pill.

Implants

99 percent effective. **Implanon** is a narrow flexible rod about the size of a match that is inserted under the skin of the upper arm.

Pros: The rod releases a constant amount of **progesterone** to provide contraception for up to three years, but this effect is reversed soon after the implant is removed.

Cons: Periods can be irregular or stop altogether, and health considerations are similar to the pill.

The Coil and IUS

Both 98–99 percent effective. The old-fashioned intrauterine device ("IUD" or "Coil") is now being offered alongside Mirena, the newer intrauterine system (IUS), a small, plastic T-shaped device that contains progesterone. Both these devices need to be fitted and removed by a professional.

Pros: The IUD works for three to ten years, depending on the type: the IUS works for five years, and has the added bonus of improving heavy, painful periods.

Cons: The IUD can cause heavier periods and there's a small risk of contracting an infection. For the first few months of use, some women using the IUS have slight irregular bleeding and can suffer temporary "PMS"-type side effects, as well as small ovarian cysts which disappear on their own. Your periods can also stop altogether. The IUS is not recommended for women with health conditions, including liver disease or certain heart problems, and some women find themselves sensitive to progesterone, leading to breast tenderness and other side effects. Ask your doctor for more details.

Permanent Sterilization

Almost 100 percent effective. If you are sure your family is complete, this might be an option. Under general anaesthetic a doctor clips your fallopian tubes, to stop the sperm meeting the egg.

Pros: You never have to worry about contraception again.

Cons: This is not a flippant decision. You can't change your mind – reversals have a low success rate. On the other hand, in very rare cases, the tube can rejoin and you can still get pregnant. It's also wise to consider the emotional repercussions of sterilization. You may begin to feel that part of your female identity has been sabotaged. It's a good idea to see a counsellor before taking such a large step.

You might also want to speak to your partner about having a vasectomy (almost 100 percent effective) – a more straightforward procedure, done under local anaesthetic, where the tube that carries the sperm from his testicles to his penis (the *vas deferens*) is cut, sealed or blocked.

I'm confused about breastfeeding and fertility. Can you explain?

When your baby sucks, he stimulates the body to release the hormone **prolactin**, which suppresses ovulation. According to established scientific research, as long as your periods have not returned, the baby is less than six months old, and you are exclusively breastfeeding (ie on demand, and for every meal), you should not get pregnant. However, if one of these conditions is not being met, the prolactin levels will rise, and your fertility will gradually return. It's also worth bearing in mind that some women get pregnant again the first time they ovulate, with no intervening periods.

These are the agreed scientific facts – but as most people know someone who has got pregnant while breastfeeding, it's a personal decision about whether you should take them as gospel or not.

Getting back: Your career

Whether you take six weeks, six months, a year or decide not to return at all, the subject of going back to work (or not) is a very personal decision and also the ground for febrile debate by outsiders.

Ours is the first generation where it's more usual for a woman to return to work after having a baby than to stay at home – two-thirds of mothers now return. How you feel about it depends on so many variables. You might be going back because you simply don't have a choice – your partner's income isn't enough, or he doesn't work, or you are a single parent. You might be going back because you never dreamed of an alternative – after years of university, hard graft and career building, you're not willing to "throw it all away". Or you might just be craving mental stimulation, adult company and the ability to put a cup to tea on your desk without a baby threatening to pull it all over himself.

MATERNITY LEAVE

All women are now entitled to 26 weeks of **Ordinary Maternity Leave**, regardless of how long they have been with their employer. With some exceptions, most will get **Statutory Maternity Pay** (SMP) for the whole of this period, or **Maternity Allowance** if they haven't worked continuously for their employer up to fifteen weeks before the week in which the baby is born. SMP is ninety percent of your salary for six weeks, followed by twenty weeks at £106 a week (or ninety percent of your earnings if you earn less than £100 a week). Many employers have more generous packages than SMP. If you have worked for your company for six months by fifteen weeks before the week in which your baby is born, you are eligible to take a year in total off work, although the second six months is usually unpaid.

It hardly needs pointing out that you'll have needed to save in advance: £106 a week for six months sounds good but just about covers nappies and wipes. As this book went to press, the current Labour Government was planning to increase maternity leave to 39 weeks by 2007, and to twelve months by 2009. See **www.direct .gov.uk** for more details.

Your views on returning also depend on your industry: a TV presenter may well be keener to start work again than someone who spends all day packing boxes in a factory. If you've been lucky enough to negotiate part-time or flexible working (see below) you'll probably be feeling happier than someone given the "all or nothing" option.

However you feel about your job, the day you dust off your work bag and leave your baby for the first time with someone else is a traumatic experience for even the most seasoned glass-ceiling smasher. Even before that tearful day, there's the trauma of finding someone good enough (and affordable enough) to take care of your child. The labyrinth of childcare is up there with labour pains and leaky breasts when it comes to the list of secrets they kept from you before birth.

The good news is that in recent years, government policy is slowly changing to make life easier for working mothers. There is better provision for maternity leave and tax credits, which look set to improve further, plus a general mood of growing flexibility in the workplace (yes, it could always be a lot better, and depends largely on your employer). None of this completely fixes the emotional wrench you feel if you'd rather be at home, but at least it's a start.

Flexible or part-time working

There's a middle ground between the extremes of a full-time job and staying at home with your baby – and that is negotiating to work part-time or flexible hours. New research by the London School of Economics has shown that 60–70 percent of new mothers are now what they call "adaptive women" – they would prefer to alter their pattern of work to fill their families' needs.

When's the best time to go back to work?

Though the law now allows women to take a year away from work, for many, it depends on how long they are being paid/they can afford to manage without a salary. Go back at three months, and you may still be exhausted and craving more time to get to know your baby. Go back after a year, and you'll be feeling physically stronger, but your child will notice your absence and may be more upset when you leave in the morning. It goes without saying that this is a very personal decision, but most women are happy with their choice after they get in the swing of juggling their two lives.

Slowly, things seem to be changing to suit this majority. In 2000, a new law came into force, giving part-time workers the same rights as full-timers. This act also "recommends that employers give serious consideration to requests to change to part-time working, and these requests should not be unreasonably refused". It's not a right to work part-time – an employer could "seriously consider" your request, and still say no. But anecdotal evidence suggests that die-hard attitudes are changing, and employers are starting to realize the benefit of keeping women in the workplace once they've had babies – even if it is for fewer days or shorter hours. It's also true that many partners are changing their working day to help out: about a quarter, according to a recent survey.

Finding childcare

You've decided you are going back: now the real headache begins – finding decent **childcare**. There are four main options (five if you are lucky enough to have a willing grandparent or other relative): a nanny, a childminder, nursery or an au pair.

The agony of finding an appropriate carer for your precious baby is quite unprecedented. First up, there's the crippling cost. After you've paid a carer (from your taxed income) and the mortgage/rent, bills etc … there isn't a lot left at the end of the month. More worrying still is that fact that every day, the papers are full of homicidal nannies, childminders who let their charges drown in the bath and nurseries full of feckless employees who humilate the children. Even grandparents don't escape – there has been research showing that young children who stay at home with relatives suffer with their social development.

It feels like you can't win, whatever you choose. But there really is some excellent childcare out there. Whether you choose nanny, nursery, childminder or granny, the right decision will be the best "second-best" that you can find for your baby.

A nanny

Pros: Some parents rest happy in the knowledge they are leaving their baby with one constant carer, who is solely dedicated to them, in a familiar home environment. For small babies, it can seem like the kindest option. And it can be easier if you work long hours: nannies are often more flexible than other carers and can look after your baby even when the baby is ill (unlike a nursery). When a nanny comes to your house, you don't have to worry about getting your child dressed and out of the door every morning.

Cons: The expense (see below) although increasing numbers of families are "sharing" nannies. Plus the fact that there is no register of nannies and they are not police-checked – so you're not really sure what you are getting. This is less likely if you go through an agency, but their commission (£1000 or beyond) will make the cost rocket even further.

How much do they cost?
From £150 to £500 a week, depending on where you live, but you also have to pay the nanny's tax and national insurance, sick pay and maternity pay if they get pregnant. Family Tax Credit is available for families who do not earn enough to qualify for the higher rate tax bracket (£32,401 and above) but on this money, you may not be able to afford a nanny in the first place.

How do I find a nanny?
By recommendation is probably the best idea, but not everyone has this option. References are beyond essential. Look for agencies on the Internet

– you'll also find cards in local shops and church halls. *The Register* is a magazine dedicated to the nanny market (you have to subscribe) and there are also adverts in the quaintly named *The Lady*.

Three signs of a good nanny

- Your baby insinctively warms to her, and vice versa.

- She has the skills you require: driving, cooking, fluency in another language you'd like your child to learn.

- She's happy to do a "trial day" with you – paid, of course.

A nursery

Pros: Nurseries are rigorously policed by OFSTED. They are generally fun, safe places for your child to be, offering a wide range of stimulating activity – your child has carte blanche to make a mess with paint, water and sand, yet your kitchen stays spotless. The nursery also makes your baby's food (although you'll probably have to provide made-up bottles and nappies). Unlike nannies and childminders, nurseries don't go off sick or on holiday, although many do shut around Christmas or Easter. Drop-off and pick-up times are also a good way to meet other parents in your area.

Cons: Less one-to-one care than with a nanny or childminder – various studies have shown that nurseries are not ideal for children under two, and can possibly raise antisocial behaviour – other studies have shown completely the opposite. Nurseries are biological weapons institutionalized – your child will come home with every virus under the sun, so expect some days off to look after them.

You'll also have to tailor your working hours, as some nurseries charge if you're late picking up your baby. Plus, you need to be very organized from the outset – places for children under two are hot property, and popular nurseries have long waiting lists. In London, in particular, you may find yourself having to put your name on the list as early as your first scan.

How much do they cost? Again variable – the average national cost for a full-time child under two years is £134 a week. But in London, nurseries can charge £60 a day or more.

How do I find a nursery? Local authorities often keep a list – the best way, however, is to ask around on the mummy grapevine.

Three signs of a good nursery

- It feels warm and welcoming, the children seem happy (children don't know how to pretend) and staff/child ratios are within legal limits (3:1 for under-twos).

- It has an "open door" policy for people to come in and look round, but a very strict security policy as regards the children.

- It has an outdoor play area.

A childminder

Pros: If you can't afford a nanny, and aren't keen on the busyness of a nursery, a childminder is a popular choice. Many childminders remain family friends for years, and can continue to help out through the school years. Childminders work in their own homes, and can look after three children under five (though only one under a year old). They are strictly regulated by OFSTED and have yearly checks for safety and hygiene.

Cons: Less personal care than a nanny, less supervision than if your baby was being looked after by a nursery nurse and possibly less stimulation than at a nursery. Who can say if your baby is being left in front of the TV all day? You may also need to provide your child's meals, which requires an extra level of organization. Childminders also go on holiday, and often have their own children to worry about.

How much do they cost? The average cost for a child under two is £120 a week, higher for London.

How do I find a childminder? Personal recommendation is always preferable, otherwise, see the childcare link (below). Your local authority should also be able to provide you with a list of registered childminders in your area.

Three signs of a good childminder

- They have a valid OFSTED registration.

- You have a positive instinctive reaction to them, and find their home environment clean and inviting.

- They share your philosophies on discipline, TV, appropriate food and are happy to describe a typical day in their household.

An au pair

Pros: Good value for money – au pairs only need around £50 a week pocket money. Plus, they are flexible: as they are living in your house, you don't have to rush home from work to relieve them. There's loads of cheap, short-term babysitting at your disposal, emergency childcare if your baby isn't well enough to go to nursery, and some help with housework. And the advantage of bringing up your baby in a home where another language is spoken.

Cons: In general, they are officially unqualified in childcare. The fact that a stranger is living in your house; if you don't have an extra floor or annexe, you could find yourself watching TV with a Slovenian nineteen-year-old every night. You also need to consider the extra outgoings on food, bills and car insurance, plus most au pairs don't tend to stay longer than a year. According to the Home Office, au pairs aren't allowed to do more than five hours' childcare a day, must be given time to study, and need two days a week off, so you'll need to make other arrangements if working full time.

How much do they cost? The Home Office recommends a "salary" of £55 a week but you'll need to factor in household bills as detailed above.

How do I find an au pair? Through a reputable agency, small-ads or personal recommendation. The **British Au Pair Agencies Association** (BAPAA – www.bapaa.org.uk/) is a useful source of information. Agencies will charge you a fee for matching your needs to the correct au pair. For this fee they should supply you with a police check, as well as a health certificate and of course references. You should get at least two references – one official (say from a doctor or headmaster) and one from a previous employer. Always check references.

Three signs of a good au pair

- They have previous relevant experience with babies and demonstrate confidence and warmth when introduced to your child.

- They can communicate well in English and possess other skills you may require, for instance, can they cook?

- They are presentable and you have an instinctive feeling that you can bond with them – after all, they will be sharing your home for several months, if not longer.

How I felt on going back: The 5.30 pick-up is the highlight of my day

"From about three months in, I was really looking forward to going back

to my job in an art gallery, but the week before my return-date, I started to have horrific nightmares. That my daughter was being taken away from me, that I had only 'borrowed' her for six months, that she was now going to live with her real mummy and daddy. I beat myself up about it and felt incredibly guilty – none of which was helped by my mother and mother-in-law's clear disapproval of my decision to go back. The first morning I left her at nursery, I backed towards the door with tears in my eyes. Serena just started playing with a yellow ball and didn't even look round. The rest of that day was awful and I rang the nursery three times, each occasion to be told she was completely fine. As the days passed, the drop-off became easier, everything enjoyably fell back into place at work and I stopped worrying about my daughter. But nothing ever beats the feeling when, at 5.30 I approach the nursery door, and my walk turns into a run as I anticipate Serena's big smiley welcome."

Lucia, 29

The first time I stood in front of a class again, I shook with fear

"There was never any option for me, apart from returning to work full-time as a teacher in an inner-city comprehensive. My partner, Terry, was studying for a PhD and – besides – the women in my family have always worked, so it felt completely normal. I took eight months off with my son, Bob, and loved every second of it – I blocked out any thoughts of work until a couple of months before it was time to go back. Then, I started dreading it. Childcare wasn't a problem as Terry looked after Bob three days a week, and he went to a childminder (who was a family friend) the other two days. But the first time I stood up in front of a class again, I shook with fear. By the Friday I was begging my headmaster to let me go part-time (he refused). I was exhausted and felt sick when I left the house every morning, and was already planning my next maternity leave. Two months in, I started to feel better. I was enjoying the independence, the money and the status of being a 'real person'. Though I obviously adore my son, it wasn't ever in me to be 'just' a mother."

Anna G, 39

My friends who don't have babies are avoiding me, but I don't only want to mix with stay-home mums. How can I win?

If you're the first in your group of friends to have a baby, it can feel isolating. Whether they mean to or not, after an initial flurry, former acquaintances might start contacting you less because they feel you have fewer things in common. On a certain level, this is true – it's easy for a small baby to dominate most of your thoughts and conversations leaving little room for anything else. But, as time goes on, you'll find mental space for work, films and gossip about mutual friends. When you meet them, try and stick to these topics with the minimum of chat about your newborn – it will prove that the "old you" is still there, despite the new member of your household. Having said this, there is still room for your new "baby" friends – they'll prove invaluable support in the early days and, as you get to know one another, you'll see they are not just "mothers" – any more than you are.

… and the women who decided not to go back

It gives me a real thrill to see them growing up

"The other day, I was filling in a form that asked my occupation. On writing the word 'homemaker', I had to laugh, but deep down, I felt quite flat. 'Well,' I thought, 'that's me for the next ten years.' But on the whole, I love being at home with my daughters. I didn't really enjoy my job as a PA in the City, so I never intended to go back after maternity leave, and we were lucky that as a couple, we could just about afford it. There were positive reasons, too – my mother was at home for me and my brother, and I was determined to do the same for my children. It probably took three months after Sienna's birth to start enjoying myself and to meet friends I knew would stick. I lost touch with a few who went back to work later in the year, but when I saw the stress they had dealing with nannies and nurseries, I was quite relieved.

Yes, I miss the financial independence and the getting dressed-up every morning, but I love being there for Sienna, and her new baby sister, Livia. It gives me a real thrill to see my oldest dancing at a music class, or getting along with other children. If I was at work, I feel I'd be missing out on all that."

Anna V, 35

Getting back: Your free time

Sorry – bit of a misleading sentence there – "free time", as you know it, will not exist again for at least another eighteen years. But the problem with new parenthood is that you spend so much of the first bit just trying to survive, that when life does start to get easier again, you need to make a conscious effort to pick up old interests. Here are some ideas of what other people did:

- My husband and I made a pact: he would go out one night during the week, I would go out another, and we'd found a babysitter for a third night so we could take some time together.

  (Claudia, 34)

- I stopped driving to work, and started to take the train, so I could have some time to myself to read.

  (Diana, 27)

- I promised myself that I would do at least three interesting things a week. Yes, I know it sounds really contrived, but I made sure I either saw a film, saw a friend or went to the gym (you'd be amazed what becomes interesting when you're at home with a baby all day). It certainly helped.

(Laura, 29)

- Simon and I planned what we called "adults days around town" where we'd take a day off and leave the boys at nursery, then spend a day doing things for us – seeing films, having lunch in places with no buggy access, just for the hell of it.

(Justine, 35)

Further resources

Books

Eating
The GI Diet: The Easy, Healthy Way to Permanent Weight Loss by Rick Gallop (Virgin, £10.99). Definitive guide to the Glycaemic Index (GI) diet, explaining its history and how it works with an exhaustive list of the GI rating of different foods, and some simple recipes.

Outsmarting the Female Fat Cell After Pregnancy: Every Woman's Guide to Shaping Up, Slimming Down, and Staying Sane after the Baby by Debra Waterhouse (Hyperion, available on Amazon). Sensible advice on diet (but not dieting), encouraging new mothers to relax and enjoy their early days with a baby.

Exercising
Complete Guide to Postnatal Fitness by Judy diFiore (A & C Black, £14.99). Highly recommended by postnatal fitness instructors themselves, this book covers all methods of getting back your post-baby body – with reference to modern methods such as pilates, yoga and use of the Swiss ball.

Get into Shape After Childbirth by Gillian Fletcher (NCT, £10.99). Fletcher is an obstetric physiotherapist – her illustrated book contains exercises you can do from day one, for posture and pelvic floor.

Videos

Getting back by Deborah Mackin, (NCT, £12.99). Comprehensive video covering the early days after birth, the first six weeks, and beyond, with reference to workouts, eating and nutrition.

Perfect Postnatal Workout by Karyne Steben (£13.99, A & C Black). Steben is a former trapeze artist with Cirque de Soleil, who shows you a (down-to-earth!) way to exercise with your baby.

Going Back to Work

Books

I Don't Know How She Does It by Allison Pearson (Vintage, £6.99). Unusually, a fiction recommendation, but Pearson's account of one mother juggling a high-powered job and family is very entertaining – many working women will identify with the heroine.

When I Go To Work I Feel Guilty: The Working Mother's Guide to Sanity and Survival by Jenny Mosley and Eileen Gillibrand (HarperCollins, £8.99). Dealing with the guilt some mothers feel when they go back to work, with 'workbook' sections to give practical solutions.

Your Sex Life

Babyshock! Your Relationship Survival Guide by Elizabeth Martyn (Vermilion, £7.99).

The Sex-starved Marriage: A Guide to Boosting Marriage Libido and Resolving Conflicts That Get in the Way of Sex by Michele Weiner Davis (Simon and Schuster, £10). Not specifically about the post-baby period, but this book has useful advice for all relationships where your sex life is suffering.

Websites

Childcare

www.childcarelink.gov.uk. **Childcare Link** Government-sponsored website telling you about childcare options in your area, with links to finding further information. Tel: 0800 0960296.

www.ndna.org.uk. **The National Day Nursery Association** For parents and communities, as well as those who work in the childcare business. Has good sections on different types of childcare and how to choose a nursery. Tel: 08707 744 244.

Eating and Exercise

www.bdaweightwise.com (British Dietetic Association) The British Dietetic Association's consumer site. Very reader-friendly, with sections on getting started on weight loss, good eating and finding a dietician.

www.edauk.com. Eating Disorders Association The leading charity for eating disorders has help and advice for sufferers, information on how to find a counsellor, as well as a chatroom and fundraising area. Tel Helpline: 0845 634 1414 (10.30am–8.30pm Mon to Fri; Saturdays 1.00pm–4.30pm).

www.postnatalexercise.co.uk Guild of Pregnancy and Postnatal Exercise Instructors.

www.weightwatchers.co.uk Magaziney site, with details on the weightwatchers' ethos, sample recipes and where to find meetings near you.

Your Relationship and Sex Life

www.fpa.org.uk. The fpa (formerly the Family Planning Organization) Very in-depth website that will answer any query you might have on contraception, sexually transmitted diseases and unwanted pregnancy. National helpline number Tel: 08453 101 334 (9am–6pm).

www.relate.org.uk. Relate are leading UK relationship counsellors, and this website has useful information, publications, and directions of where to go for further help.

Remember me?

8

Special family situations

8

Special family situations

For anyone becoming a parent for the first time, the arrival of a baby sends their world into a tailspin. But for some people, there can be an extra layer to deal with on top of the stuff already outlined in the preceding chapters. Every year, thousands of new mothers (and some fathers) are facing life with a new baby on their own; then there are the challenges faced by disabled parents, gay parents, mixed-race parents, or those with a strong allegiance to a particular religion. Often, these challenges manifest themselves in the form of practical difficulties, whether it's a shortage of money or how to pick up or bath a baby if you're disabled; however, there can also be the harder-to-quantify emotional problems of isolation or prejudice from certain sections of society.

This chapter is a short introduction to some of these issues, with suggestions on where to find help and support should you and your baby be affected.

Lone parenting

The average lone parent is not a feckless fourteen-year-old on a high-rise estate. According to the lone parenting charity **Gingerbread**, 97 percent of single parents are in their twenties or older. Almost half have been in a solid relationship but are now separated, widowed or divorced; 41 percent had a baby while still single, and ten percent are dads on their own.

There are three times as many single parents as there were in the 70s, and this number is probably set to rise as many women of the "Bridget Jones" generation either find themselves in volatile relationships or simply decide they haven't found the right partner, yet are happy to have a baby on their own.

What's the hardest thing about being a single parent?	
The feeling that your children need both a mother and a father	8 percent
Financial difficulties	45 percent
Loneliness	48 percent

(Source: Gingerbread website)

Emotions

Parenting is tough enough for a team of two. Before you even start on the "job share" angle, there's the frustration, exhaustion and sense of loneliness that many new parents feel. Imagine, then, having to go through the whole process alone. Experts agree that **single parents**, or those who don't have the full support of a partner, are increasingly likely to suffer from postnatal depression, or to feel isolated in a world where communities are fragmented, their mum no longer lives around the corner and all their good friends are off at work all day. On the other hand, women who've been in a difficult or abusive relationship may experience a sense of relief and freedom and be perfectly content.

As all new parents, whether coupled-up or not, will testify – it's very hard to understand the feelings of a new mother or father. Some well-meaning friends may tell you "at least you've got the baby" but new babies aren't that good at conversation. He or she may grow up to be your best friend, but there's a hell of a lot of lonely slog to go through first. "Getting out there" to meet another partner has its own problems – whether they're the practical hurdles of babysitting, the perceived "baggage" of having a baby, or working out the right time to introduce a new partner to your son or daughter.

Many single parents still find that family and friends, whether they live locally or not, offer invaluable love and help, especially in the form of babysitting. If that doesn't apply to you, the good news is that there is a vast network of support organizations who can put you in touch with other parents in your situation – see Further Resources at the end of this chapter.

Money and work

Shortage of money is a critical problem for single parents, especially if maintenance has not been agreed or remains unpaid by an ex-partner. If you're the sole carer for your baby, you'll need to finance all the everyday expenses of nappies, clothes and babygear, plus bills, childcare and holidays (if you're lucky enough). Though it's an incredibly difficult decision, many single mothers find themselves going back to work simply because they have to – yet because they often need to work part-time, they are frequently forced to accept menial, low-paid jobs.

MONEY MATTERS

Financial help for single parents

There are a great many government benefits on offer to the lone parent. These are headspinningly complicated, however, and constantly changing, but it's worth fighting your way through the bureaucracy to get whatever financial help is out there. If you're struggling, organizations such as **Gingerbread** and your local **Citizens' Advice Bureau** (see below) can help make sense of it all.

The section below is not exhaustive, but provides some examples of benefits you may be entitled to:

● **Child tax credits**

This is a means-tested allowance paid by the Inland Revenue to parents, whether you are in or out of work. There's a sliding scale of entitlement: for example, a parent of three children who earns £5000 a year will get £5625 a year, but if the same parent earns £50,000, they'll receive £545 a year. Working Tax credit is also available for single parents on low earnings.

For updates and more details, see **www.taxcredits.inlandrevenue .gov.uk**

Tax credit helpline: 0845 300 3900 (7 days a week, 8am–8pm)

(Contd.)

● **Income support**

People out of work, or working an average of less than sixteen hours a week can claim income support by contacting their local **Jobcentre Plus**, or **Social Security Office**. The current amount is £56.20 a week, but claimants with more than £8000 savings are ineligible.

For updates and more details, see **www.jobcentreplus.gov.uk** or your local Jobcentre Plus.

● **Housing benefit and council tax benefit**

If you are a council tenant, all your rent will be paid, but if you are a private tenant, the local rent officer has to make a discretionary decision. A lone parent living in a property gets a 25 percent reduction on their council tax.

For updates and more details, see **www.directgov.co.uk** or your local Jobcentre Plus.

● **Jobseeker's allowance**

Payments of £56.20 a week are offered if you are unemployed and looking for work. See **www.directgov.co.uk**

● **The New Deal for Lone Parents**

This is a network of local schemes which offer personal advisers helping with job seeking and mentoring. See **www.newdeal.gov.uk**

Helpline: 0845 6062626 (7 days a week, 7am –11pm)

● **Sure Start and Home Start**

Both these organizations are government initiatives which help support children and parents in their search for work. See **www.surestart.gov.uk** and **www.home-start.org.uk**

Your baby and your ex-partner

So much depends on the circumstances under which your relationship has ended. There may be extreme bitterness, and a wrangling over access. Your ex-partner may also refuse you and the baby financial support. But whatever the situation, there's no getting over the fact that there is a permanent bond between you and your ex, regardless of what you decide to do. Research has shown that the outcome for children is twice as good if they have had a stable relationship with both parents – irrespective of whether they're together as a couple. For the sake of your baby's future, it may be advisable to encourage a relationship between your child and your ex – you don't necessarily have to be involved. If this proves impossible, take heart in the fact that there are thousands of relationships where a single partner has taken on the dual role of "mum" and "dad" to their baby highly successfully.

Somehow, life looks after me

"I have brought up two children on my own. It hasn't been easy. Unexpected motherhood meant I had to totally change my lifestyle, moving from being an independent woman with a career, living in a private flat, to being dependent on income support. Because of the way the benefits system is structured, I had no choice but to be evicted from my beautiful little flat (two weeks before my baby was due) and allow my local Council to house me in temporary accommodation. It was a terrible blow to my self-esteem and my self-confidence.

THE CHILD SUPPORT AGENCY (CSA)

The CSA was set up in 1993, with the aim of administering the system of child maintenance under which non-resident parents (often absent fathers) are required to pay towards the upbringing and support of their children. In recent years, it has been heavily criticized – by mothers reporting problems getting through to their helplines, then waiting years in financial straits for any resolution. Many fathers, too, complain that the method of calculating and enforcing maintenance is unfair and stressful. As the book went to press, the government were talking (again) about scrapping the CSA.
Helpline: 08457 133133 (Mon–Fri 8am–8pm; Sat 9am–5pm)
www.csa.gov.uk

My friends were fantastic, but as most of them live outside of London, they could only help me by talking things through. A new mother needs practical support – it's really important for your mental health, to get away from your children for a few hours, or just to rest, but there was nobody to help. It was definitely one of the contributory factors to the awful postnatal depression I suffered with both of my children. It was like loving them through a pane of glass.

My lowest point was the night I was suffering from severe gastric flu. Both NHS Direct and a visiting doctor insisted I go to hospital immediately, but I had to refuse because my children would have been taken into care. Now that they are aged eight and four, life is getting much easier.

When I was first pregnant, an aunt said to me: 'You mustn't worry – every baby is born with a loaf of bread under their arm' and I now understand what she meant. We've never had money and things have always been tight but people have been very generous, giving us baby clothes, school uniform, toys … Somehow, life looks after me and I feel very positive about the future."

Ann, 40

The middle-class mothers are the worst

"I found out I was pregnant on the very same day I received my A-level results. Though we tried hard to stay together, my boyfriend of four months was overwhelmed by the news, and we split up before Saffron was born. I was very hurt and disillusioned by this – I'd always imagined pregnancy to be a shared experience, not something I would have to deal with alone. Plus, despite what you might think, there is a still big stigma to being a young single mother – I used to wear a wedding ring to hospital appointments.

My mum was my birth partner, and we agreed that I'd move back home with her so that I could continue my plan to study law at university. The first six weeks were very tough – though mum was amazing, she works full time and I'd had a Caesarean, so found it hard to do all the washing and nappy changing. Thank goodness Saffron slept well and my mother was able to help with the feeds on alternate nights.

The worst thing for me has been the prejudice. We live in a middle-class area of Hertfordshire, and I was astonished by the reaction at mother-and-baby groups, where many women just ignored me. When I was looking round nurseries for Saffron, I'd be asked when my partner was coming – followed by a bunch of intrusive questions: why we'd split up, whether he was going to be in contact, how was I going to pay.

I been difficult financially. We decided, before Saffron was born, that we would have no contact with her father and not ask him for any money. I've been lucky to live rent-free with my mother, and the university has picked up 75 percent of my childcare. But I've had to finance all my education on a £1200 a term loan.

Five ways to make it easier on your own

- Get as much help as you can from girlfriends. Arrange a "babysitting rota" so you know you'll always be able to get a few hours away. *(Mel, 29)*
- Don't rely on your ex's word that he's going to pay maintenance – involve the CSA from day one, and you won't have the emotional stress. *(Ann, 40)*
- Don't be proud. Tell your GP and health visitor you're on your own. I was amazed at how much emotional support I was offered – and not just about breastfeeding and sleeping. *(Helen, 38)*
- Look into government schemes – I found Sure Start and Home Start really useful. *(Beth, 32)*
- Ignore other people's ignorant prejudices. It's amazing how quickly you toughen up. *(Francine, 21)*

Then there's the dating conundrum. Men my age are often initially enthusiastic about my daughter, but once the relationship develops, they become frustrated that I can't go out spontaneously, or have to be home at a certain time. I have had one relationship of a year, but we split up recently when he wanted too much control over decisions I was making for my daughter. I often attract men who either want a ready-made family, or who are ready to start one of their own. But I've got my career to think about now."

Francine, 21

Lesbian, gay, bisexual or transgender (LGBT) parenting

There have always been gay parents, but it's only in the past couple of decades that they have "come out" about their sexuality. Previously, children came from heterosexual relationships – now, LGBT couples can adopt, use surrogates or donor insemination, or "co-parent" (team up with another gay couple to conceive a baby). There aren't any statistics about how many gay parents there are in the UK, although an estimated one in five LGBT people have children.

A great many myths surround gay parenting: that the children are more likely to become gay themselves, that they will be confused about their own gender, or that LGTB people won't make good parents. All of these have been proved false – a survey in the late 80s from America showed that gay fathers were more responsive to their children's needs than straight dads. As with single and disabled parents, gay parents can be subject to prejudice from strangers, health-care workers and schools, and some have reported needing to work harder to prove how much they love their children. However, as attitudes become more enlightened, and gay families more common, this is definitely changing.

Our children are happy and well loved
"When my first daughter Penny was four and a half months old, my partner Debbie and I took her to nursery for her first day. The nursery staff were very sweet about our situation, they said that it was new for them, and they would just ask questions if there was anything they didn't understand. As we

introduced Penny to her key worker, she asked: 'does she think of you both as mummy then?' It was a good question, but it made us laugh – at four and a half months old, she probably hadn't thought about it much.

Penny's now four, and her little sister Millie is eighteen months. I gave birth to Penny and Debbie is Millie's biological mother. They were conceived with different donors, John and Alex, who are in a gay relationship together – we'd been friends with them for years before we decided we wanted to make a family together. So the girls are not biologically related, but they could not be closer as sisters. Their fathers have a big input in their lives; they are 'daddy John and daddy Alex', while we are 'mummy Kay and mummy Debbie'.

In lots of ways, we face the same problems as any 'straight family', but we also face issues they don't have to. So far, we've been lucky that we haven't encountered any prejudice but we do live in a cosmopolitan university town – a lesbian couple in a country village might not be so fortunate. John and Alex say they occasionally get funny looks if they're on their own with the girls, but they're not sure if it's homophobia, or simply because it appears unusual for two dads to be out with their kids.

Penny and Millie have eight doting grandparents, which I'm sure is a big benefit from their point of view (all those treats and sweets!). While my parents were initially astonished that I was pregnant, they treat both the girls as their granddaughters. My only real worries are about when they're a bit older at school, where children routinely hurl around insults about sexuality.

The main thing is that our kids are happy and well loved. We've worked hard to make sure everyone involved in their lives knows that we're all their parents, and to counter the idea that biological parents are privileged, so they have lots of people to love and support them. At a nursery sports day last week, three out of the four of us turned up to cheer Penny and Millie on. Well, they say it takes a village to raise a baby."

Kay, 39

Disabled parenting

How do you push a buggy if you are in a wheelchair? Or how will a partially sighted person help a toddler safely across the road? For the estimated two million disabled people who are parents (this definition includes people with learning difficulties or mental health issues) there are multiple challenges, and each of them very individual. Of course, some people may have a physical or mental impairment and not consider themselves disabled.

The disabled mother

"All parents want to be seen as doing the very best they can for their child, but for disabled people, there's an even stronger desire. I've heard of cases where other disabled parents expecting their first child are told 'aren't you being selfish?' or 'at least they'll be able to help you'. It's incredibly patronizing – based, I think, on the revelation that disabled people actually have sex. In addition, I have an able-bodied partner, and strangers often presume that he'll be the one doing the parenting.

I'm thalidomide-impaired, with shortened arms and legs. I'm very lucky that I haven't been on the receiving end of ignorant prejudice, but I have many friends who have. The problem often starts with children who have a natural inclination to stare, but their parents pull them away, which alarms the child and makes them feel disabled people are something to be feared. People also think that, with a disabled mother, the child won't have such a good quality of life. The fact is that we just parent in a different way – often better. Because I'm not rushing about between work and childcare, I have time to read to my eight-year-old daughter and to cuddle her.

I had Lois in 1996 after two years of fertility treatment. From the start, she was a 'good baby', who ate and slept well. She also adapted quickly to my disability. She developed strong neck control early on, because I couldn't cradle her head. When I picked her up, she clung on to me like a baby monkey, because I couldn't put my arms around her to support her completely. The main problem was bathtime, but my husband was usually there for that – if he wasn't, I practically had to get in the bath with her. As a toddler, Lois never asked me to peel an orange, and has learned to open things with her teeth, like me.

The thing about disability is that you have to plan absolutely everything in advance but, of course, as a new parent, you don't always know what to expect. Still, I managed to breastfeed by improvising with a U-shaped beanbag to lie her on. I also made good use of an old-fashioned playpen which was modified to have a gate – Lois was such a fast crawler, it was a necessity. She didn't feel imprisoned, she loved it in there with all her toys.

At times, being a disabled mother has been tough, but it's amazing how quickly you and your baby adapt. I'm lucky to have my partner – how single parents cope, I do not know."

Simone 43

Mixed-race or religion

According to the 2001 census, the UK has one of the highest rates of mixed-race people in the world – it grew by around 75 percent in the 90s, to over 400,000. In London and other urban areas, no one bats an eyelid at people from two different cultures together, but sadly that's not the case everywhere. What's more, outsiders wonder whether it can be confusing to be a child whose parents have different skin colours – or even to be a white mother with a black partner who has a black baby – but anecdotal evidence suggests that in the twenty-first century most mixed-race children and their families feel comfortable, enjoying the double dose of heritage. Our parents' generation are possibly less convinced, but even the most die-hard Middle Englanders are becoming more open-minded.

Often, greater problems arise with couples who are racially similar, but have different religions with a troubled past relationship: Protestant and Catholic; Hindu and Muslim – situations which often require sensitivity and do risk alienating families. Even if these cultural problems don't exist, the question of religious education is a tricky one: what may not seem important now might become thorny later in life. There are no right or wrong ways to sort out these issues, but it's productive to be open-minded to any possibility, whether you decide to bring up the child in one faith or the other, or "let them decide" when they are old enough (although, for this to happen, they'll need an education in both religions which demands a concerted effort from each parent).

I'm desperate they might lose their identity

"When I first got together with Sam eighteen years ago, my Indian parents had more of an issue with our different races than his white, rural Christian family. Oddly enough, since we've had children, that situation has become the reverse. Sam is now embraced as an honorary 'special Indian', whereas, just the other day, my mother-in-law was talking about the 'irresistibility' of blonde, blue-eyed babies, while cradling my dark-skinned, dark-haired son on her lap.

Both my children have English first names as well as surnames, though their middle names are Asian. We came to that decision because it would be 'easier', although now, I sometimes wish I'd decided differently. I'm desperate for them not to lose their identity – although they do both look Indian – but I don't want to ram it down their throats. We had a Hindu naming ceremony for them both, with Indian costume. My son, who's almost three, has an understanding of colour already. When he sees a brown-skinned person on TV, he shouts 'like nana' or 'like grandpa'.

In many ways, I think life will be easier for them as mixed-race children than it has been for Sam and me as mixed-race parents. Our getting together, however, has scuppered any plans we might have had to move outside London; the other day we went into a pub in Devon, and everyone turned around and stared."

Geeta, 35

Compromise is the key

"I'm Jewish, and my husband Ed is (lapsed) Church of England. Luckily, neither of us feels too strongly about our religions, so it has been easy to compromise. We had a blessing from a rabbi when we got married, and when we went to meet him, the rabbi asked about our future children, and what religion they would practise. That freaked us out a bit – I was still choosing my wedding dress. My son is now a year old, and my daughter almost three – thus far, there have been no problems. Before Jonah was born, Ed told me that he was adamant he didn't want him to be circumcised (a Jewish tradition). I was happy to go along with this, because I knew it would have upset Ed, and I didn't mind too much either way. I guess we are lucky that both our families are very accepting of us as a couple. We celebrate Christmas, and we have Passover at my parents' house. It recently crossed my mind that my daughter may want to get married in a church one day, which would make me feel uncomfortable, but these are fleeting moments. Though my children aren't old enough to understand they have a choice of two separate religions, a blend of both – or neither – I'd like to think that at some point they'll be pleased to reflect on the richness of their family heritage."

Miriam, 32

Further resources

Single parents

Books

How to Succeed as a Single Parent by C. Baldock (Sheldon, £6.99). Supportive and practical advice on how to handle bringing children up on your own.

How to Succeed as a Single Parent by Diane Louise Jordan (Hodder and Stoughton, £7.99). The ex-*Blue Peter* presenter tells how she coped when she became a single mother overnight. Readable book with practical advice and other real-life stories.

Find Your Way Through Divorce by Jill Curtis (Hodder and Stoughton, £6.99). Down-to-earth practical advice on this wider subject, which also covers how to help your children through a difficult time.

Websites

www.citizensadvice.org.uk. Citizen's Advice Bureau A volunteer-run charity, which helps people resolve legal, financial and other problems. There are 3400 branches nationwide.

www.dads-uk.co.uk. Dads UK Set up by a father whose children went to live with him, the website covers many of the practical and emotional difficulties of being a single dad. **Helpline: 07092 391489/390210 (Mon–Fri, 11am–10pm; Sat 2–6pm)**

www.gingerbread.org.uk. Gingerbread The UK's largest organization for lone-parent families, Gingerbread offers on-line advice, detailed information on benefits and self-help groups, and even organizes holidays for children. **Helpline: 0800 018 4318 (Mon–Fri, 10am–4pm)**

www.mama.co.uk. Meet-a-mum association (MAMA) 0845 120 6162 (see Further Resources, Chapter 2)

www.spanuk.org.uk. Single Parent Action Network (SPAN) An informal, chatty website with sections on work, money, health and support groups. **Helpline: 0117 9514231 (Mon–Fri, 9.30am–4.30pm).**

Gay parents

Books

Families Like Mine: Children of Gay Parents Tell it Like it is by Abigail Garner (HarperCollins, £7.19; from Amazon). Garner was five when her father "came out" and this is her experience, plus that of other children from gay families.

The Guide to Lesbian and Gay Parenting by April Martin (Rivers Orham Press, £12.99). An easy-to-read compendium about all the issues of gay parenting, from artificial insemination to adoption, and relationship problems.

Websites

www.pinkparents.org.uk. Pink parents Website supporting LGBT families, with support, workshops and a place for children to share their experiences. Tel: 01706 849979

www.proudparenting.com. Proud parenting (US site) Chatty, in-depth US website which reflects the more established culture of gay families across the Atlantic.

Disabled parents

Books

Disabled parents: Dispelling the Myths by Michele Wates (NCT, £8.95). Disabled parents talk about the obstacles they overcame to have children and share their experiences – for good and for bad.

Parenting and Disability: Disabled Parents' Experiences of Raising Children by Olsen and Clarke, (Policy Press, £18.99). The results of a UK study examining the views of 75 families about disabled parenting: both children and their parents are interviewed.

Websites

www.disabledparentsnetwork.org. Disabled parents' network A national organization for disabled people who are, or hope to be, parents, and their families. Has newsletter, resources and advice about where to get further support.

www.remap.org.uk. Remap. Make special equipment for disabled people eg cots or playpens.

Mixed marriages

Books

Mixed feelings: The Complex Lives of Mixed-race Britons by Yasmin Alibhai-Brown (£11.99). Left-wing journalist Brown discusses the history of Britain's mixed-race population, and the issues that they continue to face.

Websites

www.mixedmarriage.net American website with several forums where people in mixed marriages share their opinions and experiences.

www.pih.org.uk. People in harmony An anti-racist organization, which sets up workshops, discussion groups and social events in the South East. PIH offers advice, support and information and publishes newsletters, papers and resources.

9

What's normal, what's not

What's normal, what's not

In this whole child-rearing business, there is one word that endlessly crops up in the thoughts or conversations of new parents: the word "normal". Is it normal for my baby to throw up some milk after a feed? To get through a pack of nappies on a single weekend? To scream inconsolably when I leave the room? These questions, and others, are hopefully answered throughout the course of the book (and you've probably realized by now that the answer to most of them is "yes").

There are two particular areas where this "normalness" is of greater particular concern to parents. The first is their baby's development, as regards things like smiling, sitting, crawling and talking. Secondly, and most crucial of all, are worries about their baby's health – especially the questions of when they should see a GP, or even rush to A&E.

Both of these concerns are covered in the following chapter, although they are a guide only, and can never be promoted as a substitute to visiting a doctor or asking other professional help.

Is it normal?

Your baby's development

Babies don't understand your hurry to make them walk so you can proudly make your first visit to Clark's. Nor the fact that you want them to roll over because all the other NCT babies are flattening the grass. A baby does something only when she, or he, is ready. And when she finally achieves this goal, she has the gall to look surprised when you cheer and clap with excitement, with a look that says: "what's the big deal? I knew how to do that all along."

Having said that, after years of observation, researchers have been able to pinpoint *average* ages at which certain physical and mental skills are mastered (they're often referred to as "milestones"). It can't be reiterated enough that you should not be upset or worried if a baby is lagging behind in one or more area, even if all his friends are competent. A case in point: my daughter didn't walk until almost nineteen months of age and we started to despair that she ever would. Then, one day, she simply picked herself up, marched the length of the kitchen and up the stairs, leaving her parents open-mouthed with disbelief.

As long as your baby is hitting most of the major milestones within a few months of the dates indicated here, all is likely to be well. If you are at all worried, a doctor or health visitor should put your mind at rest, or, in the unlikely event of a problem, refer you to seek appropriate advice. Premature babies tend to reach their milestones slightly later than their fully cooked peers, because their age is "corrected" for the number of weeks they are born early. For example, you would expect a baby born eight weeks early to be eight weeks behind full-term babies developmentally. The good news is that these babies eventually catch up.

Baby timeline

Your baby is one month old

Believe it or not, the little bean in your arms that seemed so fragile and unresponsive is quickly developing his own personality. Slowly, he will start to find his own rhythm of eating, sleeping and waking (although it might not be your preferred routine). By the end of this month you'll start to feel more in control of your day – despite possibly being more exhausted than ever before.

You may start to see your baby ...

- Focus on things close to his face, and lose the goofy cross-eyed look.

- Lift his head briefly when placed on his tummy (other babies simply collapse in a puddle of their own saliva).

- Make his first cooing sounds.

Brain development
Your baby:

- Starts to watch you as you talk – and may even imitate your facial expressions.

- May start reacting to the sound of a bell as his hearing develops, by crying or startling.

- Will still have some newborn reflexes – try holding him in a standing position and you will see his feet start to step.

- Uses crying as a way to communicate his needs.

Get involved

- Encourage your baby's eyes to focus by bringing your face close to his as you talk, or by hanging a mobile 20–35cm away from his eyes.

- Start making repetitive actions to see if he will copy you – like smiling, making "o" shapes with your mouth or even poking your tongue out.

Where you come in

Make sure you allow your baby to rest properly during the day by putting him in his moses basket, cot or fully reclined chair on a regular basis. Don't be fooled into thinking that keeping a young baby awake will help him sleep longer at night – you will generally find the opposite to be true.

Your baby is two months old

And isn't she growing fast? From now on, many babies put on about 250g (half a pound) a week. That means a lot of eating to keep up with the growth spurts. Daytime naps start to shorten as your baby becomes more alert and aware of her surroundings and your interaction becomes more rewarding. On the other hand, sleepless nights (see Chapter 5), or colic (see Chapter 6), sore breasts and a landfill site of dirty nappies may be taking their toll on you. But as your baby gives you that precious first smile, all the hard work starts to feel worthwhile.

You may start to see your baby …

- Have more control over those jerky body movements.

- Hold onto a rattle or small toy.

- Develop more neck control.

- Respond to noises nearby.

- Give that wonderful first smile in response to yours.

Brain development
Your baby:

- May focus on objects 17–20cm away and even watch them move from side to side.

- Start to notice her own hand – this is the first step towards reaching out to grab objects. It will also keep her entertained for hours.

Get involved

- Babies don't see pale colours at this age so use simple, bold, black and white images to grab her attention. Just remember that all noises and sights are new and stimulating so don't feel pressured to "educate" your baby at this stage.

- Now is the time for your baby's first injections (see p.277). Although some babies have no reaction at all, be aware that they can make other infants sleepy, clingy and sometimes feverish. Plan a quiet day at home and talk to your GP or health visitor about how to deal with any side effects or symptoms.

Where you come in

For many women, the two months, mark can be the low-point of the postnatal period. The euphoria has worn off, the sleep-deprivation is becoming chronic – postnatal depression may begin or peak at this point. Bear this in mind, and don't be Superwoman when planning your day. Say "yes" to babysitting, rest when you can and try to get a couple of hours alone with your partner if you have one.

Your baby is three months old

This is a month of true discovery as your three-month-old enjoys a surge of brain activity. The world is suddenly more visible, sounds become more distinguishable and, as his parent, you are the centre of the universe. It's time for fun, for interaction and for stimulation. You should find it much easier to go out and about together with confidence, albeit with a huge bag in tow.

You may start to see your baby …

- Lift his head up 45° or even 90° when lying on his tummy.

- Uncurl his hands from a tight fist to a loosely clenched one and, eventually, open.

- Bring his hands together.

- Kick more forcefully and with more control.

- Laugh out loud.

- Need less food overnight (you hope).

Brain development
Your baby:

- Follows vertical and horizontal movements with his eyes – try holding out a toy and moving it slowly up and down.

- Starts to recognize your face rather than just your voice and may start to turn towards you when called.

- Is stimulated by moving pictures and music.

Get involved

- Be silly. Your baby will love your out-of-tune nursery rhymes and stupid dancing – just make sure the curtains are closed.

- Start to introduce a predictable thirty-minute bedtime routine so your baby winds down before sleep. Bath, book, breast or bottle all help to relax your baby into a better night – in theory.

Where you come in

You may have been resisting them, but **mother and baby groups** are a really good way to meet other women going through the same stuff as you are. (See p.104 for more suggestions on activities to do with your baby).

Babies of this age also start to respond to new toys, faces and situations – a bored and grizzly infant should perk up with a change of surroundings. If you're not a coffee morning kind of gal, look for library sessions, swimming lessons or even baby massage courses. Contact your local council for a list of activities in your area.

Your baby is four months old

Miss Sociable has arrived and is ready to meet her public. Watch with joy as your baby spreads her love around the room with smiles, coos and giggles. Familiar faces are welcomed, but Mummy and Daddy still get the best response. Your four-month-old starts to learn how to play more independently, and can even be propped up to a "sitting" position with a bouncy chair or cushions, so life becomes easier all round. Enjoy these few months of relatively static baby time, though, because she will be on the move before you know it.

You may start to see your baby ...

- Push her chest up off the floor when lying on her tummy. Don't be disappointed if this doesn't happen – the flipside of babies sleeping on their backs now is that they are less happy on their fronts.

- Roll over one way (usually front to back). Once she's mastered this skill, she may not bother again for a few weeks. On the other hand, some babies don't roll until much later in the first year.

- Squeal with happiness.

- Hold her head steady when pulled into a sitting position.

Brain development
Your baby:

- Starts to develop a perception of depth and shapes and so is able to grab at toys and rattles when held close.

- Is getting more coordinated: you might see her lift her legs to touch her knees and feet.

- Will be able to distinguish colours by the end of this month, and her eyes will be able to focus on people and objects across the room.

Get involved

- Take advantage of her social nature and hand her around the room to anyone who wants a cuddle. The more familiar your baby becomes with arms other than yours, the better.

- Despite pressure from family and friends, stick with a milk-only diet if you can. Experts now recommend that babies are not weaned onto solid food until six months.

Where you come in

For mothers planning a return to work, now is the time to further explore your childcare options. If you have your name down for a favourite nursery, pick up the phone and check that you are still near the top of the list. If you are hoping to use a childminder, be sure to call now to confirm your dates and times. Start easing your baby into childcare with short trial sessions in the weeks before you go back, and make a comprehensive list of her daily needs to pass over to her new carers.

Your baby is five months old

And getting ready to move. Although most babies won't start crawling until at least eight months – and some not until around the year mark if at all – they are already developing the muscles and coordination they'll need.

Watch as your baby starts to lift his head and shoulders off the floor, arch his back and stretch out his arms and legs. Babies have usually doubled their birth weight by this stage, and their downy baby hair is being replaced by a thicker new thatch.

You may start to see your baby ...

- Hold his head steady when sitting or held upright.

- Start rolling more frequently.

- Bear some weight on his legs, and possibly start to bounce on your lap.

- Touch everything in sight and lean out to grab smaller objects.

- Chew anything he can put in his mouth – keep little items like stones or grapes out of the way – they're choking hazards. If you have an older child, watch out for marbles and bits of lego. See p.257 for what to do if you think your baby's choking.

- Make basic sounds like "da" or "ba".

Brain development
Your baby:

- Wants to communicate and will try using movements, gestures and noises to get your attention before crying.

- Is becoming more proactive and will do anything possible to work out how to reach for what he wants.

- Might start to whine when you take a treasured toy away from him.

Get involved

- **Door bouncers** are a great way to encourage babies to feel their toes on the floor for the first time – and are very entertaining to watch. Your baby will love it if you clap, cheer or play music. Adjust the bouncer so the baby isn't bearing any weight on his legs.

- As your baby starts to make new sounds, help him along by repeating his noises to show you've "understood" and introduce new ones.

Where you come in

Start looking to buy a **high chair** to safely feed your baby from next month. There are many different types – from retro wooden chairs to large plastic chairs that recline or even rock. Some have trays and some pull up to your table. Decide what suits your set-up and try your baby in a few whilst shopping. If your baby's head control is still weak, you may prefer to start feeding solids in a bouncy chair, car seat or held on your lap. See Chapter 10 for more information on buying a high chair.

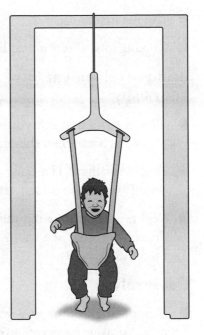

Door bouncer

What's normal

Your baby is six months old

Grub's up. It is time to introduce solids to your baby's diet. Formula or breastmilk is still the most important fare, but start adding small amounts of baby rice, vegetable and fruit purees. See Chapter 4 for more information on feeding.

You may start to see your baby …

- Pass a toy from one hand to the other.

- Hold onto cup handles and attempt to drink.

- Hold toys in one hand rather than two.

- Roll over in both directions.

- Use fingers in a raking motion to draw a tiny object towards her and try to pick it up (watch for those little choking hazards).

- Cut his first tooth.

- Making lots of new noises like tongue clicking and blowing raspberries.

Brain development
Your baby:

- Now realizes that everything disappears when her eyes are covered, but it all comes back when she can see again. Not only is this fun, but reassuring.

- Discovers that "The baby in the mirror" is jolly good fun, even if she doesn't realize it's herself yet.

- Will now be expressing more extreme emotions – loud frustration if she doesn't get what she wants, bouncing for delight and a quivering bottom lip for uncertainty.

Get involved

- Play peek-a-boo behind your hands or using a muslin draped over her head. As your baby gets used to the game, she'll start to pull the cloth off herself, to her great amusement. In a couple of months time, she'll start to initiate the game.

- Bear in mind that it can take several attempts before your baby accepts a new taste so don't give up on the greens yet. Leave it for a few days and then try again, or mix new tastes with old favourites to make them more palatable.

Where you come in

It's easy and cheap to make your own baby purees at this stage. Lightly steam or boil fruit and vegetables then puree with a little of the cooking water or your baby's usual milk. Rather than wasting time cooking small amounts of puree each day, make larger batches and freeze in ice cube trays for use later on. If time is short or you're too tired, jars can be just as nutritious.

Your baby is seven months old

This is an exciting month for your baby. Suddenly he can see the world from a different angle as he masters sitting up alone – or wobbling precariously between cushions. Some babies think it's boring to sit still so watch yours roll, twist and possibly creep across the room. Always curious, seven-monthers want to know what everything is – from the buttons on remote controls to the lock on the bathroom door.

Babies become mobile at different times, and some are more adventurous than others. One ten-month-old may happily crawl past an open bottle of bleach; another might know where the bleach is kept, how to get inside the cupboard and attempt to twist off the lid. However, at some

time in the first year, you'll have to start babyproofing your house. Here are a few pointers, although none of these is a substitute for the permanent state of vigilance you'll also have to adopt:

- Put stairgates on any flights that your baby could tumble down or climb up.
- Move all cleaning products, medicines and electrical appliances that your baby could get hold of and with which he could potentially harm himself. Ideally, move them to a high shelf, or put special "childproof" locks on doors and drawers.
- Don't let your baby play with scarves or string for fear of strangling when he's on the move.
- Move electrical cords out the baby's reach, and put socket protectors in plugs to stop fat little enquiring fingers.
- Cover sharp coffee table corners, and move rickety furniture. Glass-topped tables may also need to be covered.
- Put up fireguards, or better still, live without an open fire until your baby is old enough to understand the dangers.

Stairgates, door locks, table-corner covers etc, can be bought from babycare shops such as Mothercare and John Lewis (see Chapter 10).

With this sudden independence comes a fear of being alone. Don't be surprised if your sociable baby briefly turns into a clingy, emotional wreck when you are out of sight. Fortunately this behaviour – known as "separation anxiety" – usually passes any time between the ages of six and eighteen months. See Chapter 6 for more details.

What's normal

You may start to see your baby...

- Sit unsupported, possibly pushing up to sitting from lying.

- Poke at objects to make them move.

- Use one hand to reach for small objects like wooden blocks and both hands together for large things.

- Babble with ba-ba-ba, ga-ga-ga and da-da-da. Ma-ma comes later. Sadly these noises are still meaningless.

- Discover noise by clapping hands and banging surfaces.

- Blow kisses or lean in with an open mouth when prompted.

Brain development
Your baby:

- Recognizes and responds to his own name with a big grin.

- Reacts to familiar faces aside from parents' and looks warily at new ones.

- Starts to develop emotional understanding, and may smile or clap when prompted.

Get involved

- Recent studies have shown that since the "Back to Sleep" SIDS campaign, infants are not flipping over as they once did and they tend to crawl later. Some even miss out crawling altogether. But don't worry too much – crawling is not considered a developmental milestone and non-crawling babies will almost always sit up and walk at similar times to crawlers. "Back to Sleep" should be countered by "front to play" so encourage your baby to spend time on his tummy by getting down to play on the floor with him. For more on SIDS and the "Back to Sleep" campaign, see p.174.

- Start giving small amounts of finger foods like toast, peas, lightly steamed vegetables or pieces of soft fruit. Your kitchen (and baby) will look a fright but your baby will get better at conveying food to mouth with those chubby fingers.

Where you come in

Some babies are inexplicably drawn to fireplaces, TV sets and loo brushes. Others are happy just to sit and look around. If yours is on the move, it's time to babyproof your house (see box on p.245).

Your baby is eight months old

This month is all about discovery and independence. Some babies start to move more proficiently – either by crawling, rolling or bum-shuffling their way around (often backwards, first), while others are content to admire the view from the comfort of their well-padded bottoms.

You may start to see your baby ...

- Pull, tug and yank anything loose – from curtains to spectacles, table cloths to electrical wires.

- Move more proficiently.

- Clap hands together.

- Wave bye-bye.

- Eat solid, cut-up and mashed food rather than puree.

- Pick up finger foods with a "pincer grip" (finger and thumb, as opposed to in his fist) and feed himself more effectively.

Brain development
Your baby:

- Will start to mimic the tone of your voice – even if the right sounds aren't quite there yet.

- Might begin hiding behind his bedroom door, trying to suss out how it opens and closes, so take care when coming through.

- Will be able to see almost as well as you can.

Get involved

- Expensive toys are unnecessary – get out the wooden blocks, spoons and saucepans and encourage your baby to bang them together. Making noise is fun and it also helps their hand/eye coordination.

- Nursery rhymes with actions are a great way to introduce new words, music and signs to your baby. You'll be surprised how quickly they learn to anticipate a favourite action or sound.

Where you come in
You may be more concerned about what dirt and germs your baby is picking

up when he rolls on the floor. Don't be. According to allergy experts, a little dirt helps to build up immunity – one explanation for the rise in asthma and allergies is that modern homes are far too pristine. As long as your home is generally hygenic, he won't come to any harm by chewing on dropped toys or food. However, bacteria breeds rapidly in water so keep him away from things dropped in puddles and sandpits that pets may have visited. Ditch any food that he has sucked on or half-eaten.

Your baby is nine months old

Can you believe that this little person has been in the world as long as she was in your womb? It's time to show-off now as your baby discovers she can make people laugh by doing certain things. So she'll do them again, and again … and again! Nine-monthers are also rapidly understanding what you're saying and able to respond to simple commands.

You may start to see your baby …

- Throw her toast off the high chair and watch it land, watch you pick it up and throw it off again. Ad infinitum.

- Pull up on furniture at every opportunity, in preparation for "cruising".

- Adjust the shape and size of her hand to pick up an object.

- Work out how to put one toy on top of another.

- Comfortably get into sitting from lying – a major milestone for independent play.

Brain development
Your baby:

- May well now respond to simple instructions like "clap your hands" or "wave bye-bye".

- Could well even say "mama" or "dada" to the right person by the end of this month – or to the wrong one.

- Will attempt to hold a cup and drink from it without your help.

Get involved

- Always include your baby in anything you are doing by talking it through in simple sentences. She will listen intently and slowly recognize familiar words and phrases.

- Mealtimes should be more interesting now as you can share your family food with your baby – see Chapter 4 for what to introduce, and when.

Where you come in

From now on, your baby will get most of his nutrients from food rather than milk, possibly losing interest in his afternoon bottle or cup of milk. To ensure he is getting enough iron, try to include a portion of iron-enriched cereal into his diet. If she goes off foods at this point, just keep offering a range of foods and let him tuck into what he wants. Of course, sneakily adding fruit to his favourite cereal, or smearing cheese spread or marmite on toast is an easy way to a balanced diet.

Your baby is ten months old

Babies don't need assertiveness training. Your ten-month-old knows exactly what he wants and he will let you know in no uncertain terms – and very loudly. Now that most babies have mastered moving around one way or another, this month they might want to climb. Unfortunately, a desire to climb does not mean an ability to get down safely – so watch out.

You may start to see your baby...

- Copy gestures and expressions.

- Roll or drop a ball when asked.

- Stand whilst holding onto something and start to climb up it – often getting stuck or tumbling back down.

- Play happily *alongside* other children; playing together comes later.

Brain development
Your baby:

- Will start to understand, copy and ignore 'no'.

- Might be scared of loud noises or objects that he used to tolerate ie the vacuum cleaner or dishwasher. Just reassure and comfort him until the fear has passed.

Get involved

- Baby singing or baby gym classes are great ways to help stimulate your child's language and physical development. Classes will be advertised in local papers, the library or on the Internet.

- If your baby's kneeling or standing, lower the cot mattress to avoid unexpected tumbles. Even if he isn't, anticipate he soon will – babies learn skills quickly and with little warning.

Where you come in

The ideal footwear for babies learning to walk is bare feet, but when your little one starts to totter outside for the first time, you'll need to buy his first shoes. It is best to have shoes fitted professionally at a specialist children's shoe shop. You will have a choice of "cruisers" that are softer and more flexible for younger babies; "walkers" have harder soles and are more supportive when a baby is up and walking properly. Cute as they look, hard-soled shoes are not needed in the early months as they can restrict the healthy development of your baby's feet.

Your baby is eleven months old

Here comes trouble. You'll be amazed at how ingenious some babies are this month – nothing will defeat their attempts to clamber into cupboards or reach up to shelves or open doors. However, don't worry if you seem to have a chilled-out baby, who doesn't look remotely interested in moving. Some won't start walking until sixteen, seventeen or even eighteen months.

You may start to see your baby …

- Point his finger.
- Hand over toys – and grab them back again.
- Get physical – pushing, throwing, crashing into everything.
- Walk or "cruise" around furniture.
- Try to feed himself with a spoon.

Brain development
Your baby:

- Starts to work out how far away things are by how big they look.
- Still needs reassurance from his mummy so will always come back for a hug, kiss or even just to touch your leg after venturing off.

Get involved

- If you haven't already, start reading to your child. You may find she starts to point at familiar images and can concentrate on the page for longer. Although most babies don't say many words for a few more months, they are soaking up every word they hear.
- Mealtimes are getting very messy, but that's all part of the fun. It's also important for development. Encourage your baby to feed himself by hand, or try with a spoon.

Where you come in

At twelve months, a baby can move onto cow's milk rather than breastmilk or formula, and now is a good time to introduce a beaker or a cup. You might meet resistance if you leave it too much longer; babies become very attached to the breast or to bottles. Be sure to brush your baby's teeth *after* the last milk feed – never leave a bottle in the baby's mouth as he falls asleep or you will damage his teeth.

Your baby is twelve months old

Happy Birthday! Can you believe it? The "terrible twos" are legendary, but you may have a sneak preview of a tantrum as your one-year-old continues to assert her independence. The world looks very different from a more upright position and a few babies even take their first steps around now. Separation anxiety can revisit with a vengeance over the next six months so be prepared for a clingy child in new situations.

You may start to see your baby …

- Stand alone for a few seconds, possibly even trying to take a step or two.

- Use gestures to get what she wants.

- Easily pick up a very small object – like a pea – with just the tips of her finger and thumb.

- Say a word other than "mama" or "dada".

- Perform simple actions to order – try asking her to point to her nose or show you where the dog is.

Brain development
Your baby:

- Is now developing a stronger sense of her own identity. She knows what she likes and dislikes, when she wants to be held and when she wants her freedom, when she wants to eat or sleep

- Has, alongside this independence, a renewed anxiety about keeping you within sight. Your baby may already have a favourite soft toy or blanket but now it acts as a true "comforter" to help with separation anxiety.

Get involved

- Talk, talk, talk … your little one is desperate to learn what things are, so keep up your commentary on the everyday world. Describe colours, shapes, point out animals (a perennial favourite), share your thoughts. It all helps enrich her early vocabulary and understanding. By this age, your baby will understand about fifty words.

- Stimulate your one-year-old with shape sorters, pushalong toys and imaginary play. You may need to show your baby how to master a new game but she will soon catch on.

Action point

Over the next few months, your baby is likely to start venturing further afield, and your childproofing may need a revisit. Get down to her level and move around the house to spot danger zones. Pay particular attention to the cupboard under the sink and outside doors – you'd be surprised how easy they find it to open a handle (even operate a key) and walk outside.

Your baby is eighteen months old

Welcome to fully fledged toddlerhood – an action-packed, fun-filled stage of increased independence and assertiveness. Your child is discovering his place in the world and starting to communicate more effectively through gestures, actions and those first few words.

You may start to see your baby ...

● Being far more confident on his feet, possibly even starting to run.

● Speak a few simple words or at least babble as if conversing with you.

● Build a tower of three to four blocks.

● Stack toys into each other and understand the concept of "cleaning up" or putting away.

● Feed himself with a spoon or fork and drink from a cup.

● Help you turn the pages of a book and suss out how door handles work.

IF YOU ARE WORRIED ABOUT ANYTHING

Remember, all babies develop at their own pace, so use this chapter as a rough guideline, not a foolproof timeline. However, occasionally a severe delay in reaching some milestones can be cause for concern. You may wish to have a chat with your GP or health visitor for more advice and reassurance if your baby doesn't:

● Support his head when you pick him up from lying, bring objects up to his mouth or reach for toys after four–five months.

● Sit up – even when propped up by cushions or in a supporting chair – by six–seven months.

● Bear any weight on his legs or sit independently by eight–nine months.

● Stand for a few seconds without support by thirteen–fourteen months.

● Totter a few steps by eighteen months.

- Take an interest in scribbling pictures on paper, walls and sofas, etc.

- Become more aware of other children.

Brain development
Your toddler:

- Has now developed a more acute memory and will happily join in hide-and-seek games with his favourite toys.

- Shows possessiveness, independence and self-confidence – all part of being a toddler. Sharing is not.

- Becomes creative – using his imagination to make his teddy an aeroplane or his beaker a shopping basket.

Get involved

- You will be amazed at how much energy and stamina your little toddler has. Whatever the weather, bundle yourselves up and visit the park for a swing or just turn up the stereo and dance.

- Stimulate your child's natural imagination by making up play scenarios. It doesn't matter what you do, your child will soon become more and more confident about joining in.

Where you come in
Toddlers love to draw over walls so why not paint one section of your baby's room with blackboard paint. Supply the chalk and an eraser and let him scribble away as he wants. Not only can you control the mess, but it also helps him learn about boundaries and still have fun.

Is it normal?

Your baby's health
To reiterate, this section is not part of a medical textbook, nor can it take the place of a doctor's opinion. This is the professional help available:

GP: Most GPs have "emergency appointments", are happy to see babies at short notice, and an increasing number give over-the-phone advice.

Out-of-hours primary care: If you have a pressing health query that's not in surgery hours, your GP will have an "out-of-hours" service. This is staffed by doctors or nurses who will take your details over the phone, offer advice, give details of where you can see a doctor, or send someone to see you if necessary.

NHS direct: A 24-hour, government-run national helpline with nurse advisers. Tel: 0845 4647.

A&E: The emergency department of the hospital, and the best place to take a child whom you suspect to be seriously ill.

Note: As with all sections of the health service, NHS Direct is overstretched and under-funded. Many people are perfectly happy with the advice they get, but there have been reports of patients waiting around for a return phone-call, of serious conditions being missed, or of parents being given inadequate advice. If you are worried, it's far better to actually see a doctor, either during surgery hours, or at your nearest A&E.

Condition: Bronchiolitis

A relatively common viral respiratory tract infection suffered by babies up to the age of two; there are winter epidemics every year. The infection inflames the tiny bronchioles, or airways, that lead to the lungs, filling them with mucus, making it more difficult for your baby to breathe. A very few babies are admitted to hospital for treatment, which is usually help with feeding, and sometimes oxygen. Bronchiolitis usually lasts ten days, with the middle period being the most severe.

What to look for:

- A common cold with a worsening wet cough accompanied by wheezing, rapid shallow breathing and flaring of the nostrils.

- Fever and sleeplessness.

- Loss of appetite either because your baby's nose is blocked (and babies need to breathe through their nose) or because he is using his energy to breathe.

What you can do:

- Give plenty of fluids.

- Keep quiet and away from smoky environments.

- Administer saline nose drops to ease a blocked nose (available from the chemist).

Contact your GP or out-of-hours service if your baby:

- Is drinking less than half the usual amount.

- Shows signs of respiratory distress, ie his nostrils are flaring when he tries to breathe, he's breathing rapidly, or using his chest muscles excessively to draw breath.

- Has an increasingly bad cough.

- Appears dehydrated – has a sunken fontanelle – the "soft spot" on the top of the head – is lethargic, has dry nappies or very dark yellow urine.

- Has a persistently high fever over 38°C (100.4°F).

Condition: Chickenpox

An extremely contagious viral infection that usually only affects you once in life. The characteristic chickenpox blisters can last up to ten days (new spots only appear for the first five days) but your baby will be infectious

If your baby is choking

It can be terrifying to see your baby struggle for breath or start to turn blue because they have something lodged in their mouth or throat.

What to do if your baby is conscious:

1. Stay calm and call for help.
2. Don't put your fingers in her mouth to try and dislodge the object – you are more likely to shove it further down and cause more problems.
3. Lay the baby face down along your forearm, so her head and neck are supported by your hand, with her head lower than her body. Sit down if you need to.
4. Use the palm of your hand to give up to five sharp slaps on her back.
5. Turn her over to check her mouth – and pick out any obvious obstruction from the *front* of her mouth.
6. If there is still an obstruction, keep her on her back, measure one finger's breadth down from the centre of her nipple line (to the lower breastbone) and use the tips of two fingers to give five chest compressions by pushing downwards and forwards towards her face. Push down to the depth of one third to one half of her chest.
7. Check her mouth again.
8. Repeat steps four to seven up to three times.
9. Call an ambulance and continue until help arrives.
10. If she stops breathing, follow the instructions below for CPR.

If your baby is unconscious:

1. Call for help.
2. Stay calm.
3. Tap her foot or call her name to check if you can rouse her from sleep.
4. If she is still unconscious, call an ambulance.
5. Lie her flat on her back and gently tilt her head back with one hand on her forehead.
6. Pluck out any obvious obstruction from the *front* of her mouth. Do not use your fingers to try and dislodge a trapped object.

(Contd.)

7. Check your baby is breathing – put your ear next to her face and look at her chest for ten seconds. If she is breathing, hold her in your arms, keeping her head lower than her body, until help arrives.
8. If she is not breathing – begin **CPR** (see below).

CPR for (choking) babies who are not breathing:

1. Call for help
2. Follow the **ABC**:
   A. Airway – Check it's clear.
   B. Check breathing – If the baby's not breathing give two breaths with your mouth over the baby's nose and mouth, or in an older child pinch his nose and blow into his mouth. You should see his chest rise with your breath.
   C. Check circulation – Feel for your baby's pulse in his elbow or groin for ten seconds. If there's no pulse or it's very slow, start compressions at a rate of one hundred a minute with ratio of five compressions to one breath.
3. Follow steps above for chest compressions.
4. Give five chest compressions then stop to give one breath, with your mouth covering baby's mouth and nose. Compress chest at a rate of one hundred a minute over middle of chest.
5. After each breath give a further five chest compressions.
6. Continue until the baby shows signs of life or help arrives.

from 48 hours before they appear and until the last one is crusted over. These are very itchy and can scar if the scabs are knocked off. Incubation is a tedious ten to 21 days while you wait to see if your baby is infected. Chickenpox is common and rarely a problem, though it can be serious in the first seven days of life. It's more serious in adults, so make sure everyone your baby comes into contact with has had the illness.

What to look for:

● Small, red spots that develop into blisters filled with a clear fluid that then turns cloudy. They usually start on the tummy and back, spreading all over the body (including the scalp, soles of the feet and even inside the eyes).

Once these blisters burst they leave open sores that eventually scab over.

- Fever – occasionally stomach pain and nausea.

What you can do:

- Gently sponge down the spots with cool or lukewarm water to help the itching. Frequent bathing can also help as can sodium bicarbonate added to the bath water.

- Pat, never rub dry. Applying calamine lotion to the spots seems to soothe some babies, although others hate it.

- Some babies will have spots inside their mouths so prepare easy-to-eat, soft and bland foods.

- Use a baby analgesic such as Calpol or Nurofen (see box p.276).

See your GP for initial diagnosis, or see a doctor if your baby:

- Has an ongoing fever or if the symptoms worsen to include a severe headache, cough, aversion to light or difficulty breathing.

- Seems dehydrated (see section on Bronchiolitis).

Condition: Colic (see Chapter 6, p.192)

Contact your GP if your baby:

Behaves this way for several days, you feel you are not coping, or if you are concerned that the colic is masking a more severe problem.

Condition: Common cold

A viral infection of the upper respiratory system. Almost all colds clear up in less than two weeks without complications but expect children to have as many as eight colds per year or more.

What to look for:

- Tickly throat, runny nose and sneezing.

- Slight temperature.

- Mucus becoming thick and green or yellow.

What you can do:

- Try saline drops to help relieve nasal congestion.

- Smear a little Vaseline under his nostrils to soothe any soreness.

- Keep up fluids and food.

Contact your GP if your baby:

- Seems to be getting worse rather than better after five days.

- Has other symptoms or an ongoing fever.

- Has difficulty breathing, swollen glands or can't keep down food and drink.

Condition: Conjunctivis

This tends to cover a multitude of minor eye complaints in babies, including a milder "sticky eye" that doesn't need treatment. Conjunctivitis is an infection of the clear membrane that covers the white part of the eye and inside the eyelids. It can either be caused by bacteria or viruses and, especially in the newborn, by a blocked tear duct that just needs gently massaging to clear up. None of these cause long-term eye damage. More seriously, newborns exposed to chlamydia, gonorrhoea or herpes in the birth canal can develop conjunctivitis in their first two weeks which leads to serious eye problems.

FINDING/CHANGING YOUR GP

It's a legal requirement that you and your baby have a GP. If you are moving into a new area, all you need to do is register at your local surgery. Note to London readers: you may find that all the GPs in your area say that their list is "full". In this case, the local authority is obliged to find you a surgery, although sadly it may not be your first choice.

If you are unhappy with your doctor for any reason, it is possible to change without giving a reason. You'll need to contact your health authority, who have a duty to send you a list of doctors and details of how to change within two days, and to forward your records within six weeks.

What to look for:

● Red, weepy eyes.

● Some pus discharge – often leading to eyelashes being stuck together when your baby wakes up.

What you can do:

● Regularly clean your baby's eyes with warm, recently boiled water, starting at the bridge of the nose and wiping outwards. Always use each piece of gauze or cotton wool once so as not to re-infect the eye. "Sticky eye" should then clear up without further treatment.

● Wash your own hands thoroughly after touching your child's eyes, and throw away cotton balls after use.

Contact your GP if your baby:

● Has the above symptoms for longer than a few days or they increase significantly – especially if accompanied by fever.

● Seems sensitive to light.

Condition: Constipation

Constipation does not refer to the amount of times your baby poos, but the dry texture of the stools that are produced. Breastfed babies rarely suffer from constipation. A few bottlefed babies sometimes find it difficult to process some brands of formula and therefore do. However, you are most likely to notice a problem once your baby is eating solid food.

What to look for:

● Your baby is struggling to open his bowels, squirming or arching his back in pain.

● Stools that are hard and pebble-like.

What you can do:

● Ensure his diet includes plenty of fresh fruit, vegetables and wholegrain foods.

● Give small sips of water on a regular basis.

Contact your GP if your baby:

● Has blood in his nappy.

● Seems in distress when opening his bowels.

● Has recurrent bouts of constipation.

Condition: Cradle Cap

A common scalp complaint for young babies. It is not infectious, harmful and can be easily treated.

What to look for:

● Scaly yellow patches on the scalp.

What you can do:

● Gently brush your baby's hair to see if that removes any of the cradle cap.

● If not, rub a little baby or olive oil into the affected areas to loosen the scales. Leave on skin overnight and wash out with a mild shampoo the following day (some stubborn patches may need several days of oiling before they come loose).

● Regularly brush your baby's hair to get rid of flakes and to stimulate the scalp's natural oils.

● There are also some medicated shampoos available to treat cradle cap.

See your health visitor or GP if your baby:

● Also has red, scaly patches on other parts of her body. This could be a sign of infantile **seborrhoeic eczema**, which occurs in areas of the body where there are large clusters of oil glands such as the scalp (cradle cap), eyelashes and eyelids (blepharitis) or the external ear canal (otitis externa). It is also common around the groin, ears and nostrils and is easily treated.

Cradle cap

Condition: Croup

If your child suddenly sounds like a barking dog when she breathes or coughs then she's probably suffering from a bout of croup. This sound happens when a baby's windpipe is constricted and she has inflamed vocal chords; croup is usually followed by a viral upper respiratory tract infection. Although croup sounds terrifying, most cases are mild and can be treated at home.

What to look for:

- A barking cough.
- Wheezing or laboured breathing.

What you can do:

- Stay calm – any panic you feel will panic your baby and make it harder for her to breathe.
- Keep your baby upright.
- Open a window and expose her to damp air. Exposing your baby to steam is *not* a good idea, as babies occasionally get scalded by the hot water.
- Give Calpol or Nurofen (see p.276) if your baby has a fever as lowering the temperature often improves croup.

Contact your GP if mild, but go to A&E if your baby:

- Has signs of respiratory distress mentioned (see bronchiolitis).
- Changes skin tone to blue or grey.
- Has noisy breathing (called stridor) coming from the upper airway.

Condition: Diarrhoea

Remember that unweaned babies will always pass copious liquid stools. However, once they are eating solid food, so their stools will start to firm up and become less frequent. If your baby has a bout of diarrhoea, he will revert to loose, watery stools on a very frequent basis. This can be a result of too much fibre, a reaction to certain fruits or an infection.

What to look for:

- A change in your baby's bowel movements – to frequent, loose, watery stools.

What you can do:

- Ensure your baby is drinking enough liquid to keep him hydrated.

- Always ensure your hands are washed after changing every nappy or before preparing food and drinks.

- Sterilize bottles, teats and dummies

- Don't give your baby more "bowel-loosening" foods like soft fruit or prunes for 24 hours.

Contact your GP, but go to A&E if your baby:

- Has been suffering from diarrhoea with other symptoms such as fever or vomiting for more than six hours.

- Is showing signs of dehydration (see Bronchiolitis).

Condition: Eczema

Eczema is a group of skin conditions, each of which needs specific treatment. In mild cases the skin is dry, hot and itchy, whereas some sufferers have broken, raw and bleeding skin. Although it can look unpleasant, eczema is not contagious. **Atopic eczema** is the commonest form of eczema and usually runs in families.

What to look for:

- Overall dryness of skin, redness and inflammation.

- Infected eczema where the skin may crack or weep.

What you can do:

- Use an emollient or aqueous cream whenever you wash your baby, avoid soap.

- Keep the baby's nails short and use scratch mitts for tiny babies to prevent the skin from splitting or weeping.

- Use washing products for sensitive skin.

- Reduce exposure to allergy-inducing foods. A reaction to milk, dairy, wheat and eggs may be a factor in some children. This is a process of trial and error and needs a lot of patience.

See your health visitor or GP if your baby:

- Has recurrent bouts of dry, itchy skin that look like eczema.

FEVER

If your baby has a raised temperature of over 37.4°C, she is said to have a fever. This is the body's defence mechanism to fight infections and is a symptom of an illness rather than an illness in itself. It is uncomfortable for the baby, but when doctors come to diagnose your child, they will also look at other symptoms, eg how alert she is, the colour of her skin, her heart rate, how she's been feeding, and how often she passes urine.

There can be a variation in a child's normal "temperature" – one baby can be different from another. It's a good idea to record your baby's temperature when they are well, so you have a benchmark to compare.

According to Rough Guides' medical advisers, you should consult your doctor if your baby has a persistent temperature of over 38°C. A fever of over 39°C in a baby under a year old, especially under three months, where there is no obvious cause (eg chickenpox, a cold) requires medical attention. The first month after delivery is important as babies can have **perinatally (around birth)** acquired infections.

If your baby has a mild fever, start by undressing her and putting her to bed with just a light sheet. If the fever remains high, sponge her down with tepid, not cold, water, as this can further raise the fever. Calpol and Baby Nurofen can also help.

NB: Some children between six months and six years respond to a rapid rise in temperature by having a **febrile convulsion**, where the baby loses consciousness, goes stiff, then their body goes into spasm. This is obviously very frightening, but most episodes last less than ten minutes. You should give your baby an analgesic such as Calpol or Baby Nurofen, undress her to lower body temperature, then take her directly to hospital. This usually does not mean that your child will have epilepsy. However, she may have a further convulsion with a high fever in the future, especially if there is a history of such attacks in the family.

Failure to gain weight

In the first few months after birth, your baby should put on weight rapidly, although a ten percent weight loss is not uncommon in the first week and many babies (especially breastfed) can take three weeks to get back to their birth weight. The best way of making sure she's thriving is to make frequent visits to your local health clinic. However, in some cases, mainly due to initial feeding difficulties, the baby doesn't put on enough weight, and your health visitor or GP may want to investigate.

What to look for:

- Your baby drops down two or more centile curves on the chart in your "red book" over a short period.

- Your baby loses weight for no apparent reason, or fails to gain any weight for two weeks.

- Any other health problem that may signify a loss of weight, eg diarrhoea, urine infection, excessive vomiting.

What you can do:

- Increase the amount of formula you are giving, for a bottlefed baby.

- Up your breastfeeds, or speak to a breastfeeding counsellor if you are having problems with positioning or latching on. Health professionals occasionally support a switch to formula feeding.

See your health visitor or GP if your baby:

Is failing to gain weight in the expected way. As long as you visit clinic regularly, the problem is likely to be picked up early, and dealt with accordingly. Babies who persistently fail to gain weight may need to be admitted to hospital for investigation.

Condition: German measles (rubella)

A mild but contagious disease with an incubation period of fourteen to 21 days. Although your baby will rarely suffer any serious symptoms, pregnant women who contract the virus can find their unborn child goes on to develop birth defects.

What to look for:

- A raised temperature along with enlarged swollen glands at the back of his neck.

- Tiny pink or red spots that look more like a patch of redness than separate spots. These will start behind his ears and spread to his forehead and then the rest of his body.

What you can do:

- Keep your baby away from pregnant women or public places.

- Treat any temperature as usual and report his symptoms to your GP.

See your GP for initial diagnosis, but go to A&E if your baby:

- Seems to develop a stiff neck or headache.

Condition: Hernia

Some babies are born with a small, painless bulge in the skin caused by soft tissue protruding through a defect in the abdomen muscular wall. An "**umbilical**" hernia is most common and occurs near the belly button. This can be left untreated, and usually resolves at two and occasionally up to five years. Some boys develop an "**inguinal**" hernia lower down in the groin, once the testicles have dropped into the scrotum. This needs to be corrected with minor surgery. Girls can also develop inguinal or **femoral** hernia (in the thigh).

Any hernia (apart from an umbilical hernia) should be seen by a doctor.

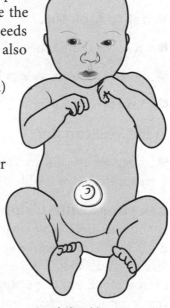

Umbilical hernia

What to look for:

- A bulge near the skin's surface that gets bigger when your baby coughs, sneezes or cries. Gently apply pressure to it and it should pop back into the hole.

What you can do:

- Check it regularly to make sure it doesn't get bigger or harden.

See your GP, but go to A&E if your baby:

● Is in pain or vomits, or if the hernia won't pop back with gentle pressure. This is an emergency.

Condition: Jaundice

One third of babies – especially those being breastfed – will develop physiological jaundice during their first week. When your baby is growing in the uterus, she has very high levels of red blood cells to help process oxygen. Once the baby is born and breathing oxygen directly, these excess red blood cells must be broken down and eliminated from her system. A by-product of this breakdown is **bilirubin**, which gives that characteristic yellow tinge to the eyes and skin. Some jaundiced babies will have a spell under a **phototherapy lamp** before leaving hospital to help break down the bilirubin.

Jaundice can also occur if there is incompatibility between your blood group and the baby's, eg **ABO incompatibility** and **Rhesus incompatibility**. You will have received anti-D antibodies to counter the Rhesus incompatibility during pregnancy and after delivery (for the next pregnancy). If your baby looks very yellow, the doctors or community midwife may wish to check the bilirubin level by means of a heelprick. This will help decide whether phototherapy is needed or not.

What to look for:

● Yellowish skin tone and whites of the eyes.

● Loss of appetite, pale-coloured poo and dark brown urine.

● Excessive drowsiness.

What you can do:

● Keep an eye on her colour and mention any darkening or worsening to your doctor or health visitor.

Ask your health visitor, or see your GP if your baby:

Is still jaundiced after two weeks. This is usually due to breastfeeding and is not a problem. However, your midwife may suggest that the baby has a blood test to check that the jaundice is not due to a rare liver or blood disorder. Only a blood test can distinguish which of the two it may be. In the case of a rare liver disorder (congenital biliary atresia) you may notice that your baby's poo is very pale or white. Only a blood test can distinguish which of the two it may be.

Condition: Measles

A very contagious childhood disease with an incubation period of between eight and fourteen days. A slower uptake in the **MMR vaccine** (see p.303) has seen an increase in measles cases across the UK.

What to look for:

● Cold symptoms – runny nose and dry cough – with a fever that could get as high as 40°C.

● Small white spots inside her cheeks.

● Sore red eyes and an intolerance of bright lights.

● A rash of small, brownish red spots appearing three days later, usually starting behind the ears before spreading across the face and body.

What you can do:

● Bring down any fever by sponging your baby down with tepid water.

See your GP if your baby:

● Has the symptoms of measles for an initial check.

But go to A&E

● If she gets worse having seemingly recovered.

● Has breathing difficulties.

● Seems more sleepy or agitated than usual.

Condition: Meningitis and septicaemia

Every parent's worst nightmare. **Meningitis** is the inflammation of the lining around the brain and spinal cord, whereas **septicaemia** is the blood-poisoning form of the disease. These conditions are life-threatening and can kill within hours if not treated. Knowing the signs and symptoms and acting quickly to get medical help could save your baby's life. There are two forms of meningitis – **bacterial** (the more serious) and **viral** (not life-threatening) but you should always seek emergency help if you suspect meningitis.

SYMPTOMS OF SEPTICAEMIA AND BACTERIAL MENINGITIS:

Not everyone will get all these symptoms and they can appear in any order.

	Septicaemia	Bacterial Meningitis
Tense or bulging fontanelle	•	•
Blotchy skin, quite pale or turning blue	•	•
Refusing to feed	•	•
High pitched/moaning cry/irritable especially when being held	•	•
Rash (see tumbler test box)	•	
Floppy, difficulty supporting own weight	•	•
Fever and vomiting	•	•
Confusion and drowsiness	•	•
Cold hands and feet	•	
Rapid breathing	•	
Abdominal/joint/muscle pain	•	
Diarrhoea	•	
Severe headache		•
Stiff neck		•
Dislike of bright light		•
Body stiffens/jerky movements		•

(*Source: The Spencer Dayman Meningitis UK information pack*)

The tumbler test

Some people with septicaemia develop a rash due to bleeding into the skin. The rash of tiny red "pin prick" spots develop rapidly into purple bruising marks.

To identify the rash, press a glass tumbler against the spots. If the rash does not fade when the glass is pressed down then it could be septicaemia. If this is the case, go straight to A&E or call an amblulance.

I refused to believe it was meningitis

"It was a normal October evening: my husband was at work, and I was getting my fifteen-month-old daughter, Rachel, ready for bed. She drank her milk as usual, but when she had finished, she was a bit sick, which was unusual for her. Still, I didn't think too much of it, so I put her down in her cot. Later, while I was having a bath, I heard her coughing and then she was violently sick all over me. In hindsight, Rachel felt clammy to the touch, and moaned when I picked her up, but it didn't really hit me at the time. I rang our doctor out-of-hours service, but they told me it was just a 'bug'. But instinct told me it was something more than that, especially as her breathing became progressively more raspy.

I knew about meningitis, but there was no reason to think Rachel had it – there was no rash, and she didn't seem sensitive to light. But I was still worried, so I called the service four or five times throughout the night. Finally, at 9am, they sent a doctor out.

We'd brought Rachel into bed with us, and when I drew back the covers to show the GP, she was covered in a violent, purple rash – it looked like a road map. I don't know what came over me, but I said to the doctor: 'Oh, it's not what you think.' He calmly told me I had ten minutes to get dressed. We were rushed to hospital by ambulance, and I was dazed to see twenty doctors waiting for us. It was like an episode of *Casualty* – Rachel hooked up to monitors and drips, people rushing around all over the place, on the phone to London for expert advice. A bell sounded – my little girl's heart had stopped. I was in such shock that I just wanted to walk away and be told to come back later when everything was okay.

Later that day, Rachel was transferred to Great Ormond Street. She was still critically ill, and they persuaded us to allow them to use trial drugs. The fantastic consultant there told me that 'it wasn't good' but that he had 'a good feeling'.

We stayed in hosptial for ten days, and Rachel was critical for five, but amazingly, she pulled through. We were incredibly lucky. The rash showed where she'd developed septicaemia or blood poisoning, and because of the way it was distributed, she didn't lose any limbs, but just has scarring on her thigh and chin. She didn't lose her eyesight or hearing, but we won't be 100 percent sure about learning difficulties until she starts school.

Three weeks after leaving hospital, Rachel was back on her feet again, but it's taken three years to get my feisty little girl back. It's impossible to realize how lucky we've been. My advice to parents is: don't panic, but be aware of what could happen – and always go to A&E if you are the slightest bit worried. It's better to be wrong than endanger your baby's life."

Sarah, 29

Condition: Mumps

A viral infection with an incubation period of fourteen to 21 days that rarely occurs in infants and young babies under the age of one. Although most cases have mild symptoms, a small number can develop into encephalitis – a very serious inflammation of the brain – or meningitis, and some children will suffer swollen testes or ovaries, which can lead to fertility problems as an adult. A slower uptake in the MMR vaccine (see p.303) has seen an increase in mumps cases across the UK.

What to look for:

● Swollen glands at the side of his face and just below his ears and chin.

● Difficulty in swallowing without pain.

● Fever.

● Dry mouth.

● Swollen and painful testes in boys or abdominal pain in girls.

What you can do:

● Treat a fever as usual.

● Puree food and ensure he is taking in plenty of liquids.

See your GP for intial diagnosis, but go to A&E if:

● The symptoms worsen after ten days, your baby has an intolerance of bright light, a severe headache and pain when the neck is stretched. This could signify the onset of encephalitis or meningitis.

Most hospitals now have a paediatric A&E, separate from the adult emergency department. On arrival, you'll be assessed immediately by the "triage" nurse, who will gauge how seriously ill your baby is. Critical cases will be seen immediately, but if your baby isn't very sick, you'll probably be given some appropriate medication and asked to wait. Depending on how busy the hospital is, you might be there some time, although there will probably be a play area if your baby is old enough (and well enough) to take advantage.

Condition: Nappy rash

● See your health visitor.

Condition: Reflux (the medical term is gastro-oesophageal reflux)

Although many babies will "posset" or regurgitate a small amount of milk after a feed, this is normal and a separate entity to babies with **GOR**. Some babies with GOR can suffer from regular and continous vomiting. (Although some babies with reflux don't vomit but show signs of distress from the resulting oesophagitis.) GOR is caused by various things, including a lax muscle at the top of the stomach. This means milk is mixed with stomach acid, regurgitated and burns the oesophagus, which can be painful. Some babies will be in pain, fretful, have difficulties feeding and settling or sleeping as a result.

What to look for:

● Recurrent vomiting, not just confined to immediately after a meal.

● Pain and distress when feeding, classically arching their back.

● Difficulty sleeping or settling.

What you can do:

● Elevate the head of your baby's cot or moses basket.

● Hold her upright for thirty minutes after feeding.

What's normal

- Use a thickened or specialist milk formula, or **infant Gaviscon**, but only if prescribed by a doctor.

See your health visitor or GP if your baby:

- Develops the above symptoms.

Condition: Teething

Even months before the first tooth appears, you baby might dribble, cry and start chewing everything in sight. Expect the first tooth around the six- to eight-month mark, or as late as a year. The last tooth is usually through at around two and a half. Many babies are untroubled by teething.

What to look for:

- A clingy, irritable, crying and fretful baby who doesn't seem to have any other symptoms of illness.

- Swollen red gums, sometimes with the white edge of a tooth visible.

- Constant chewing on any object – or her hands.

What you can do:

- Breastfeed or comfort on demand.

- Gently rub the gums with your finger to relieve pressure.

- Cool the area with chilled teething rings or give a weaned baby cold foods to chew on.

- Use homeopathic teething granules or, on the advice of your doctor, topical gels or baby analgesic.

Ask your health visitor for advice, or see your GP if your baby:

- Refuses to eat for a prolonged period of time or develops other symptoms unrelated to teething.

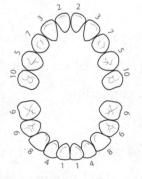

1	1st incisors
2	1st incisors
3	2nd incisors
4	2nd incisors
5	1st molars
6	1st molars
7	Eye
8	Eye
9	2nd molars
10	2nd molars

Common order of tooth appearance

COMMON ORDER OF TOOTH APPEARANCE

Upper:

10	5	7	3	2	2	3	7	5	10

Lower:

9	6	8	4	1	1	4	8	6	9

1. 1st incisors
2. 1st incisors
3. 2nd incisors
4. 2nd incisors
5. 1st molars
6. 1st molars
7. Eye
8. Eye
9. 2nd molars
10. 2nd molars

Condition: Undescended testicles

Although testicles actually develop inside the abdomen, they will move down into the scrotum shortly before birth. Sometimes one or both fail to descend. This will be discovered at birth. Many will go on to descend by the time your

baby is one year old. If not, minor surgery or hormone injections may be required.

What to look for:

- Whether there is a pea-sized lump inside his scrotum. Do warm your hands before checking (or check after a warm bath when they are most likely to be descended) or you may cause it to temporarily retract into the abdomen.

What you can do:

- Check progress regularly.

See your GP if your baby:

- Still has undescended testicles after one year of age.

Condition: Umbilical cord infection

The cord stump usually withers and drops off naturally about ten days after birth. Sometimes it can become infected but this is easily treated.

What to look for:

- Weeping fluid or pus from the stump that then crusts over.

- The surrounding skin area looking red and swollen.

THE BABY ANALGESIC (PAINKILLER) – MOTHER'S LITTLE HELPER

When faced with some of the common conditions in this chapter, you may be tempted to bring out the bottle containing a baby analgesic. In the short term, this can bring blessed relief to both your child (and you) in the form of a lowered fever, respite from pain and a better night's sleep. Look for **paracetemol** or **ibuprofen**-based remedies (such as the lurid-pink Calpol or baby Nurofen – aspirin is not recommended for babies) and be sure to read the packet for full instructions – paracetamol overdose is particularly dangerous.

What you can do:

- Leave the stump exposed to air when you can.

See your GP if your baby:

- Has signs of an infection (see above).

Vaccinations

Why our babies have them

Diptheria, polio, whooping cough – don't they sound quaint, Victorian, irrelevant? But until the introduction of immunizations in the 1940s, many children didn't make it beyond toddlerhood because of these common but fatal illnesses. To illustrate: in 1942, when the diptheria jab was introduced, over 40,000 cases were reported, with almost two thousand deaths. But there have been no reported cases of diptheria since the early 1950s.

The goal of a vaccination is "herd immunity". This means that if most people in a community are immunized against an infection, the spread of that infection is significantly reduced and even unvaccinated people are at much less risk of catching the illness. Herd immunity in measles (and mumps) has recently been compromised because of the drop-off in the uptake of the MMR (see p.305).

How do they work?

When a person catches an infection, the body produces chemicals called **antibodies**, which make us immune from that particular virus, ie it's unlikely we'll ever catch it again. A vaccination is a controlled way of stimulating this immunity by introducing an altered or "killed" non-infectious version of the disease into the body, which will cause the production of antibodies, without the actual illness.

Are they safe?

In certain circles there has been a lot of muttering about the safety of vaccinations – especially since the MMR controversy. This, in turn has focused attention on the other jabs, including the new "five in one" jab that

THE NEW JAB

As this book was going to press, the government released plans to introduce a vaccination against pneumococcal meningitis, to be given to the baby at some point during the first year. The injection, which is said to give 80 percent protection, could save 30–50 lives a year and stop 200 children becoming disabled from this particularly lethal form of the disease. To allay fears of 'vaccination overload', the government is planning to reduce the number of jabs routinely given against menigitis C, or 'Hib', though no specifics about this have yet been released.

your baby has at eight, twelve and sixteen weeks of age, against **diptheria**, **tetanus**, **whooping cough**, **polio**, **Hib** (an infection that can lead to meningitis), and **meningitis C** (given separately).

Some critics have argued that this vaccine can overload a baby's immune system, but health officials reply that it is in fact safer than the old "four in one" jab – it doesn't contain mercury, which one (largely disproved) American study linked to **autism**, and it doesn't have "live" polio of the old immunization which carried a tiny risk of the mother (or whoever changed the nappy) catching the disease.

The overwhelming argument is that it's the safe, responsible decision to take your baby to his early immunizations to stop the resurgence of these previously fatal diseases. While diptheria and polio are largely eradicated, there are still isolated cases of whooping cough in babies under six months old (and one in five hundred babies die). For this reason, it's important that herd immunity is maintained through high vaccination coverage.

On the day of the jabs, or possibly a couple of days after that, your baby might suffer mild side effects – usually some swelling or redness at the place it was given, or a slightly raised fever. Your GP might suggest a dose of Calpol. Always see your doctor if your baby's reaction seems severe.

Baby timeline

 At birth: BCG in areas with a high risk of tuberculosis.

 Eight weeks: The "five in one" jab, usually in the thigh – for diptheria, tetanus, whooping cough, polio, Hib. Meningitis C is also given as a separate jab.

 Twelve weeks: The "five in one" jab, and meningitis C.

 Sixteen weeks: The "five in one" jab, and meningitis C.

Twelve to eighteen months: MMR jab.

 Three to five years: Pre-school booster: diptheria, tetanus, pertussis, polio and MMR, but not Hib.

The MMR debate

The dilemma:

When your baby is around twelve–eighteen months old, a slip will come through your letter box informing you that it's time for your baby's MMR (mumps, measles and rubella) jab. Of all the issues you have to face and the choices you have to make in early parenting, for some, this is one of the most perplexing. The main reasons for this are the acres of newsprint that have been published in recent years about the MMR controversy – chiefly because of a purported link between the vaccine and autism, a disorder characterized by problems with communication, showing emotion and excessive attachment to ritual.

The background

In 1998, Andrew Wakefield, a doctor at London's Royal Free Hospital, published a paper in the esteemed medical journal *The Lancet*, suggesting that there might be a connection between the MMR, an inflammatory bowel disease, and autism. His study focused on tests carried out on twelve children who had been referred to the Royal Free for gastrointestinal problems (they also had autism). Wakefield suggested that further research was needed but, in the meantime, rather than have the "triple jab" as offered at GP surgeries, parents should opt for single jabs against mumps, measles and rubella instead.

The press coverage following his comments was huge, sparking off a large, and understandable panic amongst new parents. By autumn 2004, the national uptake for MMR had fallen to 80 percent (even lower in London) as parents either decided to give their children single jabs, which were pretty much available only privately, or decided not to immunize their children at all. The latter choice has lead to an alarming increase in cases of measles – a disease which, in rare cases, can be fatal (measles caused one hundred deaths a year until vaccination brought it under control in the 1960s). And even the single jabs were not an ideal option – often expensive, hard to find and, in certain cases, unlicensed and ineffectual.

Then, in late 2004 and early 2005, a series of findings seemed to discredit Wakefield's research. In November 2004, the editor of *The Lancet* told a journalist that they regretted printing the article. He claimed that Wakefield had a conflict of interest – that while working on the original study, he was also being paid to find out if parents who claimed their children were damaged by the MMR vaccine had a case. Some children were involved in both studies. More pertinently, perhaps, the UK's medical research council published a study of 5500 children finding no link between the MMR and autism. This was followed in March 2005 by a large Japanese study of 30,000 children which claimed that replacement of the MMR with single jabs made no difference to the number of children diagnosed with autistic spectrum disorders.

So what should you do?

The prevalent view seems to be that the benefits and protection of MMR outweigh any tiny theoretical risk that hasn't even been established. On the other hand, you can read statistics, research, newspaper columnists and the views of academics until your head spins, but if you are concerned that there is the teeniest, tiniest risk of an injection harming your perfect baby, of course you are going to think twice. That said nearly all medical advisors strongly recommend having the MMR. However that has not deterred some parents from attempting to go the route of using single jabs for each disease something the same experts strongly advise against and government health policy has done all it can to discourage. Anyone considering single vaccines should take great steps to ensure that it is a reputable clinic administering them and that the full course is completed. Doctors for instance have advised that there has been a recent minor epidemic of mumps, which might have been helped by the fact that MMR uptake rates have fallen (though now appear to be rising again) and some parents often get measles vaccines, but not mumps and rubella.

Most people agree on one thing, however, – a parent really does have a duty to their child, and other children they know, to immunise their child.

Further resources:

Books

Development

What to Expect – The First Year by Heidi Murkoff, Arlene Eisenberg & Sandee Hathaway (Simon & Schuster, £12.99). Reviewed on p.39, but worth mentioning here for its development section at the start of each chapter, explaining what your baby "should be able to do", "will probably be able to do", "may possibly be able to do" and "may even be able to do".

Websites

www.babycentre.co.uk. Detailed week-by-week updates on your baby's development. Subscribers get a regular bulletin sent to them by email.

Health

Books

Baby First Aid by Dr Miriam Stoppard (Dorling Kindersley, £5.99). An excellent reference book to have in the house: small enough to go in a first-aid box, but full of practical, easy-to-follow advice on how to cope with an emergency, and remain calm.

Birth and Beyond: The Definitive Guide to Your Pregnancy, Your Birth, Your Family – From Minus 9 to Plus 9 Months by Yehudi Gordon (Vermilion, £20). Reviewed on p.39, but mentioned again here for its excellent health reference section.

The Great Ormond Street Guide to Baby and Child Health by Jane Collins (Dorling Kindersley, £20). Comprehensive guide to your baby's health from birth to age eleven, which covers preventative, orthodox and complementary medicine.

Websites

www.webmd.com American website with news, experts and articles on health for the whole family. On the downside, it's packed with American pharmaceutical adverts.

Immunization

Books

MMR and Autism by Michael Fitzpatrick (Routledge, £15.99). Michael Fitzpatrick is a GP with an autistic child who believes the anti-MMR campaign was misguided. His book is feted by doctors and parents alike as one of the few balanced accounts of this contentious issue.

Websites

www.immunisation.nhs.uk. The government-run website has comprehensive sections on each jab, plus articles and FAQs on the illnesses being immunized against.

www.mmrthefacts.nhs.uk. A reassuring overview of the MMR jab (although bear in mind it's published by the government trying to get anxious parents back to the doctors' surgeries).

www.wddty.co.uk. "What Doctors Don't Tell You" is a website run by people cynical about the medical establishment. They have published several articles and a book about the MMR vaccine.

Meningitis

Websites

www.meningitis.org. Meningitis Research Foundation. Charity at the forefront of fighting death and disability caused by meningitis and septicaemia. The website is packed with useful information and support for sufferers and their families. Tel: 0800 880 3344 (24-hour free helpline).

10

Baby budgeting and buying

10

Baby budgeting and buying

There's no getting away from it: having a baby punches a big hole in your bank balance. Before you've even started shopping, there are the several months you're likely to have off work on maternity leave – unless you're lucky enough to work for a company willing to pay a full wage for the entire time. Then there's the whole range of gear you need to buy for a newborn – cot, buggy, car seat, etc... Finally, for those women going back to work, there's the astronomical cost of childcare, which can leave you with just enough for your bus fare and a couple of pairs of tights (and for those women who aren't going back, the loss of a wage). A recent survey in a parenting magazine* has estimated that it costs over fifty thousand pounds to raise a child up to the age of five.

With clever planning, however, it is possible to minimize the amount you spend, despite the attractions of the latest three-wheeled buggy sported by the latest celebrity mother. As you'll see in this chapter, a baby doesn't actually need all that much (until she reaches two and starts demanding Barbie tricycles) and doesn't use what she does need for that long. A lot of stuff can be bought second-hand or begged from relatives. And for low-income families who do find themselves struggling financially, there is help out there in the form of benefits and government initiatives.

With the general pennilessness that accompanies a new arrival, it's probably just as well you're no longer able to go out to eat or take flash holidays and are too miserable about your weight to buy the new season's wardrobe. How the hell would you afford any of it?

Pregnancy and Birth magazine

Baby budgeting

Seven ways to save the pounds

• Buy second-hand

In most areas, the **National Childbirth Trust** holds "Nearly New" sales where you can pick up amazing bargains – parents are often getting rid of hardly used gear or unwanted presents. Less reliable, but still useful if you're cautious, is an on-line auction house like ebay. Then there are jumble sales and car-boot sales, but make sure you inspect the items carefully and ask the right questions about their history (whether they've been damaged, how old they are). Second-hand sales are often a good place to pick up items like buggies and toys.

www.nctpregnancyandbabycare.com For details of Nearly New sales near you
www.ebay.co.uk
NB: Does anything *have* **to be brand new?** Yes – your car seat (unless you are absolutely sure it's 100 percent safe and fits the model of your car), and a cot or moses basket mattress. Research shows that second-hand mattresses can raise the risk of SIDS (Sudden Infant Death Syndrome, or cot death).

• Think ahead

Babies grow quickly, and in the blink of an eye, they're through many of the newborn must-haves. For example, most new parents find themselves buying both a cot *and* a moses basket and/or carrycot. Moses baskets are only suitable for tiny babies up to about three months, so you may want to skip this stage altogether, and invest in a cot from the very beginning. As long as your newborn is happy with this arrangement (and some do feel quite exposed in a big, open cot) there's no reason why you can't start off here, or keep your baby in bed with you for the first few months (see p.172 on co-sleeping).

• Have a "baby list"

If you're married, chances are you had a wedding list, so why not take it a stage further? No one will be offended: people rush to heap gifts on new parents, and it will save your guests the embarrassment of turning up with the fifth squashy little book about farmyard animals. Tiny babies don't need toys: ask your family and friends to buy clothes for different ages (eg newborn, 0–3 months, 3–6 months). Keep it simple for the newborn stage – basic white vests and babygros will suffice. A newborn grows so quickly that he may well wear a designer outfit only once (and probably puke all over it). Don't be shy about taking anything back and exchanging it.

• Don't be seduced by brands

The thought of a Gucci-coo baby may fill you with pride, but the fact is that designer gear is an

Baby expenses to age five*

Pre-birth food and books: £1217

Maternity clothes: £980

Antenatal classes: £320

Nursery furniture and cot: £899

Pushchair and baby sling: £617

The birth: £170

Formula milk: £1733

Solid food: £2935

High chair and feeding kit: £470

Nappies: £1126

Baby toiletries: £755

Clothes: £2450

Childcare: £30,150

Toys and presents: £2650

Parties and presents for friends: £1500

Childproofing home: £205

Suncare: £108

Playgroup: £570

Will, life cover, savings: £3750

Five year total: £52,605

Source: Mother and Baby magazine survey

enormous extravagance for babies – even Baby Gap is surprisingly expensive. As explained above, babies grow out of their clothes really quickly, and there isn't really a huge amount of difference between a £500 Bugaboo Frog pushchair and a £70 Graco buggy, except you'll need a bigger boot to carry it in. Cheaper buggies, cots and car seats have to pass the same safety regulations as more expensive brands, so are just as good. And, for smaller purchases like clothes, the supermarket brands are really coming into their own, with shops like Tesco and Asda selling fabulous and reasonably priced items.

• Choose reusable nappies

While a debate is currently raging over whether reusables are actually more environmentally friendly than disposables, there's no question that they are cheaper, saving you up to £500 a year.

• Breastfeed

Yes, often easier said than done (see Chapter 4) but if you do find yourself with the choice, think of all the cash you will save on bottles, sterilizers and formula – about a thousand pounds a year, once you've added it all up.

• Cook your own

It's oh-so tempting to crack open a jar of babyfood, but oh-so much more expensive. Cooking up huge batches of pureed meals, then freezing them, can help keep your bank balance in the black.

Baby benefits

For all new parents

• Maternity pay (and paternity pay)

See p.46 new fathers.

• Child benefit

This is a tax-free benefit paid to parents of children up to sixteen (or up to nineteen if they're studying for A-levels in full-time education). Parents get child benefit for each child they are responsible for, and as this book went to press, it was £17 a week. You'll get a form when you register your baby, which you then send off with his birth certificate and your national insurance number. Child benefit can be backdated for three months.
www.direct.gov.uk

THE CHILD TRUST FUND (OR "BABY BOND")

All babies born after 1 September 2002, whose parents are claiming child benefit, now get a payment of £250 from the government (those earning less than around £14,000 a year will get a further £250). This comes automatically in the form of a voucher, which needs to be put into a special account run by a bank, building society or other financial provider. There are three different types of account – deposit, stakeholder or non-stakeholder – run by lots of different providers, and you'll need to choose (as if you don't have enough to think about at the moment). The website below clearly explains types of fund, and gives a list of providers.

You (or a grandparent, or godparent) can also contribute up to £1200 a year, the start date for each year being your baby's birthday. Your child will be not be able to access the account until they reach eighteen.

www.childtrustfund.gov.uk Tel: 0845 302 1470

• Free prescriptions and dental charges

These apply to both you and your baby for the first twelve months after birth: your child will have free exemption from prescription charges until the age of sixteen.

Means-tested benefits

• Tax credits

Couples with a gross income of around £50,000 can still get tax credit, a payment which applies to parents whether they are in or out of work. There is a complicated sliding scale depending on your earnings, which will be worked out for you when you fill in the form.

To apply call 0845 300 3900 (England, Wales, Scotland) and 0800 6032000 (N Ireland)

www.inlandrevenue.gov/taxcredits. Working tax credit is also available for parents on a low income, and can include help with childcare.

For further information try:

www.directgov.uk/parents
www.dwp.gov.uk

www.jobcentreplus.gov.uk

www.surestart.gov.uk. "Sure start" maternity grants of around £500 are available for parents on Income Support or Jobseeker's Allowance.

Maternity alliance
Information line Tel: 0207 490 7638

www.babygoes2.com
Tel: 01273 230 669
www.maternityalliance.org.uk
www.takethefamily.com
www.travellingwithchildren.co.uk
Tel: 01684 594831

Work that money

Five ways to make the most of what you have
To get through the pennypinching first few years (and beyond, if you're considering private education), you may have to take a fresh look at your financial affairs. Here are some suggestions:

• Make a budget
When you have a baby, your in- and outgoings are subject to enormous change. It's a good idea to sit down with a pen and paper to factor in what the baby is going to cost you on a monthly basis (for nappies, formula etc …), but balance this with what you are saving on expenses (train fare to work etc …). Then you can work out your monthly requirements – if nothing else, this exercise will make you more aware of your spending, and show how you might need to shop around for bargains.

• Returning to work: cover all bases
It might be too early to make a decision about when you're going to return to work (or whether you are going to, at all). How you feel now may be very different from six, or nine months down the road. However, it's worth thinking now about how you'll manage financially in a variety of different scenarios (eg if you go back, if you don't, if you go back part-time) – then, when you come to make the final decision, you'll have hard facts at your fingertips.

• Maximize the Child Trust Fund
All babies now get a £250 "baby bond" from the government (see above). As explained, there is provision for parents (or other friends of the baby) to

save a maximum of £1200 a year (2005 figures) in the baby's name. It's worth taking advantage of this: though you may not be able to imagine your useless newborn packing himself off to university with a big old rucksack, he'll have a nice little nest-egg to take with him if you have the imagination to plan ahead. So, if well-meaning grand- or godparents ask if you need anything, point them in the direction of the baby bond.

• Manage your accounts

Say you are taking a year off work: you may need to dig into your savings. It's worth looking into this before you withdraw money: some savings plans (eg ISAs) are more tax-efficient than others. Moreover, if you are now in a lower-tax bracket because you are earning less, and your partner remains a higher-rate tax payer, it's worth considering moving money from any joint account into your own, so the interest would be taxed at your lower rate.

• Consider taking a mortgage or pension "holiday"

Many companies offer breaks of several months (or "holidays") from regular financial commitments. You'll have to make them up in the long-run, but this is an unusual and unique time in your life: why not relieve the pressures you're already facing?

Thanks to financial adviser, Anna Sofat

Baby buying

What you do and don't need

To run the risk of repetition from the first chapter of this book, here is a list of the items you'll definitely need for your baby at the kick-off:

- A car seat
- Some way to carry your baby about – whether a buggy or a sling
- A moses basket or carrycot *and/or* a cot
- Something simple for your baby to wear, and a hat
- Bottles, formula and sterilizing equipment, if bottlefeeding
- A supply of nappies (disposable or reusable, see p.74)

315

- Older babies (six months+) will need a high chair

If you really set your mind to it, there are endless amounts of kit you can buy for a newborn but here's a guide to the staples:

Car seat

The first, and probably the most important purchase you will make. Even if you don't have a car, you may need to take a taxi at some point, and it's illegal for a baby to travel in a car without the proper protection.

There are two types of newborn car seats: (note these fit into your car so the baby faces *backwards*.)

- The infant carrier (from birth to about 10kg–around 9 months, and the most common)
  (Labelled by manufacturers as "group 0" or 0+)

These are characterized by a handle, and can often be fixed into a "travel system" with a buggy or pram. Some click into a specially provided base in your car, and some are free-standing, attached through the seatbelt.

Pros: You can remove your baby from the car without waking them up, although it's not good to leave your newborn in a car seat for too long, because it doesn't offer proper support for her spine.

Cons: When your baby reaches nine months to a year (or 10kg) you'll need to buy a new, forward-facing car seat.

- The combination car seat (from birth to 13 kg–about 18 months, which can then be converted to last up to about the age of four)
  (Labelled by manufacturers as Group 0+, converting to Group 1)

A NOTE ON SAFETY

Always follow the manufacturers' instructions carefully when fitting and using the seat. It is crucial that your car seat is suitable for the model of your car, and fits properly: for example, some cars have shorter seatbelts than others. There should be no "give" or movement once you've fitted the seat, and the seatbelt buckle should not rest on the car seat frame. Rear-facing seats should *never* be used in the front seat if you have an airbag.

Your local authority will have a road safety department that will be able to answer any questions: See **www.childcarseats.org.uk** for details.

These tend to stay fixed in one car.

Pros: The same car seat can be used for much longer.

Cons: You can't take the baby out of the car in the seat, and it can't be transferred easily to another car or taxi.

Buggies and prams

The sheer choice that faces you when buying a vehicle for your baby is enough to make you collapse to the floor, weep and regret getting pregnant in the first place. Before you venture to the buggy showroom, it's wise to start acquainting yourself with what's on offer, so you can discount certain options before you get there. Things to think about include:

● The number of babies you are having.

● The size of your boot, if you use a car (the buggy will have limitations if it doesn't fit inside).

● Whether you live on the ground floor (or have steps to contend with).

● Whether you live in the country, and will be walking on uneven paths or fields, or whether you'll be using a lot of public transport.

● How important it is to look cool and use the latest model.

• Forward-facing buggies (pushchairs)

The most common purchase. There are two types:

● Flat-folding buggies

These are all suitable for newborns, with seats that lie flat to support the baby's spine correctly. Depending on how expensive the model, they come with extras including shopping basket, rain cover and adjustable seat.

Pros: Sturdy, yet comfortable.

Cons: Your baby lies facing away from you (compared with a pram) and you'll probably trade in for a lighter, umbrella model in six months or so.

● Umbrella buggies

Most are more suitable for older babies (of around six months old) than newborns because the seats don't tend to recline flat. However, some of the newer models do offer this feature – ask in the shop.

Pros: Lightweight, easier to collapse and cheaper than flat-folding buggies.

Cons: Even if the seat does recline, the buggy is not as substantial: you may feel your baby is less well protected than in a flat-folding type.

• Travel systems

The "hip" alternative, these have provision for a car seat or carrycot to "click" into the chassis.

Pros: Your baby lies facing you, and can be moved even when sleeping from buggy to car.

Cons: They're expensive and bulky. And though the car seat attachment sounds attractive, it can be tricky to use.

• Old-fashioned prams

The "Mary Poppins" model which our parents used is enjoying something of a revival.

Pros: Your baby faces you and has plenty of room to stretch out in the Rolls Royce of baby transport.

Cons: The most expensive option: not good for travel by car or public transport, only useful for the first few months.

• Three-wheelers

The equivalent of a four-wheel-drive car – a sturdy, don't-mess-with-me attitude.

Pros: Genuinely good for families who live in the country, near a beach or who go jogging (it's easy to steer with one hand).

Cons: Heavy and bulky, although newer models do collapse down to fit into the boot. Pricey. Are the streets of Notting Hill *really* that bumpy?

• Double buggies

If you have twins, or find yourself pregnant again before your first child is walking confidently and not yet ready for a "buggy board" (a sort of platform that a toddler stands on, attached to the back of the pushchair), you'll need one of these. There are two varieties:

● Side-by-side buggies

Pros: The most common, and therefore with the most consumer-friendly choice. Some of the newer models are surprisingly light and manoeuvrable.
Cons: Hard to get through narrow spaces – you may need to plan high-street shopping trips according to the width of the doorways. The seats are also quite thin.

● Tandem buggies (one baby in front of the other)

Pros: Easier to get through doors, with wider seats for older babies.
Cons: Bulkier, heavier and harder to steer and collapse than side-by-side models.

• Slings

• Front-carriers

Strictly speaking, a "sling" is a swathe of material that is knotted over one shoulder and acts like a hammock, but most parents use the term to describe baby front-carriers, where the baby hangs in front of you in a harness. You'll see many a proud dad marching down the high street with his achingly cute newborn's feet sticking out of the holes. Newborns start "face in", but as your baby grows, he can be turned around to take in his surroundings.
Pros: Gives a baby more warmth and security than a buggy, especially in the early days. Leaves your hands free to carry things. Marching around with a baby may help you lose weight (or not). If you have an older child and don't want a double buggy, you can carry your newborn in a sling for the first few months. Slings are also a guaranteed way to send a fretful baby to sleep.
Cons: Can be fiddly to put your baby in until you get used to it – you might need an extra pair of hands. May also give you backache after long walks.

● Slings

The hippy alternative, as described above.
Pros: Baby lies in a "sleeping" position, and you can often breastfeed discreetly.
Cons: No real safety mechanism, the baby could fall out.

Moses baskets, carrycots, cradles and cots

As discussed above, you may decide to skip the "tiny baby" stage altogether and go straight to a cot. However, after the snugness of the uterus, some babies feel overwhelmed by the vast expanses of a cot (some also feel overwhelmed by the comparatively vast expanses of a moses basket!) and prefer starting life in a smaller bed.

• Moses basket

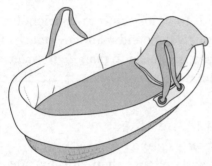

Moses basket

Generally made of wicker or cheaper palm, moses baskets are a picturesque way to present your baby to visitors in pride of place in the front room. They normally come with a fabric-covered hood, and a wooden stand.

Pros: Baskets are very portable – because of the handles, you can take your baby into another room, or even to other people's houses (but she will have to travel in a car seat). Also useful to "rock" your baby with gentle swinging if she's upset.

Cons: Only generally big enough for babies of about three months old (or younger, for bigger babies).

• Carrycot

Carrycots fit into pram and pushchair bases, but can also be used for night-time sleeping.

Pros: Similar to the moses basket, and handy if part of a "travel system".

Cons: Possibly time-consuming to fit on and off the travel system or pram base. And again, only useful for three months or so.

NB: Some carrycots are designed to be used in the car, but most experts agree that, while they comply with current safety standards, they do not offer the same level of protection as a rear-facing infant car seat.

• Cradle or crib

It's sometimes hard to resist a picture-book baby in a cradle, especially if you have the offer of a nostalgic or antique hand-me-down.

Pros: Bigger than a moses basket or carrycot, with a built-in rocking motion for fretful newborns. Some find this upsetting, however.

Cons: Not portable, and more expensive than the other options if bought new.

> **BEDTIME SAFETY**
>
> No harm in reiterating this: never buy or borrow a second-hand mattress for your baby, because of the increased risk of SIDS, and make sure it fits well (the gaps between the mattress and the sides and ends of the cot should be less than 4cm). A second-hand cot should always be stripped and repainted, because of the risk of paint which contains lead – this can be poisonous.

• Cots

Whatever you decide, at some point in the first three months or so, your baby will need to move to a cot, which will be her bed until she's about two and a half (or earlier, if she's a proficient climber). The best cots have drop-sides (easier to put a baby down to sleep) and adjustable bases (which you can lower as she learns to sit up and stand).

Pros: A good sleeping arrangement for a baby over three months – you can also save money on a second-hand cot, as long as it's in good condition.

Cons: Babies grow out of them. To save shelling out on a bed when your baby hits two or three, you might want to consider a cotbed (see below).

• Cotbeds

Similar to cots, but bigger and wider.

Pros: Will last for several years, as they'll accommodate your older toddler.

Cons: Most don't have drop-down sides.

High chairs

When your baby is on solids, and starts sitting up, it's time for them to join you for mealtimes. Unlike the other big buys, the high chair will be in the kitchen, in your face, and you may want to consider the aesthetics as well as the practicalities of your choice. On the other hand, you may well admit that your battle against the relentless march of gaudy plastic monstrosities into your home is lost at this point.

Here's a rundown of the main types:

• Free-standing high chair with tray

The traditional version – baby sits in his own "space" apart from the table.

High chair with tray

Pros: Adjustable and portable, giving your baby room to experiment with eating – tray can also be used for playing with (and eating) playdoh etc ...
Cons: Often not as stylish as "without tray" varieties (see below).

• High chair without a tray

Growing in popularity – often seen in fashionable restaurants.
Pros: Your baby sits at the table and feels more part of the proceedings. These chairs are usually made of wood (often with a choice of finishes), blend better into a "grown-up" kitchen, and can adapt as your baby gets bigger.
Cons: Lack of a tray means more mess on the floor.

Ask the old hands – parents tell us their best (and worst) buys

The three best things I bought ...

- A "Medala" electric breast pump – the manual one was really fiddly, and I kept losing a vital part down the waste-disposal unit.
- A "Baby Mozart" DVD which has children's toys and puppets dancing to classical music – Alice watched it most days, and I didn't feel guilty because it was "educational".
- The Mamas and Pappas "Aria" double buggy for when my son came along and Alice wasn't walking well – really light and easy to open and shut.

Caroline, 36

- The "Bébé Confort" pram I bought on ebay – I could see Cecily as I pushed her, and really loved it.
- A baby gym – the perfect place to put a baby while you have a cup of tea and read a magazine.
- A set-top box: *Cbeebies* is telly you can trust!

Leah, 42

- A "Grobag" for bedtime – I could just zip Luca up, and he couldn't kick the covers off.
- A "Shade-a-bub" sunshade which ties onto the buggy – no messing around with fiddly parasols.
- A box of wooden blocks from the Early Learning Centre – perfect for chewing on, banging together and knocking over Mummy's towers.

Rebecca, 31

- The "Tripp-trapp" high chair – because it doesn't have a tray, Ben could sit at the table with us, and it was relatively stylish.
- A towelling "bath-support" – he could safely recline so I didn't have to crane over the bath when holding him.
- A door-hanging "Tippytoes" baby bouncer, so he could practise "dancing" and "standing" safely.

Sarah, 32

... and the three worst

- A baby bath – completely pointless: you can use the washbasin at first, then move up to the big bath.
- A baby breathing monitor – it just made us paranoid and keep on checking.
- Fancy newborn clothes – most of them lay unused in their boxes.

Caroline

- The pushchair I ordered on-line – it turned out to be ideal if you are 5ft 1, but I'm 5ft 8. Try before you buy!
- A white-noise tape. Completely pointless as it didn't make Henry sleep and you had to play it really loudly, which was annoying.
- A sterilizer – our dishwasher is really hot, which gets the bottles just as clean.

Leah

- A manual breast pump: painful, undignified and useless.
- A "kit bag" with lots of pockets and zips. It cost £50, and irritates me every time I look at it.
- An underarm thermometer. A total false economy. It was cheaper than the digital ear thermometers, but useless – I ended up getting different readings every time. I have now bought the digital and it is brilliant.

Rebecca

- An umbrella buggy that didn't lie completely flat – I soon swapped it for a flat-folding one that lasted most of the first year.
- A sling without a strap around the waist – it made my back and shoulders ache.
- A children's wardrobe: it seemed a good idea at the time, but would have been cheaper and more stylish to have just got a grown-up one.

Sarah

Baby budgeting

• Clip-on seats

As they sound – non-free standing chairs that attach to the table.

Pros: Allows the child to feel part of things, and are easily stored away. Also cheaper.

Cons: Can be uncomfortable.

For information on breastfeeding and bottlefeeding buying, see p.134-137.
For information on nappies, see p.72.

Shops and websites

If you are buying the big items from new, it's probably wise to use the big retailers, such as Mothercare and John Lewis, or a trusted local babycare shop. The advantage of these, as opposed to buying on-line, is access to a "nursery adviser" and also the chance to try things out – collapsing a buggy, seeing if a car seat is right for your car. That said, Internet shopping is fantastic for the smaller items (feeding gear, clothes, toys) as you're no doubt discovering that going to the shops with a newborn requires as much planning and preparation as an Arctic expedition. www.babycentre.co.uk

Some shopping resources:

www.bloomingmarvellous.co.uk
For clothes, toys and other items. Tel: 08707 518 944

www.bumpto3.com
For grobags and other items. Tel: 0870 6060 276

www.greenbaby.co.uk
For environmentally friendly gear. Tel: 08702 406 894
www.johnlewis.co.uk Tel: 08456 049049

www.kiddicare.co.uk
Everything from buggies to toys. Tel: 0906 170 2999
www.mothercare.co.uk Tel: 08453 304 030
www.mumsnet.com

www.verbaudet.co.uk
Stylish and surprisingly reasonable baby gear.

Travelling with a baby

The thought of taking your baby further than the end of the road, let alone to some far-flung foreign location, may understandably fill you with horror. But, in many ways, the months before your baby starts running around are the very best to take off. New babies usually travel for free (you usually have to start paying a substantial fare after the age of two) and, depending on the airline and the length of flight, you might be able to get a "skycot", or at least a bulkhead seat.

Just make sure you've thought of everything in advance – eg whether cots and car seats are provided, if there's a shop nearby to buy nappies (it'll fill your whole luggage if you take your own). It's worth asking your doctor about the health implications of visiting exotic countries.

I couldn't sunbathe, but we took her to restaurants in her car seat

"When Esther was three months old, we took her to Cyprus. It all started off smoothly – our 'bucket shop' airline let us get on the plane first because we had a young baby, although we had to check the buggy in at the desk, which was annoying. Esther screamed on take-off, because her ears were popping, but once we gave her a bottle, the sucking motion made her feel better, although she did have her moments of crying intermittently. I felt very tense, however, and kept looking nervously at the twenty-something child-free couples, and their 'can't you control your baby?' scowls. Once we arrived, all was fine. We'd double- and triple-checked that the car company would provide an infant car seat, and they did, and the hotel gave us a travel-cot – but I have heard of friends who were promised both and left stranded. I suppose I was a little restricted in what I did – for example, endless hours of sunbathing were out, for obvious reasons, but we ate out *en famille* every lunchtime and some evenings, taking Esther in her car seat. Some nights we had dinner in the hotel – our baby monitor worked in the restaurant – so we could hear her if she woke up. On the flight home, she conked out completely, which was something of a relief."

Sue, 40

Further resources

Books

How Can I Ever Afford Children?: Money Skills for New and Experienced Parents by B. Hetzer (Wiley Personal Finance Solutions, £8.95). This is an American book (so it's all about paying for college and medical insurance etc ...) but there are still some general principles about budgeting that hold true for an international readership.

Travelling Abroad With Children by Samantha Gore-Lyons (Arrow, £7.99). This book helps a new family choose a holiday destination, with tips on the right time to take your baby away, where you should go and the best ways of getting there.

Your Child's Health Abroad by Matthew Ellis and Jane Wilson Howarth (Bradt Travel Guides, £8.95). Tips, advice and check lists – especially useful if you're going to a far-flung destination.

Websites

General

www.maternityalliance.org.uk. Comprehensive website telling women all they need to know about their rights and benefits during pregnancy and beyond. Information line Tel: 0207 490 7638

Travel

www.babygoes2.com. Great website with location reports, ideas for last-minute travel, and ideas for single parents. Tel: 01273 230 669

www.travellingwithchildren.co.uk. Full of information – eg packing guides and health and safety tips. Holiday destinations are also helpfully broken down into newborns, 6–12 months, 1–3-year-olds, etc ... Tel: 01684 594 831

11

Looking ahead

11
Looking ahead

The future is bright – brightly coloured plastic with flashing lights and electronic noises, as Mr Fisher and Mr Price set up permanent residence in your front room. As your baby blows out his first birthday candle (or, rather, watches incomprehensibly while you blow it out for him) it takes quite a feat of time-travel to return to that maternity suite, where you were sitting in bewilderment twelve months earlier. Who'd have thought that in this time, you'd have learned a whole new language (perineum, "let-down", Calpol), made yourself into a temporary dairy cow, perhaps even struggled back into last year's jeans? Most importantly, could you really have dreamt up this small person standing up against the table, clapping their fat hands together, who lights up like a firefly whenever you enter the room?

Many parents agree that the first year – or at least the first half of it – is the most gruelling in terms of sheer physical exhaustion. However, by now you probably have an inkling that new and glorious challenges await as your baby learns that he has needs, wants and impulses which sadly don't always mirror your own. No different from this time last year, you may think. But this time last year your child didn't have the skill to put his desires into action, by reaching, standing or trying to rush headlong into the road when you're unloading the shopping from the car. Or to throw a fully-fledged wobbly when thwarted.

Then there are the strange tricks that nature plays on us. As in "labour pains? I don't know what all the fuss was about". And, "three months without sleep? Oh, it wasn't that bad". These feats of forgetfulness, coupled with a visceral sense of longing when you smell the soapy head of a friend's newborn, often conspire to start couples thinking about having a second baby. Personal note from the author: it can happen more quickly than you think. Before you throw caution to the wind, there is no such thing as a "safe" time of the month;

moreover, the fact that you are taking a risk on your daughter's first birthday counts for nothing in the Russian Roulette of "natural family planning".

Whether you're making a brother or sister for your baby or not, this is the bit where parenting starts to get very … interesting. Bring on the stairgates, move the plant-pots and watch with joy as your polite little baby turns into a toddler: riotous, infuriating, rabble-rousing and wonderful.

Tantrums and tiaras: to toddlerhood and beyond

"Toddlerhood" is a rather vague definition, covering the ages of approximately one to four, although it's true that some babies don't even walk until around eighteen months and that some are still toddling about uncertainly at four. Still, when people refer to toddlers, there's a lot of chat about the "terrible twos", and rather less about the "wicked ones". World-renowned paediatrician and writer **Dr Christopher Green** puts it perfectly. "At this age," he writes in his book, *New Toddler Taming*, "little ones discover that they have the muscle to manipulate and challenge and are not backward about flexing it. This stage starts gradually after the first birthday with senseless and unthinking acts predominant up to the age of one and a half years, when more considered forms of manipulation take over." Your child's behaviour at this point can be embarrassing and verge on the sociopathic, as she refuses to share toys, is unwilling to play with other children – she may even prefer to bite them – and goes out of her way to put her life in danger by eating small stones and sticking her finger into plug sockets. This is normal. On the other hand, however, the "ones" are also rather marvellous as your baby's development accelerates apace: by eighteen months, she'll probably be able to feed herself (and her hair, her clothes and the kitchen floor), say simple words like "duck" and point to her nose, feet and tummy.

Four things you may need to think about

Discipline
At some point soon, all those "Supernanny" and "Tiny tearaways"-type programmes are going to become scarily relevant. But for now, it's too early

to think about the merits of "Naughty Steps" because your child simply won't understand what it's all about. With a young toddler, the best practice is to wildly, theatrically play up behaviour you approve of with whoops and cheers, and to firmly discourage things you don't want them to do with a disapproving tone of voice, moving them away from the scene. Many experts insist that merely saying "no" to an older baby is bad because it leads to negative behaviour in the child, and that you should explain the reasons for your decision. But in the real world, it's the automatic response to a toddler who's about to a) hurl himself down the stairs b) pick up a bee or c) pull the television set down on his head.

Tantrums

Some parents report that their child's temperament remains mild and sunny all through the second year, and it is true that for many older babies, this is a delightful time. The moment will come, however, when the switch will be flicked, and you'll witness your baby's first tantrum. Tantrums are a bit like labour contractions: you keep thinking – is this one? And then, when the first one really kicks off, there's absolutely no mistaking it. The sight of your

baby rigid on the floor, purple with rage, screaming, banging fists, feet and even her head is a typical scene. If it wasn't so alarming, it would be hilarious.

Tantrums are caused by a number of issues: hunger, tiredness or a desperate need for the baby to exert some control over her pretty powerless situation. Mainly, though, tantrums are caused by frustration, the inability to be understood, or to do something (whether a "good" thing, like put on their socks, or a "naughty" one, like chew through your iPod wire). In the same way bonfires thrive on twigs, tantrums thrive on attention – toddlers generally don't bother if there's no one to watch the display. Best advice is to ignore tantrums as much as possible, which isn't always practical if you're in the egg aisle of the supermarket. So, stay calm, speak softly and leave the room (as long as the child is safe and not able to harm herself. If she is trying to hurt herself, hold her in a firm cuddle until she calms down.) Some child psychologists suggest taking your child to a "time-out" zone in a bedroom until she calms down in her own time. When the storm has passed, which it invariably does, most experts agree it's vital not to bear a grudge and to "welcome your baby back" with a kiss and a cuddle, though not behaviour which rewards the tantrum, ie giving them the biscuit that the screaming fit was over in the first place.

Fights over food

The probability is that up to now, your ravenous baby would eat everything presented to him. However, from this period on, it's also normal for your little one to become less amenable at mealtimes. One reason for this is a desire to be independent – to learn that they can say "no". It's a way of displaying power (and all toddlers learn to shake their heads and say "no" before they say "yes").

This coincides with a slowing of growth, and thus a need for fewer calories than before – in the first year, your baby will have probably tripled his birth weight, gaining nearly as much as in the next four years put together. Do your best to ensure your toddler has a balanced diet, but don't make a big deal over it – if he gets the equivalent of 700ml (a pint and a quarter) of full-fat milk a day, that should cover most of the nutrition "holes". Also bear in mind that toddlers who are ill or teething sometimes go off their food temporarily.

Bedtime struggles

When they reach toddlerhood, many babies rebel against going to bed, because it's *boring*. If you've had a bedtime routine since the early days, it's important to keep this up. It might also be worth looking at your child's daytime sleeps: babies of a year to eighteen months old only need about an hour and a half of sleep during the day, so you may want to drop a nap, or perhaps move bedtime a little bit later. Once you've decided it really is bedtime, you'll need to be tough, though. Tell the stories, give kisses, but when the curtain falls, it falls.

At the other end of the day, many children this age decide that 5.30am is time to get up – especially during the lighter mornings of the summer. Hints include: investing in black-out blinds, trying a slightly later bedtime and ditching the morning nap, if it's still in place. Sometimes you can "con" your toddler into falling asleep again after their milk, or put some toys in their cot to keep them busy and postpone the inevitable by a few minutes.

Should I allow my toddler to watch TV?

Open any newspaper, and the message seems clear: TV causes obesity; TV causes your toddler to become a playground bully; TV makes your child commit mass murder. And while it's generally accepted that plonking your baby in front of the box all day is patently a bad idea, a closer look at relevant research shows that used judiciously, a maximum of two hours of TV a day, can actually help a child's development (as well as allowing you ten minutes to have a shower). The Child Literacy Trust say that age-specific programming eg "CBeebies" and especially the repeated watching of appropriate videos, can foster familiarity with, and help with the learning of words.

The best way to use TV is to watch *with* your child, so you can talk about what you've seen, and to switch it off when the programme is over, rather than leaving it on in the background all day.

Two things you don't need to think about yet

Toilet training

In our parents' days, babies were toilet-trained rather sooner than they are now – at eighteen months, or even earlier. It's hard to imagine the misery for both parents and their children. These days, experts accept it's not worth putting your baby on the potty much before the age of two or two and a half; your child needs first to know what doing a poo or a wee feels like, to be able to tell you that he wants to go, and also have the necessary bladder or bowel control. The later you leave toilet-training, even into the third year, the easier and less painful the process will be for everyone.

Reading (or at least formal "education")

With the proliferation of super-nurseries, infant gym classes and music lessons for babies, it's not surprising that many parents feel under pressure to "hothouse" their children. Well, you may consider your toddler a genius, but most children's mental powers simply haven't developed enough to learn to read before the age of five or six. However, from the time your child was around six months old, he will have loved looking at simple primary-coloured books with lots of big pictures. Between the ages of one or two, children start to appreciate rhyming and books with lots of repetition – animals and animal noises are always a big hit. And the child who grows up in a house with lots of books, who is frequently read to, and sees his parents are reading, is bound to have a great start when it's time for formal education.

Thinking about "number two"

Some readers, flicking ahead from the early chapters, may choke on their tea when it comes to this section. *Another baby*? But we haven't even sussed out how the first one works yet. Apologies for the shock, but ... it's a pretty fair statement that most parents will at some point think about adding to their family, even if they ultimately decide not to, or find themselves unable to ("only child" families are on the increase: according to a recent Mintel report, seventeen percent of UK families stop at one baby).

Following on from this is the natural question: "when's the best time?" Most parents of two or more would agree that there is no "best time" as each has its own special rewards and challenges, although medics do agree that having babies close together or too far apart can have its drawbacks (see below).

When's the best time: medically?

- **Not before six months** – according to a University of California study of 300,000 women, which suggests that babies conceived this soon are more likely to have lower birth weights, possibly because mothers haven't had the chance to replenish all their nutrients and are still stressed from the first baby.

- **Not after ten years** – because there's a greater risk of premature birth.

- **Between 24 and 35 months** – was shown to be the ideal time for the baby's overall development.

How do I get my son used to the idea that he has a sister on the way?

For someone who's only ever been the centre of attention, your toddler may not meet the news of a rival with unequivocal glee. It's up to you when you tell your son that he has a sister coming: but experts suggest not too early in your pregnancy, as the concept of waiting is alien to small children, and not so late that he "guesses" from the size of your tummy or any new purchases, and thinks a secret is being kept from him. If there are any big changes to be made (eg moving your son to a bed so the baby can have his cot or starting him at nursery) do them some time before the birth so he doesn't feel he's being "punished" in any way. In the run up to the birth, get him used to spending more time with other family members (eg his father, grandparents) because the reality is you'll be preoccupied with the new baby for a while, especially if you need to spend time in hospital.

When the baby does arrive, ask guests to make just as big a fuss of your older child – the odd judicious present flying his way will also make the transition easier.

When's the best time: for your family dynamics (and mental health)?

Clearly, this a very personal decision. So much depends on your family's domestic situation – the state of your finances, the size of your house, what you've decided to do with your career, how demanding your firstborn might be. It's also worth bearing in mind that older mothers might find it harder to conceive, so "timing" is less of an exact science. But here's what some other parents found:

The gap: thirteen months

What was good about it?

- I was still in baby mode: nappies, sleepless nights, baby vomit etc …

- The practicalities: they wear the same nappies, read the same books, bath together, go to bed at the same time.

- It's a talking point – I can beat all those competitive mothers – even those with twins as they didn't have eighteen months of pregnancy and two labours!

And not so good?

- Being pregnant with a little one around was very hard. At the start of my pregnancy, I had morning sickness, and at the end, carrying him around gave me backache.

- Having two sets of equipment: cots, a double buggy, two high chairs.

Mel, 35

The gap: twenty months

What was good about it?

- A sense of "getting it out of the way" – I feel like I'm out of the woods while my friends are starting again.

- There was no jealously at all – at twenty months old, Alice was too young to feel she'd been supplanted.

- They're very good friends. I get such joy watching them howl with laughter at each other in the bath.

And not so good?

- The exhaustion. They were both such terrible sleepers that at times I thought I wouldn't be able to cope.

- Being pulled in two directions by two very needy little souls.

Caroline, 36

The gap: two years, nine months

What was good about it?

- Luke was just about out of nappies, so we didn't have both of them to change.

- He was also old enough to stand on a buggy board, so I didn't need a double buggy.

- He was actually excited about Max's arrival.

And not so good?

- As Max got older and started moving about, Luke became upset when he tried to take his toys.

- Luke was still young enough to need a sleep during the day, so there were a few tricky trips to the shops when I put the baby in the sling, and Luke in the baby's buggy even though he was too big for it.

Debbie, 42

The gap: three and a quarter years

What was good about it?

- Liam was old enough to understand what was going on, but not too old to be inflexible.

- He was in a good routine, which made it easier to fit a baby in.

- Free nursery places had kicked in by the time William was born, so I had some free care while on maternity leave.

And not so good?

- Liam was going through the boundary-pushing "terrible twos" and it was hard work.

- I'm worried they'll be too far apart to be playmates – but only time will tell, as William is only six months old.

Becky, 38

The gap: four and a half years

What was good about it?

- Plenty of time and undivided attention for the firstborn (a huge plus).

- A sense of being able to recover, both physically and emotionally, from my first pregnancy and the tiring baby days.

- Charlotte was excited about her sister's arrival, and was even able to help me a bit.

And not so good?

- I was out of "baby mode" so it felt a bit like starting again.

- It's hard finding activities to suit the different age groups and also difficult to police children in two different parts of the playground.

Debora, 28

Your second pregnancy

First time round, you were the star of the show. This time, you'll be regulated – quite literally – to a supporting role by your family and friends and a deeply unimpressed older baby. Pregnancy this time round is likely to be more tiring because of the lack of "me time", long lie-ins, and the physical toll of rushing around after and carrying an active toddler. You might also feel like time whizzes by far more quickly, because you're preoccupied with number one.

You may also get bigger much more quickly, because your abdominal muscles have already been stretched: you may find yourself back in those maternity jeans almost as soon as the blue line appeared on your pregnancy test. On the other hand, second-time-rounders generally find themselves more relaxed, less neurotic and not as likely to be "Googling" every tiny symptom for fear it betrays a sinister message.

This time around, there's more chance of:

- Piles, heartburn, anaemia, cramps.

- Backache and pelvic pain, from already loosened joints.

- Morning sickness (tiredness can make it worse).

- Miscarriage, or chromosomal problems such as Down's Syndrome (the rate rises for older mothers).

- Gestational diabetes, if you had it first time round.

But less chance of:

- High blood pressure and pre-eclampsia, unless you had them first time.

- Going overdue and hence being induced.

- New stretchmarks – you'll just add to the old ones.

Your second labour

No amount of reading or research is a substitute for "been there, pushed, screamed and got the T-shirt". In other words, as far as labour goes, knowledge is power, and the fact that you've already done it once is a huge bonus. And while there are refresher courses for second-time mothers, many women don't even think about their second labour (or spend a great deal of time trying not to think about it) until their waters have broken and they're realizing they haven't even packed the bag.

The good news is that second labours are usually easier and shorter – though by no means always. Your cervix tends to dilate with fewer contractions, and the pelvic ligaments and muscles open more easily, so the baby will be easier to push out. Because labour is more likely to start spontaneously, you're less likely to be induced, which in turn makes it less likely you'll have need an **epidural** (though go ahead, if you want one!), and intervention such as ventouse, forceps or episiotomy.

I had my daughter by Caesarean. Can I try and give birth "normally" this time around?

It depends on the reason. If you've had more than one Caesarean, or a less common type of incision on your uterus (such as a vertical one) most obstetricians would recommend a repeat Caesarean. In addition, if your section was because of an ongoing health problem, such as heart disease, or because your pelvis was too small to let the baby through, then it's also unlikely. However, if your surgery was because of a "one-off" eg your baby was in distress, was in the breech position, or you had placenta praevia, and these are not repeated, then there is no reason not to give birth naturally (experts call it a "trial of labour"). It's generally a safe procedure, although there is a small risk (less than one percent) of your scar rupturing with the effort. This is a potentially serious complication, so you'll probably need to be in hospital.

Having been through one Caesarean, you'll no doubt understand only too well the benefits of avoiding one this time, especially with an older child to look after. But if things don't go according to plan, and you end up with another section, it's vital not too feel guilty or disappointed – a healthy baby (and mother) is the ultimate goal.

If you've had a Caesarean first time round and there's no reason not to try for a vaginal birth (vaginal birth after Caesarean, or VBAC), most hospitals are very encouraging. Research shows that over half of women can have a VBAC, and some studies suggest that the rate is far higher than this. On the other hand, if you had an emergency Caesarean and fear the same complications, you may be able to arrange an elective Caesarean. This depends on your hospital's policy. In a climate where doctors are trying to bring down the high Caesarean rate, it isn't necessarily automatic.

This time around, there's more chance of:

- A shorter, easier first and second stage.

- The feeling of being "in control".

- A quick recovery from a vaginal birth, though more difficulties getting over a C-section, with two small children at home.

- Bad "afterpains" as your uterus contracts.

But less chance of:

- Being pushed around by bossy midwives.

- As many presents for your newborn.

Further resources

Books

The Best Friends' Guide to Toddlers by Vicki Iovine (Bloomsbury, £9.99). If you enjoyed the jolly, anecdotal style of her pregnancy and baby books, you'll love this tale of stories from the real world of bringing up a toddler.

From Contented Baby to Confident Child by Gina Ford (Vermilion, £9.99). The next stage in the Gina method, for parents who enjoy this writer's firm approach. Want to potty train your child in a week? Gina promises it shall be so.

New Toddler Taming: A Parent's Guide to the First Four Years by Dr Christopher Green (Vermilion, £12.99). A world-renowned paediatrician, Green's books are written with warmth, humour and the benefit of his long professional experience.

Three Shoes, One Sock and No Hairbrush by Rebecca Abrams (Cassell, £9.99). There are surprisingly few books on what happens when baby number two comes along, and Abrams book is well researched, empathetic and readable.

What to Expect, the Toddler Years by Arlene Eisenberg, Heidi Murkoff and Sandee Hathaway (Simon and Schuster, £12.99). The Q and A formula that characterizes their first books continues successfully here, with a chronological look at how your toddler develops up to the age of three.

Websites

www.babycentre.co.uk.
www.mumsnet.com.

www.onlychild.com. American website catering for those who *are* only children, and those who *have* only children. Packed with articles and book references.

www.nctpregnancyandbabycare.com (for refresher courses). See p.40.

www.vbac.org.uk. Aimed at women thinking of having a "Vaginal birth after Caesarean", this site goes into the pros and cons, addresses worries and has lots of further resources.

Epilogue

When you're sharing a home with a new baby, you may occasionally start to wonder what on earth you've let yourself in for. As someone who's recently been there – twice, within two years – I can testify how utterly exhausting the first year with small children can be. The lack of sleep, the amount of gear you have to carry, the ping-pong effect as my baby son chose to do an "up the back" poo while his sister screamed in the prostrate position because she wanted a Noddy story for the fifteenth time that afternoon. But, as you're no doubt discovering, slowly, imperceptibly, it gets better. I am back at work, (as you can see) mainly from home. I've even bought a pair of this season's "skinny jeans" – though they don't quite look the way they should. My husband Mark and I have started going out again, thanks to fantastic babysitting grandparents, and last summer we went away for a weekend without the kids.

Best of all is the way the children are growing and developing daily in front of our eyes, in truly magical ways. At the time of writing, my daughter Annabel is just three. She chooses her clothes every morning (mainly clashing shades of pink; trousers will not do, only skirts), insists on "The Three Bears" every night before bed, and has learned to say "I love you". My son, Jacob, nearly eighteen months, is currently tottering around the living room, gabbling into a TV remote control that he thinks is a telephone. He can touch his nose, laugh throatily and say "mamma", "dadda" and "allo".

Will you ever enjoy motherhood? You bet. The journey is only just beginning.

Looking ahead

flicks   Samantha Cook

he songs • The solo years

THE BEATLES

atles

Chris Ingham

A DIGITAL MUSIC GUIDE FOR MAC & P

THE ROUGH GUIDE to

iPods
iTunes & music on

3 RD EDITION:
COVERS IPOD NANO, VIDEO IPOD & IPOD SHU

ROUGH GUIDES

THE ROUGH GUIDE to

THE DA VINC
Co
TOTALLY UNAUTHORISED

Michael Haag and Veronica Haag

UGH GUIDE to

nexplained
nomena

e filth • the fury • the fashion

"The brilliance of the Rough Guide concept is breathtaking"
BBC Music Magazine

ROUGH GUIDES

BROADEN YOUR HORIZONS

COMPUTERS Blogging • The Internet
iPods • iTunes & music online
Macs & OSX • PCs & Windows
Website Directory: Shopping Online
& Surfing the Net
FILM & TV American Independent Film
British Cult Comedy • Chick Flicks
Comedy Movies • Cult Movies
Gangster Movies • Horror Movies
Kids' Movies • Sci-Fi Movies • Westerns
LIFESTYLE Babies • eBay • Ethical
Shopping • Pregnancy & Birth
MUSIC Classical Music • Heavy Metal
Hip-Hop • Jazz • Opera • Punk • Reggae
Rock • Soul and R&B • World Music
Vol 1 & 2 • Book of Playlists
The Beatles • Bob Dylan • Elvis • Frank
Sinatra • Pink Floyd • The Rolling Stones
POPULAR CULTURE Books for
Teenagers • Children's Books 0-5
& 5-11 • Cult Fiction • The Da Vinci Code
Lord of the Rings • Poker • Shakespeare
Superheroes • Conspiracy Theories
Unexplained Phenomena
SCIENCE Climate Change
The Universe • Weather

www.roughguides.com

GH GUIDE to

unk

THE ROUGH GUIDE to

Soul and R&B

THE ROUGH GUIDE to

The Rolling Stones

Sean Egan

ROUGH GUIDES

THE ROUGH GUIDE

Blogg

Index

Index

Index

index

Index

Index